ACQUISITIONS

ACQUISITIONS

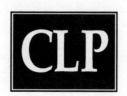

Published by

College of Law Publishing,
Braboeuf Manor, Portsmouth Road, St Catherines, Guildford GU3 1HA

© The University of Law 2024

British Library Cataloguing-in-Publication Data

A catalogue record for this book is available from the British Library.

ISBN 978 1 915469 56 4

Typeset by Style Photosetting Ltd, Mayfield, East Sussex

Tables and index by Moira Greenhalgh, Arnside, Cumbria

Preface

This book provides an introduction to the legal and taxation implications of buying and selling a business enterprise. It considers the purchase of a business as a going concern by purchasing all of its assets, as well as by acquiring the entire issued share capital of a private company. The book highlights the various areas of the law that may fall to be considered during an acquisition transaction, focusing on the issues and legislative provisions which are most commonly relevant, and taking in the extra considerations where the transaction is an international one.

Part I of the book deals with factors relevant when planning an acquisition. Part II provides detailed explanations of the main terms of agreement and how those terms may vary according to the type of transaction. Part III examines the particular concerns specific to an asset purchase and a share purchase, as well as issues relevant where the target is, or is to become, part of a corporate group. There is also a chapter highlighting the main implications for an acquisition where the purchaser is a private equity fund.

Although most of the principles described in this book are of general application to all acquisition transactions, it is worth noting that the additional obligations involved where the seller, the buyer or the target company is a public company listed on the Stock Exchange are not covered. For a detailed explanation of those further issues, the reader is referred to *Public Companies and Equity Finance*.

This book will prove a useful guide for trainee solicitors in corporate seats, and for lawyers and advisers in other areas of commercial practice who may find themselves involved in what can be extensive acquisitions teams. The fundamentals of international acquisitions are considered by reference to the law and practice of England and Wales, but with comparisons and references to the variety of differing approaches taken in other jurisdictions. Lawyers requiring in-depth consideration of the practice in particular jurisdictions outside the UK should consult more detailed sources.

The law is stated as at 1 October 2023.

Contents

Table of Cases

Table of Statutes

Table of Secondary Legislation

Table of Abbreviations

AIFM	alternative investment fund manager
AIFMR 2013	Alternative Investment Fund Managers Regulations 2013 (SI 2013/1773)
BA 2010	Bribery Act 2010
BoE	Bank of England
CA	Companies Act
CGT	capital gains tax
CMA	Competition and Markets Authority
CTA	Corporation Tax Act
DBT	Department for Business and Trade
DOJ	Department of Justice
EA 2002	Enterprise Act 2002
EAT	Employment Appeal Tribunal
EEA	European Economic Area
ECJ	European Court of Justice
EIS	Enterprise Investment Scheme
ERA 1996	Employment Rights Act 1996
ERRA 2013	Enterprise and Regulatory Reform Act 2013
ETO reason	economic, technical or organisational reason
EU	European Union
FCA	Financial Conduct Authority
FPC	Financial Policy Committee
FSA	Financial Services Authority
FSMA 2000	Financial Services and Markets Act 2000
FTC	Federal Trade Commission
GAAP	Generally Accepted Accounting Principles
HMRC	His Majesty's Revenue & Customs
HSR Act	Hartt-Scott-Rodino Antitrust Improvements Act
IFRS	International Financial Reporting Standards
ITA 2007	Income Tax Act 2007
MBO	management buyout
MAC	material adverse change
OFT	Office of Fair Trading
PAYE	pay as you earn
PRA	Prudential Regulation Authority
Rome I	European Council Regulation 593/2008
Rome II	European Council Regulation 864/2007
SDLT	stamp duty land tax
SDRT	stamp duty reserve tax
SFO	Serious Fraud Office
TCGA 1992	Taxation of Chargeable Gains Act 1992
TFEU	Treaty on the Functioning of the European Union
TUPE 1981	Transfer of Undertakings (Protection of Employment) Regulations 1981

TUPE 2006	Transfer of Undertakings (Protection of Employment) Regulations 2006
UCTA 1977	Unfair Contract Terms Act 1977
UK	United Kingdom
US	United States of America
VAT	value added tax
VATA 1994	Value Added Tax Act 1994
WARN	Worker Adjustment and Retraining Notification Act 1988

PLANNING AN ACQUISITION

TYPES OF ACQUISITION

LEARNING OUTCOMES

After reading this chapter you will be able to:

- distinguish between different types of acquisition
- explain the various factors that may affect the parties' choice of acquisition structure
- appreciate the need for pre-sale restructuring of the target business.

1.1 INTRODUCTION

The term 'acquisition' is used to describe a wide variety of transactions involving the sale and purchase of either the underlying assets of an operational business, or the ownership and control of a corporate entity that operates a business. The same major concerns are common to all acquisitions, whatever the size or nature of the parties involved or the entity being acquired. The buyer must ensure that it acquires exactly what it wants (and no more than that) for the best possible price. The seller will try to minimise its continuing obligations whilst aiming for the highest realistic price. In order to achieve those aims, the terms of the proposed acquisition will be carefully negotiated. Although in a complex acquisition those negotiations may cover a whole series of smaller transactions including many different parties, the basic principles explored in this book will apply throughout.

Most jurisdictions have at least two forms of corporate vehicle; these can be broadly categorised as private companies (for example German GmbH, French SARL and UK limited company) and public companies (for example German AG, French SA or SCA and UK plc). In many jurisdictions, including the UK, there will be additional regulations that apply to a transaction where it involves the acquisition of control of a public company and where the transaction involves a company whose shares are listed on an investment market. For example, in England, public company share acquisitions have to follow a formal 'offer' process whereby all the shareholders of the company are issued with an offer document setting out the terms on which an offer will be made for their shares. This 'offer' documentation is governed by the City Code on Takeovers and Mergers and must follow a pre-determined timetable. These rules will also apply if a scheme of arrangement is used to implement a merger involving a public company. If one of the parties to the transaction is listed on the Stock Exchange then the Stock Exchange Listing Rules will additionally apply to the transaction. Such additional rules for public companies, and their jurisdictional equivalents, will not be covered in this book.

In this book the two most common types of acquisition are considered: (i) the sale and purchase of the underlying assets of an operational business (an asset acquisition); and (ii) the sale and purchase of a private company (the 'target company') by share transfer (a share acquisition).

An *asset acquisition* involves the buyer acquiring the assets (and certain agreed liabilities) that make up the business. The contract is made between the buyer and the owner of the assets of the business, who may be an individual, a partnership or a company. The assets of the business may include tangible assets, such as land, machinery and stock, as well as intangible assets, such as intellectual property and goodwill. After the acquisition, the buyer will own the business and will continue to operate it using the assets acquired.

A *share acquisition* is where the buyer acquires the shares in the company that owns and operates the business. The contract is made between the buyer and the owners of the shares. In such a transaction the ownership of the company is transferred to the buyer, but there is no change in ownership of the business. The business, with all its assets and ongoing liabilities, remains in the hands of the company.

This book will also include some comparisons with acquisitions undertaken through the means of a statutory procedure for legal merger that is available in certain jurisdictions. Comparisons will be made with both merger by absorption, whereby the assets and liabilities of one company are absorbed into another company and the shares of the transferring company are cancelled, and merger by formation, where a new company is formed which absorbs the assets and liabilities of both the buyer and the target company.

1.2 TYPES OF ACQUISITION

An asset acquisition, a share acquisition and a legal merger may all achieve the same commercial objective of acquiring a target business. However, the legal and tax consequences of each form of acquisition are very different, as highlighted below.

1.2.1 Shares

In a share acquisition where the buyer acquires all or the majority of the shares in the target company, it is the ownership of the company itself that is transferred. The sale and purchase agreement is made between the buyer and the owner(s) of the shares (the seller(s)). The target company otherwise remains in exactly the same shape as it was prior to the acquisition and, in particular, it still owns and runs the business. The target company will continue to have whatever assets, liabilities, rights or obligations it had before the acquisition.

The sellers may be individual shareholders, corporate shareholders, or a mixture of both. Many companies are owned by other companies and the businesses are therefore operated through a group structure (see **11.1**). The attraction of operating through a group of companies rather than divisions of a single company has much to do with the fact that each company within the group is a separate legal entity with limited liability. The parent company, for example, is not liable for the debts of its subsidiaries unless it has agreed to assume responsibility for them or there are other special circumstances.

If all the shares in the target company are owned by another company (its 'holding company'), the target company is called a 'wholly-owned subsidiary'. In this case, there is only one seller – the holding company.

However, a company need not hold all the shares in another company to be its holding company. Under English law, if one company effectively controls over half the voting rights in another company, the two companies are classified under s 1159 of the Companies Act 2006 (CA 2006) as holding company and subsidiary (see **11.1.2.2**). Although a sale of this controlling shareholding would transfer effective control, the buyer will usually want to acquire the entire issued share capital of the company. The holding company in this case will therefore be joined as seller in the acquisition transaction by the holders of the remaining shares. The sellers may thus comprise a mixture of both corporate and individual shareholders. The buyer of the shares may be an individual (or individuals) or, perhaps more commonly, a company. If all the shares of the target company are acquired by another company, it becomes a wholly-owned subsidiary of the buyer.

EXAMPLE 1

Steve and Andy are equal shareholders in Street Printers Limited, a small print and design company. They are approached by Big Limited, a much larger printing company, with a generous offer for the company. Steve and Andy sell all their shares in Street Printers Limited to Big Limited, so Street Printers Limited becomes a wholly-owned subsidiary of Big Limited.

A buyer will usually want to acquire all the shares of the target company; but if this is not possible, for example because a small number of shares are held by an individual who refuses to sell, the buyer may still go ahead and acquire most of the target's shares, thereby giving the buyer control, though it will have the inconvenience of a dissenting shareholder within the company.

If the target company itself owns shares in another company, ie it has a subsidiary, then ownership of that subsidiary will transfer along with the other assets of the target.

EXAMPLE 2

Street Printers Limited has a subsidiary company, Greet Limited, specialising in greeting cards. When Steve and Andy sell their shares in Street Printers Limited, the shareholding in Greet Limited will transfer to Big Limited as an asset of the target company. After the acquisition, Big Limited becomes the holding company of Street Printers Limited, which continues to be the holding company of Greet Limited.

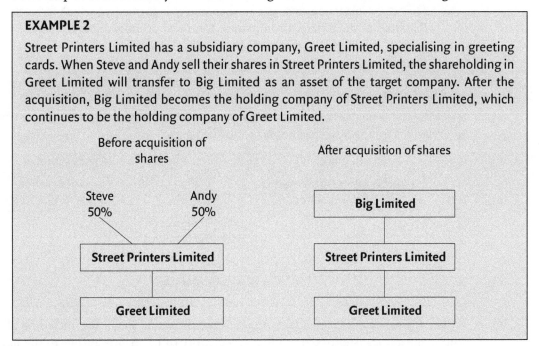

1.2.2 Legal merger

In certain jurisdictions it is possible to effect an acquisition by way of a legal merger between different corporate entities through the use of a statutory procedure. The extent to which legal merger is used varies between jurisdictions and it is probably most common in the United States (US) where acquisitions by a corporate entity are often undertaken by way of a statutory merger.

The state laws specify formal procedures for such mergers which include obtaining board and shareholder approval and in many jurisdictions include the need for court approval.

A legal merger can usually be undertaken in one of two forms:

(a)   Merger by absorption, where the assets and liabilities of one corporate entity are absorbed into another. The transferor company is formally dissolved and on its dissolution it transfers all of its assets and liabilities to the transferee company.

EXAMPLE 3

Using the facts outline in Example 1 for a share acquisition, but assuming the transaction is between US corporations, the purchase could be achieved through the use of a statutory procedure of merger by absorption. Steve and Andy, as shareholders of Street Printers Corporation, could enter into a merger agreement with Big Corporation whereby, under court approval, all the assets and liabilities of Street Printers Corporation are transferred to Big Corporation. Street Printers Corporation would be dissolved. Big Corporation would be an enlarged company with all the assets and liabilities of Street Printers Corporation. Payment to Steve and Andy for the cancellation of their shares will be agreed under the terms of the merger agreement.

~~Steve Andy~~ (shares cancelled)

| ~~Street Printers Corporation~~ (company dissolved) | → | **Big Corporation** (enlarged company) |

Automatic transfer of
ALL assets and liabilities

(b)   Merger by formation, where a new company is formed which absorbs the assets and liabilities of the different companies. Here two or more companies are each dissolved and on dissolution transfer all their assets and liabilities to a transferee company formed for the purpose of the merger.

EXAMPLE 4

Using the facts in Examples 1 and 3 above, the purchase could be achieved through a merger of companies into a newly created company.

(Shares cancelled)   (Shares cancelled)

| ~~Street Printers Corporation~~ (company dissolved) | | ~~Big Corporation~~ (company dissolved) |

Automatic transfer of
ALL assets and liabilities
↓

| **Newco Corporation** |

A key feature of a legal merger is that all the assets and liabilities, including all contracts, automatically transfer to either the merged entity (if by absorption) or to the newly formed company (if by formation). Therefore, as with a share acquisition, the whole business transfers and there is no need to effect a transfer of the individual assets that make up the business. However, unlike a share acquisition, the corporate shell does not transfer as the shares in the remaining empty shell are cancelled. The key difference from a share acquisition is that a legal merger creates a single enlarged corporate entity which has absorbed the entire target business instead of acquiring a subsidiary company.

The procedures for a legal merger are similar across European civil code jurisdictions and the US. These statutory procedures usually provide for a merger agreement, shareholders' resolutions, independent valuations, procedures for creditors to object and the need for court approval.

For companies registered in England and Wales there is no formal procedure for a legal merger but a similar result can be achieved through the use of a scheme of arrangement. A scheme of arrangement is a statutory procedure pursuant to Pt 26 of the CA 2006 whereby a company may make a compromise or arrangement with its members or creditors (or any class of them). There is nothing in the legislation that prescribes the subject matter of a scheme and it can be used to effect almost any kind of internal reorganisation, merger or demerger as long as the necessary approvals have been obtained. Under a scheme of arrangement, a target company can agree with its shareholders that the shares in the target company be cancelled in consideration for shares to be issued in the buyer. Where the buyer is a company listed on an investment market, these new shares can then be sold on that market to convert the shares to a cash price. Schemes of arrangement are not generally used for the acquisition of private companies in England and Wales as the court procedure is complex and time-consuming. Such schemes had been increasingly used in high-value public company acquisitions due to the potential for tax savings on stamp duty (see **9.4.4**) as shares are cancelled rather than transferred, although Parliament closed this loophole in 2015 by inserting s 641(2A) into the CA 2006, outlawing share cancellations in favour of share transfers. Transfer schemes of arrangement are still available for takeovers and are recognised in Pt 27 of the CA 2006, which provides that where the scheme is used to effect the amalgamation of two or more companies where one is a public company then additional provisions need to be complied with. These include the provision of a merger agreement, shareholders' resolutions, valuations and a procedure for creditors to object. In addition, the statutory code governing the acquisition of shares in public companies registered in England and Wales (the City Code on Takeovers and Mergers) and the Listing Rules for the London Stock Exchange both include provisions covering the use of a scheme of arrangement to effect an acquisition.

Although legal mergers are a common concept in a number of jurisdictions, certain issues may arise in cross-border mergers, including the need for approvals where the legal merger involves a foreign entity or where the merger is between different types of corporate entities. The European Union (EU) has taken some steps to address these issues through the Cross-Border Mergers of Limited Liability Companies Directive 2005/56/EC. This Directive requires Member States to establish a framework for cross-border mergers between limited liability companies. In the UK the Directive had been implemented through the Companies (Cross-Border Mergers) Regulations 2007 (SI 2007/2974), which provided a framework for cross-border mergers between companies formed and registered under the CAs 1985 and 2006 and companies governed by the law of an European Economic Area (EEA) state other than the UK. Following the UK's exit from the EU, the Regulations have been revoked and the cross-border merger framework that the Regulations provided is no longer available to the UK.

This procedure is consistent with that used in the UK for a domestic merger through the use of a scheme of arrangement under Pt 26 of the CA 2006 combined with Pt 27 of the CA 2006 setting out the additional requirements where the scheme involves a public company. Under the Regulations both of the companies merging must obtain pre-merger certificates from a court in their respective jurisdictions. Once the certificates are obtained, the transferor applies to the applicable court for the sanction of the merger. The assets and liabilities are then transferred and the transferor is dissolved without liquidation. In the UK, this type of merger remains limited to large public transactions, primarily due to the need for complex documentation and time constraints. However, the Regulations have led to more internal group restructuring for groups of companies operating across a range of European jurisdictions.

1.2.3 Assets

In an asset acquisition the buyer acquires the underlying assets needed to carry on the business, such as premises, plant and machinery, and intellectual property. Each of these assets must be transferred in accordance with the specific form of transfer required for that asset. For example, under English law a conveyance is needed to transfer land. If the assets will be used to carry on the business after completion of the acquisition, part of the purchase price will be attributed to the goodwill, which usually includes customer details and the right to use the business's trading name. The buyer will also be concerned to acquire important contracts that the business has concluded with third parties (for the supply of goods and services, for example). The sale and purchase agreement will specify the assets to be transferred, which may include transfers for which third party consents are required.

1.2.3.1 Acquiring assets from an unincorporated seller

A business may be operated by a sole trader or a partnership. If so, the assets required to run that business, such as the premises, stock and goodwill, are owned by that individual or partnership.

EXAMPLE 5

Marco Barr is a sole trader. He owns a motor repair business and trades under the name 'MB Motors'. He agrees to sells the business lease, tools, outstanding orders, customer details and the continued use of the trade name 'MB Motors' to Patrick Cook for £50,000. The acquisition of these assets will enable Patrick Cook to continue the trade of 'MB Motors'.

Sells identified assets and liabilities

| Marco Barr | ⟶ | Patrick Cook |
| Sole trader | | Sole trader |

Premises Tools Orders Name   Premises Tools Orders Name

EXAMPLE 6

Guy and Kate Holdsworth are partners in a grocery business trading under the name of 'Best Fresh'. They sell the assets of the business to BettaBuy Limited, and the proceeds from that sale will be divided between them in accordance with any partnership agreement. After the acquisition, BettaBuy will own the 'Best Fresh' business and will choose either to continue it in the same form, or to absorb it into its existing corporate structure.

Sells identified assets and liabilities

Guy & Kate Partnership ⟶ **BettaBuy Limited**

Acquires assets of 'Best Fresh' business

(Premises Stock Orders Name Employees)

Assets of 'Best Fresh' business

(Premises Stock Orders Name Employees)

1.2.3.2 Acquiring assets from a company

It is possible to acquire the underlying assets of a business from a company in much the same way as from a sole trader or partnership.

A business may be operated by a company either as the sole concern of that company, or as one of many businesses, or 'divisions', run by it.

> **EXAMPLE 7**
>
> Computers R Us Limited is a medium-sized company which manufactures computers and also produces a wide range of software packages. In view of the prevailing economic climate, the board of directors decides to concentrate on the software business. The board arranges for Computers R Us Limited to sell the computer manufacturing division to Avaricious Limited.

If the sale of assets involves the assets of the only business operated by the selling company then that company will usually distribute the proceeds of the sale to its shareholders post-acquisition, and the empty shell of the company will be dissolved. On the other hand, where the sale of assets relates to only one of a number of businesses operated by the selling company, the parties must be particularly careful in choosing the assets that will transfer under the sale and purchase agreement, and, once the sale has completed, the company must decide whether to distribute the proceeds of sale to the shareholders or reinvest them in new projects within the company.

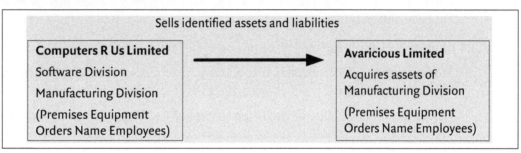

1.2.3.3 Transfer of assets that comprise a 'business'

In this book it is assumed that a buyer will want to acquire all the assets it needs to be able to continue to run an ongoing business after completion. However, there may be circumstances where the proposed sale is in relation to only some of the assets used in the business. The rules in the UK on taxation and employment protection recognise that the transfer of most of the assets of a business which enables that business to continue to trade should be treated quite differently from the transfer of just a few assets used in a business. However, this distinction can be difficult to make in practice and the precise terms of the tests under the different pieces of legislation do vary.

Employees

The Transfer of Undertakings (Protection of Employment) Regulations 2006 (SI 2006/246) (TUPE 2006), as amended by the Collective Redundancies and Transfer of Undertakings (Protection of Employment) (Amendment) Regulations 2014 (SI 2014/16), may protect employees on an asset sale. These Regulations apply to a sale of assets if that sale represents a transfer of 'an economic entity which retains its identity'. These regulations originated from European directives and accordingly similar provisions apply across the EU. The phrase 'economic entity' is defined in the Regulations and has been considered in a number of cases (see **8.3.4.1**). In general terms, if the transfer of the assets enables an identifiable business to be continued by the buyer in essentially the same form, TUPE 2006 will apply. The effect of TUPE 2006 is that the rights and obligations of the employees working in that identifiable economic entity will automatically be transferred to the buyer. In other words, full responsibility for the employees may pass to the buyer of the assets of an identifiable business, whether the parties intend this or not.

If the sale of the specified assets does not represent the transfer of an 'economic entity' then TUPE 2006 do not apply and the rights and obligations of the employees remain with the seller. If the sale of the assets means that the seller can no longer continue its own business then, unless the seller redeploys its employees, the employees' contracts will be terminated and the seller will be open to all potential claims arising from the termination of their employment, notably wrongful dismissal, unfair dismissal and redundancy.

Tax reliefs for an unincorporated seller

Two reliefs, one from capital gains tax (CGT) and the other from income tax, are potentially available where the assets of an unincorporated business (whether a sole trader or a partnership) are transferred to an existing company in return for shares in that company. These reliefs are not available on a mere sale of assets.

Value added tax

Another important factor for both seller and buyer to take into account is value added tax (VAT). If the sale involves a 'transfer of a business as a going concern' (as defined in art 5 of the Value Added Tax (Special Provisions) Order 1995 (SI 1995/1268)), the transfer is treated as a supply neither of goods nor of services (see **8.4.4.6**) and VAT is therefore not chargeable. On a mere transfer of assets though, VAT will be chargeable on the assets that are transferred, such as plant and machinery and stock.

1.2.3.4 Jurisdictional comparisons on acquiring a 'business'

In some civil code jurisdictions such as France, Germany and Italy, there are additional rules that apply where the transfer of assets is for the continuance of a business.

In France, the civil code recognises the concept of acquiring a 'business'. If the acquired assets constitute an identifiable business, then it is a purchase of a '*fonds de commerce*'. For this type of transfer, individual identification and transfer of the assets is not required other than for specified types of assets such as land. Assets which relate to the core of the business, such as employee contracts, insurance policies and any lease on business premises, will automatically transfer, although trading contracts will still need third party consents, and formalities on the transfer of creditors still need to be followed. In addition, the purchase must be publicly announced to creditors who have certain rights to oppose the acquisition or make counter offers for the assets of the business.

In both Germany and Italy, the civil code applies additional obligations where the relevant assets are transferred to enable that business to function. As in the UK, employment contracts will automatically transfer and, if the business continues to use its trading name after the sale, the buyer will become jointly liable with the seller for some, if not all, of the tax liabilities relating to the business and will take on liability for the debts of the business.

Although there is no concept of the sale of a business in the US, most US states have adopted 'bulk transfers' acts, which apply to transfers of a major part of the materials, supplies, merchandise or inventory of a business other than in the ordinary course of its business. These laws generally provide that if a buyer of these assets notifies the creditors of the seller at least 10 days in advance of the purchase, then the buyer will not be liable to those creditors for the debts and obligations of the seller. Otherwise, the creditors may trace the business assets being sold and seek recovery for unpaid debts. In addition to notifying each creditor, the buyer must also file a list of creditors and transferred property with the register of the local county in which the business is located.

These rules all highlight that if a transaction is to take place in another jurisdiction then care needs to be taken to ascertain whether the transfer will result in the acquisition of additional liabilities and whether this would impact on the choice of acquisition structure. In particular it should be noted that in some US states there is a risk that the purchase of all or substantially all of a company's assets will be regarded as a de facto merger. In these circumstances, what might have started out as an asset acquisition may result in a legal merger.

The remainder of this chapter concentrates on a comparison of asset acquisition and share acquisition where the intention is to continue the business after the acquisition.

1.3 FACTORS AFFECTING CHOICE OF ACQUISITION

Where a business is owned and operated by a company, the parties can choose whether to transfer the business either by transferring all of the shares in the company, or by transferring the underlying assets that comprise the business. The parties may have opposing views on the form that the acquisition should take. This stems from the fact that, in relation to many of the factors that influence the decision as to how to proceed, what is an advantage to one party is a disadvantage to the other and vice versa. Although this is very much a generalisation, the owners of a company will often prefer to sell their shares, whereas a buyer will often prefer to acquire the assets of the business from the company. In these circumstances, the relative bargaining power of the parties is likely to dictate the outcome.

Before analysing the advantages and disadvantages of both types of acquisition, it is worth pointing out that there will be situations where the choice may not realistically be available to the parties. This will be the case if, for example, a company has a number of different businesses (perhaps run as separate 'divisions'), only one of which the buyer wishes to buy. In this situation, the deal must progress as an asset sale unless the parties are willing to use a hive-down structure (see **1.4.2**).

1.3.1 Comparison between share sales and asset sales: seller

1.3.1.1 Clean break from business

Shares

Following the disposal of shares, the seller loses its connection with the company. The company itself continues to exist and, in particular, liabilities (hidden or otherwise) continue to be enforceable against it. It is the buyer who will now have a close eye on the state of the company and, thus, the value of its investment.

Too much can be made, however, of the share sale advantage of a clean break. The very nature of a share sale means that the buyer will make detailed investigations about the company and will seek wide protections from the seller in the sale and purchase agreement. The buyer will take every action possible to ensure that it has a right of comeback against the seller if the target company turns out to be riddled with undisclosed problems. Additionally, where the seller has guaranteed obligations of the target company, by, for example, offering a personal guarantee on bank lending or by standing as a surety on a business lease, a clean break will be possible only if the seller is able to negotiate releases from such obligations on completion.

Assets

It is a feature of any asset sale that legal liability to third parties for debts and obligations of the business remains with the seller company, although this may be subject to some jurisdictional variations (see **8.1.2**). Under English law, even where the buyer has contracted to assume responsibility for certain liabilities in the sale and purchase agreement, this will not affect third parties, who can still take action against the seller unless they have expressly released it from liability. Although the seller would have a right of indemnity from the buyer in these circumstances, this may be difficult to enforce, particularly if the buyer is insolvent. In addition, the buyer may have expressly excluded responsibility for certain specific matters for which the seller will, accordingly, remain liable, as indeed it will for any unforeseen liabilities which may materialise.

1.3.1.2 Scope of warranties and due diligence

Although the sale and purchase agreement will invariably contain warranties and indemnities by the seller in favour of the buyer, whether it is an asset sale or a share sale, it follows from what has been said above that the scope of these protections should be wider in the context of a share sale. For example, on an asset sale, there is no need for complex taxation warranties and indemnities, for the simple reason that most contingent tax liabilities will remain with the seller. For the same reasons, the investigation into the affairs of the target company will usually be more extensive on a share sale.

1.3.1.3   Transfer of title

Shares

Although the pre-contract investigation and the contract documentation will invariably be more extensive on a share sale, the actual mechanics of transferring title are much simpler. In England and Wales a stock transfer form is all that is needed to transfer title to shares, whilst in other jurisdictions this may be effected by similar documentation (albeit of varying length and complexity), such as notarised deeds of transfer. In the US, the transfer may be effected by endorsing the back of the share certificate itself. However, the terms of the company's contracts should still be checked to determine whether any of them will terminate on a change of control of the company, or whether third party consent to the change is required.

Assets

On an asset transfer, under English law, each separate asset of the business must be transferred, and this can involve complications, particularly where consents are required from third parties. Where, for example, leasehold property is involved, the landlord's consent to assignment may be required, and this can often delay the transaction significantly. Some assets, such as stock and loose plant and machinery, are transferable by delivery, but formal transfers of assets such as land and certain intellectual property rights will be necessary to transfer title.

Even under civil code provisions relating to the automatic transfer of assets relating to the continuance of a business, there are often particular assets such as land and trading contracts that can only be transferred with the consent of a third party.

1.3.1.4   Financial services regulation

Shares

In the UK, the purchase of shares, whether in a public listed company or in a private company, is classified as an 'investment' and as such is subject to financial services regulation. In 1986, the Financial Services Act introduced a regime of consumer protection to regulate persons carrying on investment business through a system of self-regulation. A single regulator, the Financial Services Authority (FSA), was created to oversee all financial and banking services, and further legislation was introduced in the form of the Financial Services and Markets Act 2000 (FSMA 2000) to regulate investment activities. The FSMA 2000 was updated in 2013 by the Financial Services Act 2012, which came into force on 1 April 2013 and replaced the FSA with the Financial Conduct Authority (FCA).

Section 21 of the FSMA 2000 restricts the issue of 'an invitation or inducement to engage in investment activity'. The definition of 'investment activity' in this context includes advising on or arranging the purchase or sale of shares, so any communication in relation to an agreement to buy and sell shares could be caught by this restriction. Importantly, breach of the restriction is an offence rendering the sale and purchase agreement unenforceable. This provision does not apply when considering the purchase of assets. A potential seller of shares who has yet to find a buyer must therefore be made aware of this legislation, though specific exemptions exist for financial promotions in the context of share acquisitions (see **9.2.1.2**).

Lawyers (or other professional advisers) who give advice in relation to a proposed sale of shares must also ensure either that they comply with the FSMA 2000 requirements for authorisation to carry out a 'regulated activity', or that the transaction falls within a number of possible exclusions under the Financial Services and Markets Act 2000 (Regulated Activities) Order 2001 (SI 2001/544).

Assets

Although the provisions of the FSMA 2000 do not extend to the sale of the assets of a business, it should be appreciated that, in relation to a target company, the decision to dispose of the assets rather than the shares may be taken at a fairly late stage in the negotiations. In other words, compliance with the provisions of the FSMA 2000 may be necessary even if the transaction ultimately proceeds as an asset sale.

1.3.1.5 Employees

Shares

On a share sale, there is no change of employer; the target company is the employer before and after the change of control, which has no direct effect on the contracts of employment of the workforce. The share sale itself will not, therefore, give rise to any potential claims by the employees, and it is the buyer, as the new owner of the company, who will be affected (at least indirectly) by any liabilities and obligations of the target company which arise in the future in relation to those employees. The seller no longer has a direct interest, except in relation to warranties given to the buyer in the sale and purchase agreement.

Assets

The application of TUPE 2006 on the transfer of assets that form a continuing economic entity has already been noted (see **1.2.3.3**). The effect of TUPE 2006 is that the transfer does not operate to terminate contracts of employment. The rights and obligations in respect of any employee working in the economic entity are transferred automatically to the buyer, who takes on responsibility for those employees. Equivalent provisions operate in all EU countries and similar provisions have been adopted by many other jurisdictions around the world. As with a share acquisition, the seller no longer has a direct interest, except in relation to warranties given to the buyer in the sale and purchase agreement.

Employees' claims

In both types of acquisition, actions by the seller or the buyer, before or after the acquisition, may result in claims by the employees. For example, the seller and the buyer may dismiss certain employees, or there may be a substantial change in the terms and conditions of employment imposed on the workforce after the transfer. These issues are explored in full in **Chapter 8** (asset sales) and **Chapter 9** (share sales).

1.3.1.6 Taxation factors

Shares: direct receipt of consideration

Where the company is owned by individual shareholders, a sale of the shares ensures that the consideration is received by them directly. The taxation consequences of a sale of shares by individuals are relatively straightforward. Shares are chargeable assets for CGT purposes and any disposal that realises a gain will involve (subject to exemptions) a charge to tax for an individual shareholder. The seller may be able to exempt some or all of the gain if the seller qualifies for reliefs.

Where the company is owned by another company, a sale of shares results in the selling company receiving the consideration directly. Any capital gain realised by the selling company is likely to be exempt from corporation tax, however, provided the seller is disposing of a substantial shareholding in a trading company. The availability of this exemption (see **9.4.2.4**) will clearly be an important consideration where ownership of the shares of the target company is in corporate hands. It should be noted that the exemption was reformed in 2017.

The reforms apply to disposals on or after 1 April 2017, and involve a widening of the scope of the exemption and a relaxation of some of the tests, subject to anti-avoidance rules.

Assets: two-tier taxation

On an asset sale, if the company owns the assets of the business then it, as the seller, receives the purchase price. For the benefit to accrue to the shareholders of the selling company further steps have to be taken, such as the company declaring a dividend or, if the sale is of all the assets of the company, the shareholders liquidating the company. Apart from the administrative inconvenience involved, this also complicates the tax position, since there are effectively two separate charging points.

First, the selling company suffers corporation tax on the sale of the assets. The disposal of the capital assets of the business may give rise to a chargeable gain; proceeds from the disposal of stock are chargeable as income receipts; and the sale of assets in respect of which capital allowances have been claimed, such as plant and machinery, may trigger balancing charges (treated as income receipts) if the assets are sold for more than their tax written-down value.

Secondly, there will be a further charge when the proceeds of sale of the assets, as reduced by the above tax charges, are distributed to the shareholders. How this distribution of the proceeds is taxed will depend on whether the shareholder is an individual or a company. If the shareholder is an individual and the net proceeds are distributed in a winding up, there is a disposal by the shareholders of their shares for CGT purposes. The alternative possibility of distribution by dividend involves an income tax charge (Income Tax (Trading and Other Income) Act 2005, Pt 4) on the shareholders (although they will have a tax credit). By contrast, a corporate shareholder is unlikely to incur a charge to tax. A distribution on a winding up is likely to attract the benefit of the substantial shareholder exemption, and a distribution by way of dividend will be covered by group relief on intra-company dividends.

Reinvesting the proceeds

Assets   Roll-over relief from CGT/corporation tax under s 152 of the Taxation of Chargeable Gains Act 1992 (TCGA 1992) is available on the disposal of qualifying assets (including land, fixed plant and machinery) used in the trade where the disposal proceeds are applied in the acquisition of replacement qualifying assets (see **8.4.2.1**). The relief operates to roll the gain into the replacement asset, thus postponing any charge to CGT or corporation tax until the replacement asset is disposed of (without itself being replaced). This relief often makes an asset sale look attractive from a tax point of view for a company which is selling a division and planning to acquire new assets to develop other businesses operated by it.

Shares: individual sellers   Shares are not qualifying assets for the purpose of the above roll-over relief. However, an individual shareholder who reinvests a chargeable gain from the disposal of shares (or indeed any gain) in subscribing for shares which qualify for the Enterprise Investment Scheme (EIS) will be able to claim a deferral relief (see **8.4.2.1** and **9.4.4.2**).

Shares: corporate sellers   Deferral relief on reinvestment in EIS shares is not available to a corporate seller which reinvests a chargeable gain in shares. However, as mentioned above, capital gains arising on the disposal by companies of substantial shareholdings in trading companies are exempt from tax.

Taxation considerations are dealt with in more detail in **Chapter 8** (asset sales) and **Chapter 9** (share sales).

1.3.2   Comparison between share sales and asset sales: buyer

Many of the points mentioned above are equally relevant when considering the matter from the buyer's standpoint. Set out below are some additional considerations for a buyer contemplating whether to proceed with an acquisition as an asset or a share purchase.

1.3.2.1 Trade continuity

The main advantage of acquiring the entire issued share capital of the target company is the lack of disruption to the trade which results. From an outsider's point of view, very little will appear to have changed, and customers and suppliers will usually be content to carry on dealing with the company as before. An asset sale, on the other hand, is more likely to prompt them to review their dealings with the new owners, who may have to work harder to build up confidence again.

Assets

The benefit of existing contracts entered into by the seller will not be transferred to the buyer automatically on a sale of the assets of the business. Under English law, these contracts must be transferred to the buyer either through assignment or novation, and the terms of many contracts require the consent of the third party for an assignment of the benefit to be effective. There may be certain contracts which the buyer sees as crucial to the continued well-being of the business, and it may be reluctant to rely on the third party continuing to honour the contract despite the change in ownership of the business. There is always the danger that, if a formal approach is made, the third party may feel inclined to seek to renegotiate the terms of the contract as a price for consenting to the assignment.

Where the assets of the business include leasehold property, it will usually be necessary to obtain the consent of the landlord to the assignment of the lease. The landlord will wish to ensure that it is not taking any greater risk by having the new owner as tenant, and will often agree to the assignment only if the buyer is able to arrange suitable guarantees. Obtaining a landlord's consent may considerably delay completion of the transaction.

The buyer must also remember that, on an asset sale, it must arrange either for all appropriate insurances to be transferred, or for fresh cover to be taken out.

Shares

On a share purchase the assets of the company and outstanding contracts remain unaffected legally by the change in ownership of the company. However, the buyer of shares does need to be careful on two counts. First, it has no guarantee that those third parties who are accustomed to dealing with the company, but who are not contractually obliged to do so, will continue to deal with it after the change in ownership. Secondly, some contracts contain clauses which permit a party to terminate the contract where control of the company changes hands. Change of control clauses are quite common, for example, in distribution and franchise agreements.

In the US, state laws differ as to whether the change in ownership of the company following a share sale would be deemed to be an assignment for the purposes of its contracts. Accordingly, consents may be required from material contracting parties of the company in connection with the sale, even in respect of contracts which contain a prohibition on assignment but no change of control clause. Care also needs to be taken if an acquisition has taken place by way of legal merger. Although on a legal merger all the assets and liabilities of the target company are transferred, including any contracts, the merger may still trigger change of control clauses. This may enable a third party to terminate that contract.

1.3.2.2 Choice of assets and liabilities

Assets

On a share sale, all the underlying assets of the company are indirectly acquired by the buyer, whether they are wanted or not. An asset purchase provides greater flexibility, in the sense that the buyer is able to pick and choose the assets it wishes to buy (subject to particular jurisdictional limitations). For example, the buyer may already have some perfectly adequate plant and machinery and may, therefore, wish to exclude certain items of the seller's plant and machinery from the sale.

Liabilities

Perhaps the major advantage to a buyer of acquiring the assets of a business relates to liabilities. On a share purchase, all the liabilities of the company (hidden or otherwise) remain with it and indirectly become the responsibility of the buyer. Extensive investigations and wide-ranging warranties and indemnities are insufficient to protect the buyer in full. The seller may not, for example, be able to meet a warranty claim, or it may prove difficult (and costly) to establish that a particular matter is covered by a warranty.

On an asset acquisition, on the other hand, the buyer acquires a bundle of identified assets and liabilities. Subject to a few statutory exceptions (notably obligations in relation to employees and environmental matters in the UK), a buyer can select those liabilities for which it agrees to take responsibility in the sale and purchase agreement. In this way the buyer can avoid the risks associated with unknown or unquantifiable liabilities.

This advantage may, in some jurisdictions be limited. For example, in some US states, 'bulk sales law' can have the effect of transferring a historic liability to creditors to the buyer of the assets of a business. Certain liabilities, such as creditors and tax, also transfer in some Continental countries such as France and Germany where the transfer of the assets relates to an ongoing business.

1.3.2.3 Integration

A buyer should consider how the new business will fit into its own commercial and organisational objectives. This will be particularly important if the buyer expects to make cost savings by integrating the new business into its existing corporate structure. The buyer must decide whether it prefers to acquire a stand-alone operational company, or whether a collection of assets will be more readily absorbed into its existing operations.

1.3.2.4 Securing finance

The buyer's arrangements for financing the acquisition may have a bearing on whether the matter proceeds as a share purchase or an asset purchase.

If the buyer is proposing to finance the acquisition through some borrowing, it may wish to offer the assets of the business being acquired as security for the loan. Many countries have enacted legislation which prohibits a company from giving direct or indirect financial assistance to a person who is acquiring or proposing to acquire shares in the company. Under the relevant provisions of English law, if the acquisition proceeds as a share acquisition and the target is a public company, such a charge over the target company's assets would be prohibited under the CA 2006 as constituting financial assistance by a company for the purchase of its own shares (see **9.2.2.1**).

1.3.2.5 Taxation factors

From a buyer's perspective, most of the taxation advantages lie with an asset purchase.

Base costs for CGT

On an asset acquisition, chargeable assets, such as land, will have a higher base cost for capital tax purposes on their subsequent disposal. In an arm's length transaction, the buyer will acquire these assets at market value. When the buyer comes to dispose of them at market value in the future, it will be charged to capital tax based on any increase in value since the date it acquired the asset.

Contrast this with the position on a share acquisition. Although the buyer acquires the shares at market value, the base cost of the assets which the company owns is the cost at which they were originally acquired by the company. It follows that on a subsequent arm's length disposal of any of these assets by the company, corporation tax will be charged based on the increase in value of the asset since originally acquired by the company. There is, in effect, a deferred tax liability, in respect of which a prudent buyer should seek a discount on the price of the shares. The importance of this consideration to the buyer will depend on its future plans for the company and, in particular, whether it is contemplating imminent disposals of any assets by the company (perhaps in an attempt to rationalise the business).

Capital allowances

On an asset acquisition, the purchase of certain assets, such as plant and machinery, will enable the buyer to obtain tax relief (as an income deduction) in the form of writing-down allowances on the price paid for them. From the seller's point of view, there may be a corresponding disadvantage if the actual price paid exceeds the tax written-down value. In that case the seller will be subject to a balancing charge – the amount by which the actual price paid exceeds the tax written-down value is treated as income profit (see **8.4.2**). However, if the seller receives less for the assets than the tax written-down value, it will benefit from a balancing allowance – the difference between the tax written-down value and the actual price paid is in this case treated as an income loss.

Apportionment of the purchase consideration

On the acquisition of the assets of a business, it will be necessary to apportion the total consideration between the various assets acquired (see **8.4.4.5**). This must be done on a fair and reasonable basis, but there is some flexibility here which can be used to gain tax advantages as the different types of assets transferred will be subject to different tax rules depending on the nature of the asset being acquired. For example, it will usually be in the buyer's interest to weight the consideration in favour of:

(a)   plant and machinery qualifying for capital allowances;

(b)   trading stock which will form a deduction against income profits for the buyer;

(c)   capital items qualifying for capital tax roll-over relief on replacement of business assets.

The apportionment is a matter of negotiation with the seller, and inevitably the parties may be pulling in different directions.

Acquiring the tax position of the company

A feature of a share acquisition is that the tax identity of the company continues. This means that, after the sale is completed, potential tax liabilities may arise in relation to activities that occurred in the company before the sale. The buyer generally seeks indemnity against such costs, usually provided by the seller in the Tax Deed of Covenant that forms a schedule to the main sale and purchase agreement.

Although the buyer must seek protection in relation to potential liabilities, a share acquisition can also enable it to take advantage of tax credits within the company. In particular, s 45 of the Corporation Tax Act 2010 (CTA 2010) permits trading losses of a company to be carried forward and set against trading profits from the same trade in the future. If the losses are made after 1 April 2017, then generally they may be set against total future profits, regardless of whether the profits are trading profits arising from the same trade. This enables accumulated tax losses of the target company to be carried forward and set against profits generated after the buyer has acquired the shares (although see **9.3.3.1** for certain restrictions on this carry forward). This may be a significant factor for a buyer who is confident that it will be able to change the company's fortunes and make it profitable, as it will view the accumulated losses as an asset.

The carry forward of losses is not generally possible on an asset acquisition.

Value added tax

A charge to VAT may arise on the disposal of business assets alone but not on the disposal of sufficient assets to enable the business to continue as a going concern (see **8.4.4.6**). Value added tax is not normally chargeable on a share sale.

Stamp duty

On the acquisition of shares, the buyer pays stamp duty at 0.5% of the purchase price rounded up to the nearest £5 (see **9.4.4**).

On the acquisition of the assets of a business, the buyer pays stamp duty on dutiable assets only (chiefly shares). Where land is being acquired, stamp duty land tax is payable at an incremental rate depending on the value of the land.

1.4 PRE-SALE RESTRUCTURING

As indicated at the start of this chapter, acquisition transactions do not always neatly fit the description of only one type of acquisition or the other. The commercial objectives of the parties to the transaction may mean that either a mixture of both asset and share acquisition, or even a whole series of related transactions, is required.

1.4.1 Creating a discrete unit

If the target company is part of a group of companies, it may use assets owned by other members of the group or hold assets that are used by other group members. The buyer may require that these assets be transferred into the company prior to any purchase of its shares or, conversely, that certain assets be transferred out of the target company prior to its purchase. Care must be taken with such pre-sale transfers as they may trigger tax charges (see **11.4**).

1.4.2 A hive-down

If the target business is one of a number of divisions but for various tax and commercial reasons the parties do not wish to proceed on the basis of an asset sale, the parties may agree that the business is first 'hived down'. This is the process whereby the target company sells some or all of its assets and undertaking to a brand new company, usually set up as a wholly-owned subsidiary of the target company. The buyer then acquires the shares of this new company. See **Figure 1.1**.

Figure 1.1   Hive-down

Following the hive-down (that is, the transfer) of the assets to the newly-formed subsidiary Newco, Target will sell all its shares in Newco to the buyer, resulting in:

The feature of a hive-down which makes it similar to an asset transfer is that only those assets (and liabilities) which the seller wishes to sell and which the buyer wishes to buy will be hived down. Unlike a normal share sale, the buyer will not need to worry about liabilities, whether known or hidden; the company it is buying will be 'clean' as it will have no history. It is principally for this reason that hive-downs are popular with receivers, liquidators and administrators of insolvent companies in the UK; they are able to attract buyers by hiving down only the profitable parts of the business to be passed on to the buyer, who need not be unduly worried about the past troubles of the insolvent company. Hive-downs are by no means restricted to this situation, however. Where a buyer wishes to buy one of several businesses owned by a company, and a straightforward share sale is therefore not possible or desirable, a hive-down structure can prove a viable alternative which may suit both parties.

1.4.3 A hive-up

The converse of a hive-down is a hive-up where, broadly, instead of acquiring a new company, the buyer purchases an existing company from which assets that the buyer does not wish to acquire are hived up (ie transferred) to the target's parent company or possibly another group company. Unwanted assets are therefore removed or disposed of from the target. This results in the target again being 'clean' insofar as it contains only the assets that the buyer wants.

Taxation factors will typically influence the nature and extent of any hive-up or hive-down pre-sale structuring.

THE ACQUISITION PROCESS

LEARNING OUTCOMES

After reading this chapter you will be able to:

- understand the roles of the advisers involved in an acquisition
- describe the impact of merger control provisions on a proposed deal
- explain the usual structure of an acquisition transaction
- appreciate the differences between a private sale and sale by auction
- explain the purposes of the various pre-contractual documents.

2.1 ROLE OF ADVISERS

At the outset of a proposed acquisition, the buyer, the seller, and even the target company, will consider the appointment of a group of professional advisers to assist in the proposed transaction. This team usually includes at least legal advisers and accountants, but often also includes other professional advisers such as financiers and business advisers, and specialist advisers such as patent agents and actuaries. This acquisition team must work as a cohesive body, and it is often the legal advisers who undertake to co-ordinate matters whilst translating specialist advice into appropriate legal documentation.

On a cross-border acquisition, there will also be advisers from other jurisdictions to co-ordinate. This process may be easier where a single firm with offices in the relevant jurisdictions has been appointed, but this may not always provide the best service for the client. On some transactions, it may be more appropriate to appoint a particular foreign firm if it has specific expertise or has a particularly close relationship with the client. In dealing with multiple advisers across various jurisdictions, certain practical issues should be addressed, such as language and time differences. There may also be practical matters arising from different legal systems, such as the effect on the acquisition timetable of a consent requirement or the need for a notarised document.

2.1.1 Lawyer's role

The extent of a lawyer's involvement in an acquisition is dependent upon the instructions of the client and varies from case to case. The objective which the parties' lawyers will be expected to achieve is the legal transfer of ownership from seller to buyer either of the shares or of the assets of the business, as appropriate. The client will also expect their lawyers to identify risks of a legal nature and to seek to protect the client from those risks as far as possible.

It is the lawyer's input into the commercial (as opposed to purely legal) aspects of the transaction which varies enormously in practice. The stage at which the client instructs the lawyer tends to be equally variable. These two factors are often linked, in that if the client sees the lawyer's role as excluding the commercial side of the transaction, the client may instruct the lawyer only at a relatively late stage in proceedings, perhaps after the substance of the deal has been negotiated.

The reality is, however, that it is difficult to isolate the legal aspects from the commercial aspects, and it is for this reason that most lawyers prefer to be involved as early as possible in the parties' negotiations. This is particularly so where the lawyer is asked to give taxation advice in relation to the acquisition. The way the acquisition is structured can have a significant bearing on the parties' tax position; if the client delays in instructing the lawyer, it may be too late to choose the most tax-effective method. The lawyer will also wish to ensure that their client does not enter into any binding commitments and that all negotiations are subject to contract. Lastly, in the UK there is a danger that, if the lawyer is not instructed at an early stage, the client may inadvertently commit a breach of the FSMA 2000 (see **9.2.1**).

2.1.2   Accountant's role

The precise roles of accountants acting for the parties in an acquisition vary considerably. Indeed, the client may instruct more than one firm of accountants and assign a different role to each firm. Accountants will often be instructed by the buyer at an early stage of a proposed acquisition to help determine the value of the target and the cost of undertaking the acquisition. In addition they will be asked to identify any potential financial and taxation risks, and may also offer advice on the most efficient way to structure the proposed acquisition from a finance and tax point of view.

2.1.2.1   Valuing the target

The seller's accountant may be asked to put a value on the assets of the target business or company, which can be used as a starting point for negotiations with potential buyers. The buyer's accountant will go through a similar exercise on behalf of their client, and the accountant's valuation will determine the parameters within which the buyer is prepared to negotiate.

The value of the business is, of course, what a buyer is prepared to pay for it, which itself depends on the buyer's motives for acquiring it. For example, the buyer's principal motive may be to prevent the target from being acquired by a competitor; or the buyer may wish to acquire a competitor in order to reduce competition, or to acquire a supplier in order to protect the source of supply. In these instances, a valuation based on established principles is unlikely to coincide with the worth of the business to the buyer. Similarly, the seller may have their own special reasons for selling which may impact more on the negotiations than a formal valuation.

A detailed analysis of the principles of valuation is outside the scope of this book. However, it is important that the parties' lawyers understand the basis on which any valuations have been undertaken, as this can have an important effect on the provisions which are included in the main sale and purchase agreement.

The two main categories of valuation are assets-based valuations and earnings-based valuations.

Assets-based valuation

A valuation based solely on the net assets of the target is rare as it will not usually reflect the true value of the target as a going concern. It is appropriate on an asset sale of an ongoing business only in so far as the valuation includes a figure for goodwill, and the valuation of this intangible asset is itself likely to be earnings based (see below).

Whether it is the assets of a business or the shares of a company being acquired, an assessment of the asset value of the business will often be included within the overall valuation. Where a company is in financial difficulty or has been making consistently low profits, an asset-based valuation may be particularly useful as the 'break up' value of the business may be more than its value as a going concern. Also, certain types of company, such as property and investment companies, lend themselves more easily to this method of valuation.

Earnings-based valuation

The potential of the target to generate profits in the future is the crucial factor in an earnings-based valuation. The main pointer towards this potential is the level of profit achieved by the target in the years leading up to the proposed earnings. Appropriate adjustments to the profit figures appearing in the accounts will be necessary, however, when using these historical figures to forecast future profits. For example, the profits may be significantly understated for this purpose if the award of large salaries to directors, who are also shareholders, has been used as the main method of extracting profits from the company. On the other hand, profits may be overstated where, for example, goods or services have been supplied to the target on favourable terms by connected persons and these arrangements will discontinue after completion.

The next stage is to apply a multiplier to the figure reached above in an attempt to capitalise the future profit-generating capacity of the target. Sometimes, in determining the appropriate multiplier, the valuer will have recourse to information published about comparable quoted companies in the same industry.

There are several other methods of valuing the target which will be appropriate in specific circumstances, and there are additional factors involved when valuing holdings of shares of less than 100%.

Valuations for auction bids – debt free/cash free

Where the target is being sold at auction, accountants may also be asked to prepare a valuation for an indicative bid (see **2.4.2.3**). The bids on an auction often have to be put forward on the basis that the buyer will have to refinance any of the company's existing borrowings that remain after all available cash in the company has been applied to the repayment of those borrowings. This is known as a 'debt free/cash free' price, and means that the auction bids will be based chiefly on the inherent value of the target as derived from profit forecasts and cash flow statements.

2.1.2.2 Completion accounts

Where the price of the target has been arrived at on the basis of either net assets or profits, the parties may not wish to rely on out-of-date audited accounts or unaudited management accounts containing this information. In these circumstances, the sale and purchase agreement will usually provide for the drawing up of completion accounts following completion. If the 'net assets' or 'earnings' are not as anticipated, an appropriate adjustment will need to be made to the price (see **4.3.4**). In addition, if a price has been agreed on a debt free/cash free basis for an auction, an adjustment will need to be made to reflect the actual amount of net debt in the company when the acquisition is completed.

Details of who will prepare the completion accounts, and the basis on which they will be drawn up, will be set out in the sale and purchase agreement. Who prepares the completion accounts will often be a point of negotiation between the parties. The buyer will want its own accountants to prepare the accounts to ensure verification of the agreed price, but the seller will also argue that its accountant should prepare the accounts as the target company's auditors. The agreement will also set out a mechanism for both the seller's and the buyer's accountants to agree upon the completion accounts and, if they cannot reach agreement, it is usually provided that the dispute be referred to an independent accountant.

Where the valuation of the target is based on its future profit-generating capacity, the parties may agree that some of the consideration will be deferred until after completion, the amount then payable being calculated by reference to profits actually achieved for specified periods after completion (this is called an 'earn out' agreement and is discussed in detail in **4.3.4.2**). These arrangements will again involve input from both parties' accountants in advising on the details of the scheme to be included in the sale and purchase agreement and, once again, in preparing and agreeing accounts for the periods concerned.

2.1.2.3 Investigation and report

The prospective buyer will often commission a full accountant's investigation and report into the affairs of the target business or company before committing itself to the acquisition. This aspect is dealt with in **Chapter 3**.

2.1.3 Engagement letters

In larger transactions, professional advisers are often appointed through 'engagement letters' clarifying the terms of their appointment. Accountants have been using engagement letters for large transactions for many years, and the practice has now extended to legal advisers, financial advisers and banks. Engagement letters may also be required by other advisers who are involved in investigating the target, such as patent agents, actuaries and environmental specialists.

An engagement letter usually has three main purposes, as set out below.

2.1.3.1 Identify areas of responsibility

The letter will usually specify the scope of the work the adviser has agreed to undertake, together with agreed procedures for co-ordinating this with the work of other advisers. There is usually a reference to one group of advisers (often the solicitors) having been appointed to co-ordinate the advice. The appointment of a co-ordinator is essential in cross-border transactions as professional advisers from various legal systems and working in various time-zones will be advising on the acquisition.

2.1.3.2 Agreement on fees

The letter will also set out the agreement as to fees. If the advice is being given in relation to an auction bid (see **2.4.2**), there may be an adjustment of fees if the bid proves to be unsuccessful.

2.1.3.3 Statement as to liability

An indemnity in favour of the adviser for losses arising from its appointment other than as a result of its negligence will also form part of the letter. This is to avoid the potentially high claims that may arise if the acquisition proceeds without a particular problem having been identified.

2.2 MERGER CONTROL

At the outset of an acquisition transaction, consideration should be given to whether there are any potential legal barriers to the proposed sale or purchase. In particular, both parties' lawyers must consider whether the proposed acquisition is likely to be affected by the provisions of EU or UK law, or the laws of any other EU Member State or non-EU state, that seek to control 'mergers'. The term 'merger' in this context covers share sales and asset sales, but it is generally only large-scale transactions that are affected. This is not to say, however, that merger control is limited to listed companies; it may well apply to acquisitions of sufficient importance involving private companies.

The parties to a merger can notify the relevant authorities either in advance of completion or post-completion. In practice they often notify in advance if referral, for example to the UK Competition and Markets Authority (CMA), is a real possibility.

2.2.1 UK merger control

Mergers are regulated in the UK by the Enterprise Act 2002 (EA 2002) (as amended by the Enterprise and Regulatory Reform Act 2013) and in the EU by European Regulation 139/2004 (if the merger has a 'Union dimension' (see **2.2.2.3**)).

2.2.1.1 When will an acquisition be controlled by the EA 2002?

The merger control provisions of the EA 2002 will apply to a transaction if:

(a)   two or more enterprises cease to be distinct;

(b)   the time limit for a reference to the CMA has not yet expired; and

(c)   either:

    (i)   the market share test, or

    (ii)   the turnover test,

    is fulfilled.

Two or more enterprises cease to be distinct

Enterprise   Section 129(1) of the EA 2002 provides that an 'enterprise' is the activities, or part of the activities, of a business. 'Business' in this context includes an undertaking carried on for gain or reward, or in the course of which goods or services are supplied otherwise than free of charge.

At least one of the enterprises must be carried on in the UK (or by, or under the control of, a body corporate which is incorporated in the UK).

Ceasing to be distinct   Enterprises cease to be distinct if either:

(a)   they are brought under common ownership or control; or

(b)   one of the enterprises ceases to be carried on at all pursuant to some arrangement entered into to prevent competition between the enterprises.

Most typical share sale and asset sale arrangements clearly come within this definition.

The time limit for a reference has not expired

If more than four months have elapsed since the merger took place then normally no reference to the CMA will be possible (EA 2002, s 24).

The market share test and turnover test

For a merger to be caught by the legislation, either of the following must apply:

(a)   the merger will result in at least 25% of all goods or services of a particular description which are supplied in the UK, or a substantial part of it, being supplied by or to the same person (or, if this was already the case before the merger, then after the merger the enterprise acquires an even greater share of the market) (the 'market share' test); or

(b)   the value of the annual turnover in the UK of the enterprise being taken over exceeds £70 million (the 'turnover' test).

The 'market share' test involves an assessment of when goods or services are of a separate description and, accordingly, form a distinct market. This makes it very difficult for the parties' advisers to be certain when the criterion is met. Where the market for particular goods or services is small, acquisitions which are relatively minor in terms of overall value may, nevertheless, be the subject of regulation.

If a target enterprise carries out activities relating to certain military sector activities, quantum technology, computer processing or certain goods subject to export control, the threshold for the 'turnover test' may be reduced from £70 million to £1 million and the 'market share test' may be satisfied by the target enterprise alone meeting the 25% test prior to the merger. It should be noted, however, that these provisions have been made largely redundant by the National Security and Investment Act 2021 (see **2.2.1.4**) which introduced wide-ranging regulation of investments in sectors such as those mentioned above.

2.2.1.2   UK merger control procedure

The UK competition law regime was reformed by the Enterprise and Regulatory Reform Act 2013 (ERRA 2013), which came into force on 1 April 2014. The ERRA 2013 amends both the Competition Act 1998 and the EA 2002.

The EA 2002 established a two-stage voluntary merger notification regime whereby the parties to a merger could first refer the transaction to the Office of Fair Trading (OFT) for an initial investigation and informal guidance on whether the deal was likely to raise competition concerns (Phase 1). Where it believed that the merger posed a real prospect of a substantial lessening of competition, the OFT then had a duty to refer the transaction on to the Competition Commission for further investigation and formal clearance (Phase 2).

Under the new regime, the two-stage review process remains but is now carried out by the CMA. The OFT and the Competition Commission were abolished by the ERRA 2013. A new statutory timetable was introduced, and the CMA has wider powers than the previous governing bodies to request information during the review process, and to make interim orders (such as suspending all integration steps until clearance has been given).

A pre-notification period of informal discussions with the CMA is both usual and advisable, in particular to establish the level of information that the CMA will require in order to conduct the investigation efficiently. Parties wishing to notify formally then do so by serving a Merger Notice on the CMA containing, amongst other details, the information mentioned in the pre-notification discussions.

Phase 1 decisions are taken by the CMA board, which has a period of 40 working days to conduct its investigation and reach a conclusion. The period starts to run when the CMA confirms that the information it has is sufficient. There is no power for the CMA to extend this deadline, but it does have the power to 'stop the clock' if parties fail to comply with formal information requests.

Phase 2 decisions are made by an inquiry group of at least three people selected from the independent experts appointed to the CMA's panel by the Secretary of State. Phase 2 investigations must be completed within 24 weeks of the date the reference is made, though this time limit is subject to a possible eight-week extension. Parties to a merger transaction that is likely to become the subject of a Phase 2 investigation will have to bear these time scales in mind when planning the transaction timetable.

At the end of both a Phase 1 and a Phase 2 investigation, the CMA has power to discuss remedies with the parties to the merger. The parties may decide to offer formal undertakings to the CMA if this will secure approval for the transaction. An undertaking to sell off parts of the target after completion, for example, may mean that the merger will no longer lead to a substantial lessening of competition and can therefore be given clearance by the CMA.

2.2.1.3   Amendments to UK merger control procedure and thresholds

Changes to merger thresholds are expected. Following a consultation during 2021, the government announced on 20 April 2022 a number of amendments that it seeks to make to the UK's competition and merger regimes, including changes to merger thresholds (namely, increasing the annual turnover test (as described at **2.2.1.1** above) from £70 million to £100 million) and the introduction of a new 'safe harbour' exemption from requiring CMA approval if each party to a merger has less than £10 million UK turnover, in order to reduce the burden on small businesses. The amendments also intend to expand the jurisdiction of the CMA by introducing a further threshold triggering review by the CMA where a buyer has both (a) an existing 33% (or more) share of the supply of goods or services in the UK, and (b) UK turnover is greater than £350 million. Specific details of the amendments are awaited as is the timeline for their introduction.

2.2.1.4 National Security and Investment Act 2021

Operating independently of the CMA's merger control rules, a new regime under the National Security and Investment Act 2021 has recently been introduced. The Act gives the UK government the ability to scrutinise and intervene in acquisitions or mergers that threaten national security. Transactions could potentially be blocked or have conditions imposed upon them. The Act came into force on 4 January 2022 and, crucially, also has retrospective effect. Transactions that completed after 12 November 2020 are caught by the new regime.

The Act applies to any business of any size in any sector and to both UK and non-UK acquirors, and so it is wide reaching. Under the new regime, a combination of voluntary and mandatory notification prior to the completion of transactions is introduced, with proposed acquisitions of target companies or businesses operating in certain 'high risk' industry sectors (such as civil nuclear, communications, data infrastructure, defence and military and dual-use technologies) requiring mandatory notification to the government, given the perceived heightened national security risks such industry sectors involve. It is understood that the first transaction to be blocked under the new regime was one involving the licensing of IP by the University of Manchester to Beijing Infinite Vision Technology Company Ltd, a transaction where vision sensing technology was considered to have potential in defence products and thus posed national security risks warranting intervention.

As further guidance on the Act is published by the government and other bodies, the extent of the Act will become better known and in turn compliance with its provisions will become a further consideration in future acquisitions of a UK company or business. For example, to assist private equity firms in their acquisitions, the British Private Equity and Venture Capital Association (BVCA) has published guidance on the impact of the Act on acquisition transactions.

It should be noted that the UK is not alone in the introduction of such an interventionist regime. In recent years, similar regimes have emerged in other countries as national security concerns have become more prominent. National security has, as a result, become an additional requirement for parties to any acquisition to consider.

It should be noted that, separately, other measures were announced by the UK government in June 2020 to amend the Enterprise Act 2002. The amendments introduced by the Enterprise Act 2002 (Specification of Additional Section 58 Consideration) Order 2020 allow the UK government to intervene on public interest grounds in any transaction falling within the UK merger control regime where a UK business that is considered important to efforts to combat public health emergencies is the subject of a takeover. Comparable reforms have been introduced in several other countries in response to the Covid-19 pandemic.

2.2.2 European merger control

2.2.2.1 European Regulation 139/2004

The EU Merger Regulation will apply if the merger constitutes a *concentration* with a *Union dimension*. Until the UK's exit from the EU, if the merger fulfilled these criteria then, subject to limited exceptions, the EU Merger Regulation applied to the exclusion of any national competition law rules and the merger fell within the exclusive jurisdiction of the European Commission. This was intended to relieve the burden on the parties to the merger, by reducing the number of regulatory authorities to which they were subject. For this reason the EU Merger Regulation is often referred to as 'the one-stop shop'. If the merger does not fulfil these criteria then it falls outside the scope of the EU Merger Regulation, but it may still be caught by domestic merger control rules (see **2.2.1**).

Following the UK's departure from the EU on 31 January 2020 (an event referred to as 'Brexit'), the EU Merger Regulation ceases to be, at least insofar as the UK is concerned, a 'one-stop shop', because the UK's CMA is no longer precluded from taking jurisdiction over UK qualifying mergers which also meet the EU Merger Regulation's thresholds (as explained below). As a result, following Brexit, UK merging parties may need to notify the CMA as well as the European Commission.

2.2.2.2 Concentration

Article 3 of the EU Merger Regulation provides that a concentration can arise where a change of control on a lasting basis results from:

(a)   the merger of two or more previously independent undertakings or parts of undertakings; or

(b)   the acquisition of direct or indirect control of the whole or part of an undertaking or undertakings.

'Control', in the context of the EU Merger Regulation, is widely defined and means more than just voting control. It includes, for example, the situation where one party can exercise 'decisive influence' over another. A 25% holding may, therefore, constitute control for the purposes of the EU Merger Regulation. Acquisition is also widely defined to comprise a direct financial purchase by contract, a purchase of shares or securities or any other resources.

2.2.2.3 Union dimension

Article 1 provides that a concentration will have a Union dimension if, subject to the two-thirds rule (see below), it fulfils certain turnover criteria. There are two alternative sets of criteria to consider, namely:

Under Article 1(2):

(a)   the combined aggregate worldwide turnover of all the undertakings concerned exceeds €5,000 million; and

(b)   the aggregate Union-wide turnover of each of at least two of the undertakings concerned exceeds €250 million.

Under Article 1(3):

(a)   the combined aggregate worldwide turnover of all the undertakings concerned is more than €2,500 million;

(b)   in each of at least three Member States, the combined aggregate turnover of all the undertakings concerned is more than €100 million;

(c)   in each of at least three Member States included for the purpose of point (b), the aggregate turnover of each of at least two of the undertakings concerned is more than €25 million; and

(d)   the aggregate Union-wide turnover of each of at least two of the undertakings concerned is more than €100 million.

Following Brexit, turnover generated in the UK will not be included as part of Union-wide turnover calculations.

Note that even if the merger does not have a Union dimension, the EU Merger Regulation provides that the parties can request the European Commission to take jurisdiction over the transaction if the merger is capable of being reviewed under the national competition laws of at least three Member States.

The two-thirds rule

A concentration will not have a Union dimension if each of the undertakings concerned achieves more than two-thirds of its aggregate Union-wide turnover within one and the same

Member State. This means, practically, that if the main impact of the merger is within one Member State, it will not have a Union dimension. It may, of course, still be caught by the national competition rules of that Member State.

Practically, it can be helpful, when calculating whether a merger falls within the jurisdiction of the Commission, to check whether the two-thirds rule applies *before* applying the Union dimension tests above. If the two-thirds rule applies, the Commission will not have jurisdiction, and so there is no need to apply the other tests.

2.2.2.4   Notification

If the merger constitutes a concentration with a Union dimension then the EU Merger Regulation provides that the parties must notify the European Commission before completion. The merger cannot complete until the European Commission clears it. The notification should answer the Commission's questionnaire, Form CO, which requires considerable information about the parties and the transaction. Form CO is annexed to Regulation 802/2004/EC, which implements the EU Merger Regulation. A Short Form CO and a simplified procedure may be followed if certain conditions are met (chiefly where the merger is unlikely to raise significant competition concerns). The European Commission widened the scope of the simplified procedure with effect from 1 January 2014 such that an estimated 60–70% of all notified mergers are now able to benefit from a more streamlined process, and a 'super-simplified' notification procedure exists for joint ventures operating outside the EEA.

From notification the Commission has 25 working days to decide that:

(a)   it does not have jurisdiction because the merger does not fall within the scope of the EU Merger Regulation; or

(b)   it will clear the transaction (because it does not create or strengthen a dominant position in any relevant Union market); or

(c)   it will investigate the transaction further (because it has serious concerns that it may create or strengthen a dominant position in any relevant Union market).

If the Commission decides to investigate the merger then, after a further period of time for that investigation, it must decide either;

(a)   to clear the merger; or

(b)   to allow the merger to proceed subject to certain conditions; or

(c)   to block the merger.

2.2.2.5   Exceptions

As mentioned at **2.2.2.1** above, until the UK's withdrawal from the EU, the EU Merger Regulation operated as a 'one-stop shop' and applied to the exclusion of any national competition laws. However, a Member State could nevertheless intervene to request repatriation of a case if it could demonstrate to the Commission that a reference back to the national authorities was necessary:

(a)   to protect legitimate interests (such as national security); or

(b)   because the merger threatened significantly to affect competition in a distinct market within that Member State (art 9).

Following the UK's withdrawal from the EU, the 'one-stop' shop' no longer applies to the UK (but does continue to apply and be available to remaining EU Member States). In relation to the UK, mergers that are caught by the EU Merger Regulation are now likely to also be reviewed by the UK's CMA.

2.2.3 Merger control in other jurisdictions

Even where the EU Merger Regulation does not apply, the proposed acquisition may still be subject to the merger control regime of one or more EU Member States or to the many other systems of merger control in countries outside the European Union. Over 60 nations worldwide have adopted a form of merger control, with more on the way. Many of these systems of merger control are based upon the EU Merger Regulation, although different substantive and procedural systems can make obtaining clearance for a multi-jurisdictional transaction complex, expensive and time-consuming.

In the US, the Clayton Act is the principal statute governing the substantive issues raised by mergers and acquisitions. It prohibits acquisitions where the effect of such acquisition may be substantially to lessen competition or to tend to create a monopoly.

The Hart-Scott-Rodino Antitrust Improvements Act (the 'HSR Act') sets out the procedural elements of the US Government assessment of mergers and acquisitions.

In the US, 'business combinations' over a certain size are subject to the HSR Act, which requires that a notification about the combination be submitted to the Federal Trade Commission (FTC) and the Antitrust Division of the Department of Justice (DOJ). The combination may only be implemented if the FTC and the DOJ raise no objection within the relevant waiting period. An initial waiting period, usually of 30 days, provides the FTC and DOJ with an opportunity to request additional information. Such a request extends the waiting period, usually to 30 days from the date on which the requested information is supplied. If the FTC and DOJ fail to raise an objection within the waiting period, the combination may proceed. In addition, sales of businesses involving industries which are important to national defence may be subject to additional requirements under the Exon-Florio Amendment to the Defense Production Act 1950 and the Foreign Investment Risk Review Modernization Act 2018.

2.2.4 Implications of Brexit

On 31 January 2020, the UK ceased being an EU Member State. However, until the end of the transition period on 31 December 2020 ('the Brexit transition period'), the UK was treated as if it remained a full member of the EU and the rules on competition law applies unchanged. The transition period is also known as the 'implementation period', and 31 December 2020 is referred to as 'implementation period completion day'. The end of the Brexit transition period on 31 December 2020 is when divergence between the UK and EU competition law systems may begin.

However, from a practical point of view, the extent of divergence may well be limited. EU rules, and in particular EU competition rules insofar as they related to merger control, will continue to govern how businesses, including UK businesses, compete in the EU. Given this, UK competition authorities may be slow to introduce inconsistencies that would make it difficult for businesses to operate across borders.

For a detailed explanation of what the potential implications on merger control could entail, the reader is referred to *Competition Law*.

2.3 PROCEDURAL OVERVIEW

No two acquisitions are the same. However, a typical acquisition – whether of assets or shares – can be broken down into the same five distinct stages: pre-contract; contract; pre-completion; completion (often referred to as 'closing'); and post-completion. In practice, though, contract and completion often take place simultaneously so that the pre-completion stage disappears. The requirements for conditional contracts are covered in detail in **Chapter** 7.

2.3.1 Pre-contract

Very few acquisitions will proceed immediately to an exchange of contracts. The buyer will usually make thorough investigations of the target business and the terms of the proposed purchase will be negotiated. The parties will follow accepted procedures for the investigations and negotiations, and often will agree preliminary documentation that governs their relationship during this pre-contract stage.

2.3.1.1 Heads of agreement (exclusivity and terms)

Before committing to the time and expense of detailed negotiations, the buyer and seller may wish to record the main points on which they have agreed and the basis on which they are prepared to proceed with the transaction. The principal commercial terms of the proposed acquisition may therefore be set out in a 'heads of agreement' (sometimes also called a 'letter of intent'), and this document may also provide for an agreed period of exclusive negotiation. The agreement as to commercial terms is not intended to be legally binding but will serve as an outline of the parties' intentions and as a starting point for negotiation of the sale and purchase agreement (see **2.5.2**).

In the US, the same type of agreement is used, but it is more commonly called a letter of intent or memorandum of understanding.

In civil code jurisdictions, for example, France, Germany and some Latin American countries like Argentina, such agreements may be entered into between the parties but these may give rise to a pre-contractual relationship resulting in a duty of good faith between the parties (see **2.5.2.1**).

2.3.1.2 Confidentiality agreement

Both parties will usually want to keep the terms of the deal (and even the existence of it) confidential. In addition, the seller must also protect any confidential information passed to the buyer during its investigation of the target. To this end, the parties will enter into a confidentiality, or non-disclosure, agreement specifying the parties' obligations in relation to the confidential information, procedures for handling it, and remedies for breach (see **2.5.1**).

Even with a confidentiality agreement in place, the seller is well advised to restrict the disclosure of commercially sensitive information. The extent to which the seller is prepared to disclose such information and the timing of the disclosure depends on the nature of the business, the type of information requested and the identity of the buyer.

2.3.1.3 Due diligence

Before the buyer enters into a contractual commitment to buy the assets or the company, it should acquire as much information about the business as is possible in the circumstances (time constraints and expense being the main limiting factors). The process by which detailed information about the target is obtained and assessed is called due diligence and is considered in detail in **Chapter 3**. The information obtained through due diligence will help the buyer to decide whether it wants to proceed with the purchase and, if so, at what price and on what terms. On larger transactions the buyer's lawyers will prepare a due diligence report highlighting the main areas of risk identified by the investigations and how such risks may be minimised by the inclusion of appropriate terms in the sale and purchase agreement (see **3.6**).

2.3.1.4 Drafting and negotiation of contract terms

The draft documents implementing the sale and purchase of the target will be negotiated between the parties until a final form of each agreement is settled. Understandably, the initial draft is likely to favour heavily the party producing it. For example, the main sale and purchase agreement, prepared by the buyer's lawyers, is likely to contain few limitations on the seller's liability for breaches of warranty; it will be for the seller's lawyers to negotiate additions to this section of the agreement.

Negotiation of the various transaction documents may involve other advisers from the acquisition team. For example, detailed amendments to taxation warranties may be made by tax specialists within the lawyer's firm, or by the accountant member of the team, or both.

2.3.2   Contract

When both parties are prepared to commit themselves contractually to effect the acquisition, they will enter into a sale and purchase agreement. At the same time, the seller will hand over a disclosure letter to the buyer.

2.3.2.1   Sale and purchase agreement

In England and Wales, the first draft of the sale and purchase agreement is usually prepared by the buyer's lawyers and is then submitted to the seller's lawyers for approval/negotiation. In the agreement, the parties will agree to transfer title to the shares (share acquisition) or the assets of the business (asset acquisition). This aspect of the agreement tends to be short; nevertheless, the agreement will invariably be very lengthy (particularly on a share transfer) as a result of the protections sought by the buyer in the form of warranties and indemnities from the seller. On a share acquisition the whole company is acquired, including its tax liabilities, and there will usually be a separate Tax Covenant by which the seller agrees to indemnify the buyer for any tax costs which arise as a result of events occurring prior to the sale of the company.

In some civil code jurisdictions, the first draft is prepared by the seller outlining the basis on which the seller is prepared to offer the shares or assets for sale. This also applies in England and Wales where the target is being offered for sale by way of an auction.

2.3.2.2   Disclosure letter/schedule

The disclosure letter, which is closely linked to the sale and purchase agreement and in many jurisdictions is incorporated into the agreement, is prepared by the seller's lawyers. The purpose of this document is to disclose matters relating to the target and its affairs which, were they to remain undisclosed, would result in the seller being in breach of warranty. The seller attaches copies of documents referred to in the letter (the 'disclosure bundle') and this can make it a lengthy document.

The disclosure letter may be written by the seller or by the seller's lawyers. In the latter case it should incorporate an appropriate disclaimer that all information has been provided by the client and that the lawyers accept no responsibility for its contents. The letter is handed to the buyer at the same time as the parties enter into the sale and purchase agreement. It has such an important bearing on the seller's potential liability under the agreement that the seller's lawyers should send it to their opposite numbers in draft form well in advance of this; a final version will be negotiated and agreed by the parties' lawyers in much the same way as the sale and purchase agreement itself. Indeed, the disclosures may prompt the buyer to renegotiate the deal (perhaps asking for a reduction in the price), or to seek to include further protections in the main agreement, usually by way of specific indemnities.

In many civil code jurisdictions, such as Germany, it is not customary to prepare a separate disclosure letter. The information contained in the disclosure letter would normally be included within a schedule to the sale and purchase agreement.

The approach to disclosure is different in the US. The disclosure letter is not used to qualify the effect of the warranties by disclosing information which would otherwise result in the seller being in breach of a warranty. In the US, the seller will include specific, stated exceptions to the warranties in schedules to the sale and purchase agreement which are cross-referenced to the warranty that they qualify (see **6.3**).

2.3.3 Pre-completion

Completion normally – and indeed ideally – takes place immediately after the sale and purchase agreement has been signed (simultaneous exchange and completion). However, there may be a gap between exchange of contracts and completion where, for example, the parties enter into the sale and purchase agreement with completion conditional upon the happening of certain events (see **7.1**). After exchange of contracts, the parties will chiefly be concerned with satisfaction of the completion conditions and confirmation that the intervening period has seen no change in the general state of the assets or the company (see **7.2**).

2.3.4 Completion

On completion, title to the assets which are the subject of the acquisition is formally transferred by the seller to the buyer in return for the buyer providing the purchase price or consideration. Completion procedures will vary from jurisdiction to jurisdiction.

On a share sale in England and Wales, the seller's lawyers will hand over duly signed stock transfer forms, and there will be a completion board meeting of the target company to deal with such matters as the resignation and appointment of directors and the approval of the share transfers (see **7.3.3**). The method by which completion takes place will normally be included as a clause of the sale and purchase agreement itself. Where the companies involved are based in multiple jurisdictions, the language of the completion clause is likely to be suitably generic, referring to such steps as are necessary in each jurisdiction concerned in order to effect the transfer of shares. Provisions dealing with what is to happen on completion are negotiated by the parties, and any documents to be executed at completion will be referred to in the sale and purchase agreement as being in the 'agreed form', and will often be annexed to or contained in schedules to that agreement (see **7.3.3**).

On an asset sale, the individual assets must be transferred in the manner appropriate for that asset. Any land which is included in the sale must be transferred by deed (assignment, transfer or conveyance as appropriate). Assignment of certain intellectual property rights (eg copyrights, patents and trademarks) is necessary. Goodwill and the benefit of contracts may also be formally assigned. On the other hand, no formal documentation is required to transfer title to assets such as loose plant and machinery and stock – title to these passes on delivery (see **7.3.1**).

2.3.5 Post-completion

On a share sale for a company registered in England and Wales, the buyer's lawyers will ensure that stock transfer forms are duly stamped; that the internal registers of the target company are updated, to reflect, for example, the change in members and directors; and that the appropriate information (eg on a change of director) is filed at the Companies Registry (see **7.4**). On an asset sale involving the transfer of land, the buyer's lawyer must make appropriate registrations at Land Registry.

The buyer may also need to take further steps to incorporate the acquired assets or company into its existing business organisation. Those steps may involve changes to the constitution of the target company, or transfer of ownership or licences in respect of particular assets.

These post-completion formalities will vary in each jurisdiction according to the required method of transfer. For example, in Germany there is no payment of stamp duty and there are no formal internal company registers (except for share registers for some AGs). The buyer's lawyers will only have to file management changes to the commercial register. In the Netherlands, similar registration requirements need to be fulfilled.

2.4 METHODS OF SALE

In some acquisition transactions the buyer and seller will already be known to one another. Usually, however, a seller will seek out buyers, or a buyer may seek out a company or business that meets its particular requirements. A seller of shares or assets must decide which is the more appropriate method of sale, there being essentially two options:

(a) *Private arrangement.* A buyer for the assets or shares may be sought either directly by the seller or by an intermediary such as a financial adviser, bank or accountant.

(b) *Auction sale.* The seller can hold an auction sale, and is likely to do so if it believes it will receive a number of competing bids. The use of the auction procedure often leads to a higher price for the seller, who may also find it has greater control over the terms on which it will sell. However, if there are only one or two potential buyers, or if the structure of the proposed acquisition is complicated, an auction sale may not be appropriate. In addition, it is clearly more difficult to keep the transaction confidential where there will be a sale by auction.

Auction sales became popular in the strong seller's market of the mid-2000s and a number of protocols were established. The accepted auction procedure is just a variation of the traditional private sale procedure. The essential elements of the pre-contract stage, such as agreeing confidentiality, investigating the target and negotiating favourable terms within the sale and purchase agreement, all remain the same, regardless of the method of sale.

2.4.1 Private sale

Where the buyer and seller are already known to each other, they will often have agreed the main commercial terms of the proposed acquisition, and possibly an agreed period of exclusive negotiations, before instructing lawyers. These main terms and any rights as to exclusivity of bargaining may be included in a heads of agreement, often prepared by the buyer or its lawyers (see **2.3.1.1**).

The buyer will also initiate enquiries about the target company or assets, often by issuing a comprehensive, and sometimes lengthy, questionnaire to the seller. Before the seller will provide the information requested, an agreement as to confidentiality of both information and of the negotiations themselves will be concluded between the parties to the transaction. As the protection of confidential information is primarily of concern to the seller, the seller or its advisers will usually prepare the first draft of the confidentiality agreement.

On a private sale, the buyer's lawyers will usually provide the first draft of the contract documentation. Negotiation of the sale and purchase agreement will often run alongside the investigations into the target, with adjustments being made to it to provide for any risks identified during the investigation. The usual procedure for negotiating the contract documents on a private sale is as follows:

(a) The buyer's lawyer prepares the draft sale and purchase agreement. They submit this to their client and, with the client's agreement, forward it to the seller's lawyer.

(b) The seller's lawyer considers the draft sale and purchase agreement with their client and amends it, returning the amended draft to the buyer's lawyer.

(c) The seller's lawyer prepares a draft disclosure letter based on information provided by the seller which, after the seller has approved it, will be sent to the buyer's lawyer.

(d) The buyer's lawyer considers the draft disclosure letter with their client, and amends it appropriately, returning it to the seller's lawyer.

(e) Both parties' lawyers agree final versions of the sale and purchase agreement and the disclosure letter (there may have been many drafts before getting to this stage).

Each stage in the process will involve discussions with the other members of the acquisition team and will take into account further information ascertained through the buyer's due diligence investigations.

2.4.2   Variations for auction sale

On an auction sale the seller has greater control of the sale process, as it is the seller who will set out the terms on which it is offering the company or assets for sale. Although there is no set procedure for the auction process and the timing or order of events may vary, most auctions will tend to follow the following format.

2.4.2.1   Advertisement of sale

When a seller has decided that it wishes to proceed by way of an auction sale, the sale will be advertised to prospective buyers. The seller must decide to whom the proposed sale will be advertised. Under English law a private company is not permitted to offer its shares for sale to the general public (CA 2006, s 755(1)). However, an advertisement issued to prospective purchasers identified by the seller falls within an exception under CA 2006, s 756(3), as the advertisement is not regarded as resulting in the shares becoming available to persons other than those receiving the offer. The FSMA 2000 must also be taken into account in drafting the advertisement of the proposed auction, if the auction relates to a possible sale of shares.

The advertisement, or notice of sale, is a key disadvantage of the auction process as it will inevitably make the proposed sale public knowledge. This may be disruptive to the target's business, and the seller may face embarrassment if the auction does not lead to a sale.

A period of time will usually be fixed in the notice of sale by which notifications of interest in the proposed sale are to be received. The seller may also require prospective buyers to provide some form of confirmation of credible interest. The seller will respond to the notifications of interest either by admitting the relevant party to the auction, or by rejecting it. The parties who are admitted to the auction process will be sent confidentiality agreements to be signed. On an auction sale there is usually little negotiation of the confidentiality agreement, which will be signed in the seller's format provided that it does not contain any unreasonable or unworkable restrictions (see **2.5.1**).

2.4.2.2   Provision of information memorandum

On receipt of the signed confidentiality agreement, the seller will send out an 'information memorandum' together with a letter detailing the auction process. This 'process letter' will be drafted carefully to ensure it does not create a legally binding contract and will invite the recipients to submit indicative offers. The basis on which bids are to be made will be outlined to ensure that meaningful comparisons between the bids will be possible. In auction sales the seller will often require that bids are made on the basis that the target will be sold without finance. In other words, valuations for the bid will be made on an artificial assumption that the target has neither debt nor cash, giving what is commonly known as a 'debt free/cash free' price (see **2.1.2.1**). The process letter may also request information from the prospective buyers to enable the seller to assess whether any regulatory problems, such as merger clearance or other conditions, may inhibit the conclusion of the transaction with particular bidders.

The information memorandum is prepared by the seller's advisers and outlines key information about the target assets or company. It will usually contain details of the corporate structure, the main assets, methods of finance, the tax position, and may even identify potential liabilities. The kind of information included is usually that which would be requested by a buyer at the outset of its due diligence investigations (see **3.4.2**).

As well as providing information about the target, the information memorandum is a sales document identifying the strengths and weaknesses of the target business. Its strengths will be emphasised to demonstrate that the target is an attractive purchase, and its weaknesses may be presented as opportunities for a potential buyer to add value.

When preparing the information memorandum, the seller and its advisers must consider the consequences of including misleading or incorrect statements. The buyer will often seek a warranty in the final sale and purchase agreement as to the accuracy of any statements of fact or forecasts contained in the information memorandum. Although the seller may resist this on the basis that the information memorandum is a sales document and therefore only generally descriptive, such resistance is not always successful. In addition, if the information memorandum relates to a sale in a civil code jurisdiction then the document will also need to comply with any relevant obligation under the duty of good faith (see **2.5.2**).

If the information memorandum relates to the sale of shares, it will be subject to s 21 of the FSMA 2000 as an invitation to engage in an investment activity. However, where an invitation relates to the proposed acquisition of control of the company, an exemption is likely to be available under the FSMA 2000 (Financial Promotion) Order 2005 (SI 2005/1529).

2.4.2.3   Indicative bids and preferred bidders

Based on a review of the information memorandum, potential buyers will put in an 'indicative bid' to the seller by a stated deadline. On the basis of these indicative bids the seller will select a small number of preferred bidders. These are not always selected purely on the basis of price, as the seller will take into account such additional factors as the proposed methods of payment and the likely speed and success of the transaction. In some jurisdictions, a seller may be liable for damages if it does not consider all the bids that are submitted (unless it expressly states in the process letter that there is no obligation to do so).

As on a private sale, the group of preferred bidders may be given some reassurances as to exclusivity of negotiations for a set period of time (see **2.5.2.2**). Preferred bidders may also be given an assurance as to fees, whereby certain costs of the preferred bidder will be reimbursed in the event that its bid is not successful. Bidders may not be prepared to pursue the potential acquisition without some protection as to costs in the event that they are not selected as the final bidder.

2.4.2.4   Further investigations and terms of purchase

Preferred bidders will be given access to additional information about the target assets or business, often through access to a data room set up by the seller (see **3.4.3**). In some transactions, preferred bidders may be given the opportunity to ask further questions of the seller, and will often be subject to further selection before any access to confidential information is permitted. One of the main advantages of the auction process for the seller is that the due diligence process is under its control, whereas on a private sale it is usually driven by the buyer's enquiries.

On some auctions the seller will also take control of the terms of the sale and purchase agreement. Preferred bidders may be sent a first draft of the agreement prepared by the seller, setting out the terms on which it wishes to proceed with the sale. In contrast to the buyer's first draft on a private sale, this will be drafted in the seller's favour, and preferred bidders must indicate any required amendments. As part of the bidding process, preferred bidders may be asked to propose draft amendments to the seller's contract to give the seller an idea of the contractual terms upon which the bidders may be prepared to make a final offer.

2.4.2.5   Selection of buyer

The preferred bidders will be asked to submit a final bid based on the results of their further investigations and an outline of the contractual terms of the purchase. A single bidder will then be selected and the final negotiations, exchange of contractual documentation and completion of the acquisition will proceed as for a private sale.

2.5 PRE-CONTRACTUAL DOCUMENTATION

Whether the transaction proceeds as a private sale or an auction, the target company or assets must be investigated and the terms of the proposed sale and purchase agreement negotiated. As already discussed in this chapter, the parties will seek the reassurance of some preliminary documentation governing their respective obligations during this process.

2.5.1 Confidentiality agreement

At the outset of an acquisition transaction, the parties will enter into an agreement to try to protect confidential information that will inevitably pass between them during the negotiations. Indeed, the parties may wish to keep even the existence of the proposed acquisition itself a secret.

When the buyer undertakes its due diligence investigations, the seller will be expected to provide a wide variety of often commercially sensitive information. If the buyer is a competitor, the seller will be particularly concerned about revealing information such as customer lists and important contracts which the buyer may be able to use to its own advantage if the acquisition falls through. The seller is therefore advised to require the buyer to enter into a confidentiality (or 'non-disclosure') agreement before any sensitive information is released. As it is the seller who is most at risk from any potential misuse or release of information, the initial draft of the agreement is usually prepared by the seller or its advisers.

A confidentiality agreement will usually follow a standard format, but there may be some scope for negotiations as to the precise terms. From the seller's point of view, the agreement should cover as much information as possible, and should provide precise procedures for the use and safe-keeping of that information. By contrast, the buyer will seek to reduce restrictions imposed, particularly those with a cost implication. Accordingly, the buyer may prefer that the restrictions apply only to the most sensitive information, and it may not wish to agree to extensive procedures for tracking information in its possession.

In general terms a confidentiality agreement will usually include:

(a) a definition of confidential information (this is likely to exclude information in the public domain and information already known to the proposed buyer). The definition will include information obtained from the seller and its advisers, and should extend to any document prepared on the basis of this information by the buyer;

(b) an obligation on the buyer not, without the seller's consent, to disclose or use such information except for authorised purposes (as defined) in connection with the acquisition. A list of authorised persons entitled to receive the information, such as certain employees and professional advisers of the buyer, may be included (with an assurance by the buyer that it will notify them of the terms of the confidentiality agreement). In addition, the seller may prevent the buyer from soliciting customers, suppliers or employees of the target for a specified period (although care needs to be taken that these provisions are not void as being in restraint of trade);

(c) an undertaking by the buyer to return or destroy such information (including copies) if the acquisition does not proceed. If the information is particularly sensitive, agreed procedures for tracking it may also be included;

(d) an agreement that the parties will not, without the written consent of the other party, make any announcement or disclosure of the fact that negotiations are taking place.

The various undertakings of the buyer may be contained in a formal agreement between the parties or, quite commonly, in a letter to the seller. Whichever form is chosen, consideration must be given for this agreement to be enforceable, the usual consideration being the provision, by the seller, of the confidential information.

A confidentiality agreement provides comfort to a seller who is in a commercially sensitive position. Nevertheless, it may prove extremely difficult for the seller to monitor breaches and, indeed, to assess the loss where it can be proved that breaches have occurred. It is therefore important that the contractual obligations are supported by monitoring the buyer's procedures for handling the confidential information. In addition, wherever possible the release of sensitive information should be restricted. Some commercial information may be so sensitive that it should not be divulged to the buyer until the moment of exchange of contracts.

The concept of confidentiality agreements is widespread in civil and common law jurisdictions. Although the content of these agreements may be similar in many jurisdictions, consideration should be given to the duration of the agreement, any liquidation clauses and the wording of the confidentiality provisions. In addition, in certain jurisdictions, such as Italy, confidentiality is protected 'by law' under specific circumstances, even without the signing of a confidentiality agreement.

According to French law, no agreement can last for an indefinite period. Usually, confidentiality agreements governed by French law include a fixed term ranging from one to three years, although some agreements stipulate a longer term. Where a confidentiality agreement has no duration clause or explicitly states that the duration is indefinite, case law has ruled that the party bound has the right to terminate the agreement at any time subject to giving the other party the required advance notice.

Liquidated damages clauses are usually drafted in confidentiality agreements to help ensure the correct performance by the other party. As it is hard to evaluate the amount of damages which will result from a breach of a confidentiality agreement, in some jurisdictions, such as Germany, it is common to agree that a fixed amount will be paid as penalty for a breach. In many other jurisdictions, in the case of a dispute a court may review the liquidated damages clause and, if the court considers the amount too high, it may modify the amount as it deems necessary to compensate the non-breaching party.

2.5.2   Heads of agreement/letters of intent

Once negotiations have reached a certain point, the parties may wish to record the main points on which they have agreed and the basis on which they are prepared to proceed with the transaction. The parties often feel more confident that the whole exercise will not prove to be a waste of time, money and effort if they are able to point to a document setting out at least some of the fundamental issues (eg price). Drawing up the document may serve to focus the minds of the parties and establish whether there is a sufficient measure of agreement between them to make it worthwhile continuing with the proposed acquisition. In practice, the heads of agreement may serve as a useful guide to the transaction for the various professional advisers involved and for those who may have been approached by the buyer to finance the deal.

Heads of agreement (often also called a 'letter of intent') are by no means universally employed in acquisitions. The parties' lawyers often take the view that the time involved in producing them can be more usefully employed in drafting and negotiating the main agreement, which – unlike the heads of agreement – will incorporate appropriate protections for their clients. Regrettably, it is relatively common for the parties to enter into heads of agreement before taking any professional advice.

Two considerations will often arise in connection with heads of agreement: first, whether the terms (or some of them) are to be legally binding; and, secondly, whether the buyer is to be granted an exclusive right to bargain with the seller.

2.5.2.1   Legally binding

It is extremely unlikely that the buyer, in particular, will want all the heads to be binding. The signing of heads of agreement will invariably precede the buyer requisitioning a detailed investigation of the target, the outcome of which may prompt it to seek to withdraw from the transaction or to renegotiate the price. The buyer will not wish to be fully committed until it has completed the investigation and is satisfied that adequate protection by way of appropriate warranties and indemnities is included in the main agreement. Indeed, if the heads were fully binding, there would be little incentive for the seller to sign a further agreement.

Where none of the provisions is intended to be legally binding, normal practice is for the document containing the heads of agreement to be marked 'subject to contract' and (because of the uncertainty as to the precise effect of this phrase) for it to include a statement that the provisions are not intended to be legally binding. 'Subject to contract' is a term which is commonly used in English law in transactions, such as a sale of land, to indicate that the document concerned precedes the binding contract between the parties.

It is likely though that the parties will want some of the provisions included in the heads of agreement to be legally binding, in which case this needs to be stated expressly. For example, provisions relating to confidentiality, exclusivity of bargaining (see **2.5.2.2** below) and liability for costs in the event of an abortive transaction should be legally binding from the outset.

Comparative position in Continental Europe

In many civil law jurisdictions, such as France, Italy and Germany, it is possible to enter into an agreement to agree. A heads of agreement may be construed by the courts as a binding pre-agreement if it contains key terms such as the parties, price and any conditions. The creation of a binding contract can usually be avoided by careful drafting of the agreement to make it clear that there is no intention to agree to agree. However, it should be noted that in some jurisdictions, such as France and the Netherlands, the contents of the letter as a whole will be considered for the purpose of assessing whether it is legally binding, and in Spain the subsequent conduct of the parties may prompt a court to decide that the intention was to create a legally binding contract.

Most Continental European jurisdictions, including France, Germany, Italy, Spain and the Netherlands, impose a general duty to negotiate in good faith known as '*culpa in contrahendo*'. This duty extends to all phases of commercial relationships, both pre-contractual and contractual. Entering into a heads of agreement, even if it is not legally binding, may help to establish a duty of good faith between the parties. An agreement setting out detailed terms would be evidence of the closeness of the parties and of what the parties expect of each other.

The exact scope of this duty of good faith varies from country to country, but usually includes the following obligations:

(a)   to inform each other where reasonable of all points which, if known by the other party, might be expected to lead it to change its views on material aspects of the transaction;

(b)   to observe reasonable diligence in the performance of pre-contractual obligations; and

(c)   to observe ethical standards of behaviour.

As this duty extends to all phases of the pre-contractual relationship, it could cover such actions as the non-disclosure of material information, changing the terms of the deal without reasonable justification or withdrawing from negotiations without reasonable justification.

In some jurisdictions, these obligations can be excluded, for example, by including in the heads of agreement an express right for each party to terminate the negotiations at any stage without incurring any obligations or liability.

In most jurisdictions, the remedy for a breach of the duty of good faith is damages which put the innocent party in the position it would have been in had the negotiations not taken place. This would usually cover professional fees and the cost of any due diligence investigations. However, in some jurisdictions, such as Germany and the Netherlands, in certain circumstances damages for loss of opportunity can be claimed.

2.5.2.2   Exclusivity

A buyer who is considering acquiring the target may be reluctant to spend the time and money necessary to undertake a full investigation into the target's affairs unless it is granted an exclusive bargaining right for a certain period, ie it is agreed that, during this period, the seller will not enter into or continue negotiations for the sale of the target with anyone else.

It is clear from the English House of Lords case of *Walford v Miles* [1992] 2 WLR 174 that such a clause (commonly known as an 'exclusivity' or 'lock-out' clause) is enforceable provided it is sufficiently certain. Lord Ackner stated that an agreement not to negotiate with anyone else for a fixed period of time is enforceable provided that the clause is sufficiently certain. In this particular case, however, the House of Lords decided unanimously that the lock-out clause in question was not sufficiently certain because it did not specify how long it would last.

By contrast, in *Walford*, it was held that agreements to negotiate in good faith (often referred to as 'lock-in' agreements), even with a time limit imposed for these negotiations, are unenforceable because they lack the necessary certainty. However, it should be noted that an undertaking for a limited period of time to negotiate in good faith can be enforceable if the obligation is sufficiently certain. In *Petromec Inc Petro Deep Societa Armanmento SpA v Petroleo Brasilerio SpA* [2005] EWCA Civ 891, it was held that an undertaking to 'negotiate in good faith' on costs, set out in a formally negotiated document as part a series of binding contracts, was enforceable. This obligation was held not to be inconsistent with the ruling in *Walford* as the obligation was narrow in context, the terms were objectively ascertainable and it was part of a series of binding agreements. The limited nature of this decision was reinforced in *BBC Worldwide Ltd v Bee Load Ltd* [2007] EWHC 134 (Comm). In this case a clause to 'consider in good faith' an extension of a contract term was stated to be merely a statement of intent and was not an enforceable contractual promise as a matter of English law.

In the context of negotiations for an acquisition, it is clear that under English law any agreement as to the exclusivity of negotiations needs to be expressed as an agreement not to negotiate with anyone else for a fixed period of time.

The exclusivity clause should include a remedy in the event of a breach, usually the recovery of costs incurred in pursuing the acquisition. There is some doubt over whether costs incurred before the execution of the lock-out agreement would also be covered by such a provision. This can be a significant amount if the agreement was entered into at a late stage of the negotiations. The English case of *Radiant Shipping Co and Sea Containers* [1995] CLC 976 provided that costs incurred before the execution of the agreement could be recovered if this was expressly provided for, as long as it did not amount to a penalty. A well-drafted provision for a remedy for breach of exclusivity should therefore allow for the recovery of all expenses, whether incurred before or after execution of the exclusivity agreement.

Lastly, consideration must be given in order to render the exclusivity clause enforceable. The usual consideration is the buyer's commitment to finance the due diligence investigation.

Comparative position in Continental Europe

In most Continental European countries, it is also common to enter into exclusivity agreements prior to the buyer's full investigation of a potential target. An obligation not to negotiate with another party (a 'lock out') will usually be enforceable unless the exclusivity binds the parties for an unreasonable period of time. Many Continental European countries, such as Germany, also permit the parties to enter into a positive obligation to negotiate (a 'lock in') although such an agreement would be unusual.

Any agreement as to exclusivity will, like other pre-contractual agreements, need to be performed in accordance with the duty of good faith. Indeed, under German law the parties will be under an obligation not to break off negotiations without reasonable cause in circumstances where the other party may reasonably anticipate that the contract to purchase will be signed. The violation of such a duty entitles the other party to claim damages, for example for the costs of the negotiations, if the negotiations are terminated without cause.

Similarly, under Netherlands law, by entering into a negotiation agreement, the parties have entered into a pre-contractual legal relationship that is ruled by the principles of good faith, reasonableness and fairness. Consequently, the parties should take into account the legitimate interests of the other party. Although the parties are free to break off negotiations, a party may be liable for damages if breaking off the negotiations would be unacceptable. According to Dutch case law, this rule should be applied reticently. This may be the case if the other party was entitled to expect that a definitive agreement would eventually be entered into or if there were particular circumstances that contributed to the other party's expectations regarding the conclusion of the contract.

In Spain, the parties have a legal obligation to act in good faith when they negotiate, even if they have not signed a pre-contractual agreement. If any of the parties do not negotiate in good faith and, due to the lack of good faith, the other party incurs damages, the bad faith party may have to pay compensation to the other party for the damages suffered. The damages will include expenses but not any benefits that the party had expected to obtain from the negotiations.

The English courts do not recognise such pre-contractual obligations of good faith.

2.5.3   Choice of law

On a cross-border acquisition, the parties to the acquisition should consider which country's law will govern the terms of the acquisition. By agreeing on a governing law for the acquisition at the outset of a transaction, the parties will have clarity and certainty about the respective rights and obligations that have been agreed between the parties. In any preliminary documentation entered into between the parties, it would be prudent to agree on a choice of law provision which specifies the intended governing law of that documentation.

For many international acquisitions, the parties will choose for the documentation to be determined in accordance with a specific jurisdiction even if the parties are not all based in that jurisdiction. By specifying a particular jurisdiction or law, a party may be protected against another country's mandatory rules. However, it should be noted that the enforceability of such choice of law provisions may be subject to international or state conventions.

Within the US, whether a choice of law provision is valid will depend on that state's choice of law rules. Generally, provisions on choice of law will be accepted, although it should be noted that where the acquisition is to take the form of a legal merger which involves a Delaware registered corporation, the statutory provisions relating to the merger will be governed by Delaware General Corporation Law even if other parts of the merger agreement are governed by a different state law. Similar provisions apply in other jurisdictions; the choice of law provision will only govern the contractual terms between the parties. The rules that relate to an effective transfer of the assets or shares being acquired or the operation of a legal merger will be subject to the national rules that apply to that particular asset or merger (see **7.3**).

European conventions on choice of law

The Rome I Regulation (593/2008/EC) (Rome I) on the law applicable to contractual obligations and the Rome II Regulation (864/2007/EC) (Rome II) on the law applicable to non-contractual obligations were introduced in order to standardise the rules by which the applicable law is determined for disputes arising on private matters within the EU. Rome I replaces the provisions of the Rome Convention on the law applicable to contractual obligations of 1980 (the Rome Convention). The Rome II Regulation expands provisions on choice of law to non-contractual obligations for those countries that have opted in (all EU Members States except Denmark).

As under the Rome Convention, Rome I reinforces the principle of the parties' freedom to choose the applicable law and governing jurisdiction. However, this freedom is subject to particular exceptions for certain types of contracts, such as consumer contracts, employment contracts and insurance contracts. Article 3(1) states the right of the parties to choose the law which governs a contract but provides, under Article 3(3), that where all other elements at the time of the choice are located in a country other than the country whose law has been chosen, the choice of the parties will not prejudice the provisions of the law of that other country which cannot be derogated from by agreement. Therefore for a choice of law to take supremacy over other relevant national laws, there should be some connection with the jurisdiction chosen; and even then, it should be remembered that under Article 9, 'overriding mandatory provisions' (meaning provisions in the public interest) cannot be restricted.

Any statement of choice of law will also determine the law under which the existence and validity of the contract will be determined (Rome I, Article 10). For example, in determining whether a letter of intent is binding, any statement as to the governing law would indicate which law should be used to determine the existence of that contract.

Indeed under Rome II, a provision on the choice of law may also determine the rules applicable to the relationship between the parties even before the contract is formally binding. Article 12 of Rome II provides that:

> The law applicable to a non-contractual obligation arising out of dealings prior to the conclusion of a contract, regardless of whether the contract was actually concluded or not, shall be the law that applies to the contract or that would have been applicable to it had it been entered into.

This provision will have an effect on the drafting of provisions on the choice of law where the agreement or commercial activity arising from the agreement may give rise to non-contractual as well as contractual obligations. It may be that the parties want to agree on the law that will govern any non-contractual obligations that arise from any pre-contractual negotiations. For example, the parties may wish to avoid any obligations to negotiate in good faith which may arise in certain European jurisdictions. In practice this means that the parties should consider whether the choice of law provisions should be drafted to include all non-contractual obligations or be limited only to contractual matters. It also raises the significance of draft provisions on preliminary documentation and the draft sale and purchase agreement because, even if they are not signed, the parties may still be subject to that choice of law in relation to pre-contractual disputes.

2.6 SUMMARY OF PROCEDURE FOR CONDITIONAL CONTRACTS BY PRIVATE SALE

If the parties are able to exchange and complete simultaneously, Stage 3 above is not necessary, although repeat searches should be carried out prior to Stage 2.

INVESTIGATING THE TARGET

LEARNING OUTCOMES

After reading this chapter you will be able to:

- explain the purpose of the due diligence exercise
- describe the factors that may affect the scope of due diligence
- discuss the chief areas of focus for a due diligence investigation
- describe the main types of due diligence report.

3.1 WHAT ARE THE BUYER'S OBJECTIVES?

During the initial negotiations on the terms of the proposed acquisition, the buyer may not have any detailed knowledge of the target. It will often be relying in these early stages on information received from the seller, what is publicly known about the target, any sales information released by the seller, any knowledge of the target's business acquired from previous dealings, perhaps as a supplier or even a competitor, and a search of the company's file at the Companies Registry or the relevant registers of the jurisdiction where the company is established.

The parties or their advisers may draw up heads of agreement to record the results of their preliminary discussions and to provide a helpful basis on which to proceed to the signing of the main agreement (see **Chapter 2**). The buyer, however, will not want to enter into a binding commitment to acquire the target until it has as much information as possible about it, and this information-gathering stage is often known as 'due diligence'. The aim of due diligence is to furnish the buyer with essential management information, to enable it to decide whether or not to go ahead with the proposed acquisition and, if so, on what terms. In particular, the results of the investigation may prompt the buyer to renegotiate the price for the target. In addition, the due diligence investigation can help to identify any consents or preconditions that may need to be obtained or satisfied.

Whilst the due diligence process can provide the buyer with an enormous insight into the business it is planning to buy, it is important to remember the basic common law principle of *caveat emptor* ('let the buyer beware'). Due to the harshness of this principle under English law, the buyer will seek to protect itself in two ways: first, like any prudent buyer, by obtaining as much information as possible on the target; and, secondly, by backing that up with extensive warranties and indemnities in the sale and purchase agreement. The purpose of the warranties and indemnities is to provide the buyer with contractual protection should the target not turn out to be as expected (see **Chapter 5**). It is important to remember that the two methods of protection are not mutually exclusive and, indeed, that a thorough investigation of the target is essential to reveal areas where the buyer is at risk and needs, therefore, to protect itself by including warranties and indemnities.

In an international transaction, the other party may be established in a civil law country. Civil law countries apply a different principle than common law countries and implement the principle of buyer protection. In many of these jurisdictions, there exist civil or commercial codes which have a broad scope of application and would apply to all purchase and sales contracts entered into in the jurisdiction. Therefore, to the extent that there are statutory provisions applicable to acquisition transactions, these underlying statutory protection provisions would also work in favour of the buyer in corporate acquisitions. Moreover, in many civil law jurisdictions a statutory duty to negotiate in good faith applies to the parties, and this includes a duty to inform. This duty is significant at all stages of the negotiation process, including the phase of due diligence investigations. Throughout the due diligence investigation, the seller will be under a duty to provide the buyer with information regarding all important matters that the buyer could not otherwise discover.

Under the statutes of some civil law countries such as Germany, for example, the seller has disclosure obligations towards the buyer. German case law has ruled that a seller is under an obligation to disclose certain material facts. If the seller does not disclose such material facts, the buyer may claim damages and in certain circumstances rescind the contract. Under French law, failure to disclose material facts could amount to deceit, and the buyer may seek rescission of the contract or claim damages in court.

The level of due diligence investigation which is normal practice in common law countries, particularly in the US and the UK, is not necessarily standard practice, therefore, in all civil law countries. In some jurisdictions, such extensive investigations may be considered as detrimental to the mutual trust between the buyer and the seller, or even an indication of mistrust on the part of the buyer.

3.2   TYPES OF DUE DILIGENCE

Depending on the size of the proposed acquisition, the investigation of the target may be undertaken by a variety of professional advisers, including general business advisers, accountants and lawyers.

3.2.1   Business advisers

When considering whether to undertake a possible acquisition, the buyer will usually want to carry out a preliminary commercial assessment of the target business. This may include a consideration of the market position of the target, its financial position and any business plan to which the buyer may have obtained access. This business assessment will often be undertaken by the buyer itself or, if the buyer is a company, by the senior management of that company. If the buyer lacks sufficient expertise in the relevant market, it will approach professional business advisers to carry out the business analysis. If the buyer is seeking to raise finances to fund the proposed acquisition, there may also be a business review by its financial advisers.

3.2.2   Accountants

The buyer may instruct a firm of accountants (if the buyer is a company, its auditors will often be appointed) to investigate the target and produce a report. Normally, this is done when negotiations are far enough advanced for the buyer to feel that the expense is justified.

3.2.2.1   Accountants' report

The accountants' report is often central to the conduct of negotiations between the parties and plays an important role in the framing of the acquisition documentation, particularly the warranties and indemnities (although it is likely that the buyer will have produced the first draft of the main agreement before the report is available). It is important that the buyer's professional advisers liaise with their client and with each other on the precise scope of the various investigations to be carried out. An early meeting between the buyer's lawyers and the reporting accountants should serve to define areas of responsibility, avoid duplication and determine a timetable which ensures that the report is produced early enough to be useful in negotiations.

The buyer should instruct the firm of accountants formally by a letter of engagement, which should set out clearly the matters on which the accountants are required to report (the initial draft of the letter is often produced by the firm of accountants after discussions with their client). The accountants will need to be in direct contact with the proprietors or management of the target, and must be informed of the terms of any confidentiality agreement between the parties.

3.2.2.2   Matters covered by the report

The matters on which the accountants may be asked to report include the commercial activities of the target, management structure and employees, taxation, profitability, balance sheet strength, accounting systems and policies, and premises.

Commercial activities

The report may include the following:

(a)   details of the past, present and planned activities of the target;

(b)   an analysis of the market in which the target operates and a description of its main customers, geographical coverage, market share and principal competitors;

(c)   details of pricing policy, terms of trade (including credit arrangements) and significant agreements with suppliers, customers, agents, etc.

Management structure and employees

The information requested may include the following:

(a)   management structure and details of the ages, qualifications and service records of the directors and senior management;

(b)   details of the service contracts of the directors and senior management, including remuneration, commission, fringe benefits, pensions, profit-sharing and share option schemes, etc;

(c)   the number of other employees (broken down into departments and locations) and details of pay structure and staff relations, including (for companies with at least 250 employees) information relating to gender pay gap reporting;

(d)   staff training schemes and recruitment policies.

Taxation

The buyer will usually want detailed information about the tax affairs of the target (particularly on a share acquisition). In the UK the tax due diligence will usually cover the following main areas:

(a)   the current tax position of the target – details of current tax liabilities, the adequacy of provisions made for tax in the accounts of the target, VAT and PAYE compliance, and whether the target's tax affairs are up to date;

(b)   if relevant, what effect the acquisition will have on the tax affairs of the target and of the buyer, for example whether the transaction will itself create any charges to tax;

(c)   the likely future tax position of the target;

(d)   the warranties and indemnities that should be obtained, including any specific indemnities to cover known problem areas.

Profitability

The accountants will usually conduct a detailed review of the audited results of a target company for the previous three or four accounting periods and any unaudited information which may be available (eg management accounts), with a view to providing a detailed breakdown of turnover, overheads and profit (perhaps in relation to each activity of the target) and analysing relevant trends.

Balance sheet strength

The accountants will report on the assets and liabilities of the target, and may include details of (and comments on) the following:

(a)   borrowing commitments, both long-term and short-term, including details of any security provided;

(b)   recent capital expenditure, outstanding capital commitments, long-term contracts and contingent liabilities;

(c)   debtors and provision for bad debts;

(d)   insurance policies (and adequacy of cover).

Accounting systems and policies

A report on the accounting systems and the accounting policies adopted by the target will assist the buyer in understanding the accounts and in determining whether changes will be necessary after completion (eg to integrate with the buyer's systems).

Premises

The buyer will usually be relying on its lawyers to provide detailed information about the properties owned or occupied by the target, but the accountant's report will often contain brief details, including location, use and tenure of each property.

3.2.2.3   Use of the report

The final section of the report, which usually sets out the accountants' summary of the strengths and weaknesses of the target, any recommendations and their conclusions on the reasonableness of the price, is often of greatest interest to the buyer, who may use the report as a lever for lowering the price.

Practice on allowing the seller to have a copy of the report is variable (and if it is given a copy, the summary and conclusion will often be omitted). The disclosure letter may deem matters contained or referred to in the accountants' report prepared for the buyer to have been disclosed by the seller (thus potentially reducing the seller's exposure under the warranties). In these circumstances the buyer may insist on a warranty by the seller as to the accuracy of the contents of the accountants' report. These are all matters for negotiation between the parties.

Under English law, the buyer will have claims against the reporting accountants if the report is negligently prepared (both in contract for breach of the implied duty of reasonable skill and care, and in tort for negligent misstatement). Most jurisdictions have equivalent provisions in relation to reliance on information prepared by a third party. It should be noted that if the buyer does not commission its own report but merely relies on the audited accounts of the target company, it will not normally have any remedy against the company's auditors if they act to its detriment.

3.2.3 Legal advisers

The buyer will expect its legal advisers to carry out an investigation into any legal issues that may affect the value or prospects of the target. Such an investigation should also identify any preconditions that must be satisfied, or consents that may be required, effectively to transfer ownership of the shares or assets of the target business. This investigation is known as 'legal due diligence' (see **3.3**) or a 'legal review' and is usually undertaken by the buyer's legal advisers.

Legal due diligence will generally focus on the constitutional framework of the target company, the terms on which the target does business, ownership of its assets and any restrictions on the free use of them, and the extent of any potential liabilities. Much of this information will be examined by junior lawyers, though the more complex areas will be reviewed by lawyers within specialist departments or other professional advisers with particular expertise, such as pensions actuaries.

On a relatively small transaction the results of the investigation will be informally communicated to the client and to those negotiating the acquisition documentation. However, on larger transactions, more formal procedures may be required to avoid overlap of investigation and to ensure efficient reporting of the results to the client and those lawyers charged with negotiating the contractual terms of the deal (see **3.6**).

Whatever the reporting process, the results of the due diligence investigation should directly inform the negotiation of the acquisition documentation.

Generally, most jurisdictions have accepted legal due diligence as a common procedure of the acquisition process. The process may, however, be limited by legal restrictions on the disclosure of information. For example, the management of a German GmbH cannot release certain corporate information without prior shareholder approval.

3.2.4 International legal team

In the case of a cross-border acquisition, the due diligence team will consist of local lawyers of various jurisdictions advising about the national laws of their respective countries. In a transaction of this complexity, a due diligence coordinator may be advisable. The coordinator will oversee the process and ensure that all members of the international team understand the scope of the due diligence, the structure of the transaction and its timetable, and lastly the kind of report that needs to be produced.

Instructing local counsel can be effected in various ways: by instructing individual non-associated firms, an alliance or association of firms that informally work together, or by instructing a firm with offices in all the relevant jurisdictions.

International acquisitions can highlight significant cultural and legal differences in the way companies and people do business and work. These can relate to differences in organisational style, management style, communication style, planning and decision-making. One of the major challenges in international acquisitions is having an understanding of the differences between legal systems and the underlying cultures, and also sometimes language barriers. In undertaking cross-border due diligence, there may be circumstances where such differences could have a significant impact on the acquisition process or the proposed timetable. For example, approvals that can be acquired quickly in one jurisdiction may require a lengthy procedure in another.

When instructing local counsel on due diligence or on any other legal subject, a number of matters which tend to vary between jurisdictions should be addressed. Lawyers in most jurisdictions have strict professional rules they must adhere to, including rules on conflict, commonly derived from principles of general law or rules of conduct handed down by professional bodies. For example, the definition of a conflict of interest differs between

Continental Europe, the US and the UK, as do the situations under which law firms are able to obtain a conflict waiver. In addition, the interpretation of client confidentiality differs throughout Europe. Furthermore, within each jurisdiction there may be important differences in approach between firms on the application of the conflict of interest rules.

There are no specific provisions governing the application of conflicts rules on a multi-jurisdictional matter. In the UK, it is general practice to apply the conflicts rules of the jurisdiction in which the work is done and so refer to the rules of the jurisdiction in which the local lawyers have been admitted. If another jurisdiction becomes involved, it is important to review the way the local lawyer handles conflicts of interest – for example whether they apply conflict procedure rules in the same way to members of an alliance or association.

Many countries have regulations laid down in the professional rules of conduct as to fee structures, and these vary from country to country. Fee scales can be based on an hourly rate or on the value of the transaction, or there may be a success or contingency fee, which is allowed in the UK but prohibited in many jurisdictions. Some jurisdictions have certain aspects of a transaction fixed by law, such as notarial fees in Germany and France.

It is becoming increasingly common practice in international acquisitions for the local lawyers to enter into an engagement letter to clarify some of the above issues (see **2.1.3**). This letter may include detail as to the responsibilities of the parties, fee arrangements, the objective, scope and duration of the assignment (ie the due diligence investigation), the form of report required, as well as information on timetables and communication lines.

3.3   SCOPE OF LEGAL DUE DILIGENCE

It is vital to determine the scope of the legal due diligence investigation with the client prior to conducting the research in order to avoid wasting time and costs. During these discussions, the format of the due diligence report should be decided upon (see **3.6**), as well as the make up of the due diligence team (see **3.2.4**).

The scope of a legal due diligence investigation can be extremely wide. In practice, the extent of the investigation will be dictated by the nature of the target business, and by the requirements and concerns of the particular buyer. A number of factors will influence both the scope and focus of a legal due diligence review, as discussed below.

3.3.1   Commercial aims

The scope and focus of the investigation will depend to a certain extent on the buyer's position and on the commercial aims underlying the transaction. If the buyer is already familiar with the target, extensive due diligence will be less important, as the buyer will be aware of the potential strengths and weaknesses of the business.

The reason for the purchase may also influence the focus of the investigations. If the acquisition is intended to allow expansion into a new market, the buyer is likely to focus on existing trading contracts for example; but if the purchase is for investment purposes, the financial stability of the target and how the investment may be realised will be of more interest to the buyer.

The most critical element when planning a due diligence investigation is for the due diligence team to understand the commercial objectives behind the acquisition. This understanding will help the team to prioritise the investigation appropriately and to determine what information is important to review, when it should be reviewed, and, also importantly, what can be left out.

3.3.2   Identified areas of risk

During the due diligence process, consideration must be given to the typical risks inherent in the market in which the target business operates. For example, if the target operates in a heavily regulated sector, the buyer must carefully explore the grant of, and any conditions attached to, any necessary consents, licences or approvals.

Any particular risk factors within the target itself must also be explored. For example, if the target has been in financial difficulties, the terms of its loan agreements should be checked carefully to ensure that no events of default have occurred which may result in claims over the target's assets.

3.3.3 Types of transactions

3.3.3.1 Shares

The scope of the investigation will usually be more extensive on the acquisition of the entire share capital of a company than on an asset acquisition. This is because the buyer of shares acquires a 'live' company with all its assets and, perhaps more significantly, its liabilities, whether actual or contingent, fixed or unquantified. There is far more involved than checking that the seller has title to the shares themselves; all aspects of the target company are of concern to a potential buyer and should, ideally, be examined.

3.3.3.2 Assets

Subject to jurisdictional variations, the buyer of the assets of a target business does not assume the liabilities of the business (see **Chapter 8**), which remain with the seller unless it is released from them by the third parties involved. The buyer will, however, often agree to accept responsibility for certain of these liabilities by giving the seller an indemnity in the sale and purchase agreement. The buyer will therefore direct its investigation at the specific assets which it wishes to acquire and at the liabilities which it is prepared to accept. It should be appreciated, however, that the goodwill of the business acquired by the buyer may be adversely affected by certain liabilities, even if these remain with the seller (eg a successful claim against the seller for manufacturing defective products). Information gained during the due diligence process will also be used after the transaction has closed by a buyer who must integrate the acquired entity into its existing business structure. Consequently, it is in the buyer's interest to discover as much about the business generally as is feasible in the circumstances.

3.3.4 Extent of contractual protection

In some circumstances, the seller may not be able (or prepared) to give much contractual protection to the buyer (see **Chapter 5**). For example, the sale may be by an insolvency practitioner, who may be prepared to give only very limited contractual reassurances about the target; or it may be by way of an auction sale, where the seller has indicated that very few contractual protections will be given. In such a case, the buyer should try to investigate as thoroughly as possible to ascertain the exact nature of the business it proposes to acquire. Conversely, if the buyer knows that it will have the benefit of extensive contractual protections, it may consider that the time and expense of a full investigation is not merited.

In the current risk-averse market, though, it is true to say that most buyers will prefer to combine a full investigation with contractual protection to reduce the level of risk as much as possible.

3.3.5 Limiting factors

Although the issues mentioned above may help to determine the scope of the due diligence investigation, the buyer is not always able to be as painstaking as it would like. A number of matters may, in practice, hinder a thorough scrutiny of the target business or company.

3.3.5.1 Time constraints

Time constraints are often the most significant factor in determining the scope of the buyer's enquiries. It is in the nature of commercial transactions that tight (and sometimes unrealistic) timetables are often agreed upon by the parties. Also, where the seller is in a strong bargaining position (perhaps because there are other interested parties), it may dictate a short timescale for the parties to enter into the contract.

3.3.5.2 Financial resources and manpower

The buyer may be unable to commit sufficient financial resources or manpower to a full-scale examination of the target. Saving money at this stage of the transaction may prove a false economy in the long term but, nevertheless, the buyer will inevitably be working within the constraints of a budget.

3.3.5.3 Confidentiality

The seller may be keen to keep the proposed sale a secret, not only from outsiders, such as competitors and suppliers, but also from its own workforce. The practical limitation which this puts on the extent of the searches and enquiries of the buyer and its advisers is obvious. The seller will often insist that all communications are channelled through one person; that a code-name is used for all such contact; and that the true purpose of any visits to the seller's premises by the buyer or its advisers (eg a surveyor) is not disclosed.

It has also been seen that sellers may, understandably, be reluctant to pass on commercially sensitive information to the buyer, such as customer lists, in advance of exchange of contracts. This problem may, in some cases, be mitigated by a confidentiality agreement between the parties.

In addition, some of the documentation that the buyer may seek to review, such as joint venture agreements for example, may themselves be the subject of confidentiality obligations. This may mean that the consent of a third party will be necessary before the buyer is able to review the information.

In some circumstances, however, such consent may not be possible to obtain. In such cases, the seller will need to take particular care to ensure it does not breach its own confidentiality obligations by disclosing information or terms of an agreement to a buyer. *Kason Kek-Gardner Ltd v Process Components Ltd* [2017] EWCA Civ 2132 illustrates this, in a case where the seller disclosed to the buyer the terms of a licence agreement which it was prohibited from disclosing, leading to the prompt termination of the licence.

In multi-jurisdictional transactions, cultural differences may arise on the confidentiality of business information, particularly when dealing with family-owned businesses. Legal restrictions on the disclosure of information under privacy or data protection laws will also vary between jurisdictions.

3.4 UNDERTAKING A DUE DILIGENCE INVESTIGATION

3.4.1 Public searches

At the outset of the acquisition transaction, the buyer's lawyers will usually review all public records relating to the target business or company. For companies registered in England and Wales, this will include information about the company held at Companies House, property details held at HM Land Registry and details of any registered intellectual property rights. In addition, the buyer may also seek information from relevant websites, the trade press, and from commercial organisations which specialise in providing corporate and financial information about businesses.

Although searching public records is a quick and inexpensive method of obtaining information, it should be remembered that the information sourced is not always up to date.

3.4.2 Questionnaire

The buyer's lawyers will often begin the due diligence process by forwarding a detailed request for information to the seller's lawyers, often known as a 'due diligence questionnaire'.

The replies to these enquiries will form the buyer's main source of information on the target business. The questionnaire should not be a pro forma document but should be tailored to the particular business involved, thus avoiding burdening the seller's lawyers with unnecessary or irrelevant questions. In compiling the questionnaire, the buyer and its advisers should give particular thought to the typical risks inherent in the market and jurisdiction in which the target operates and to the buyer's specific concerns. The buyer's lawyer should liaise with the other professional advisers representing the buyer in an attempt to avoid duplicating requests for information; the buyer's lawyer will often act as 'information controller'.

Where the target company has subsidiaries in multiple jurisdictions, it may be advisable for the buyer's lawyers to submit a draft questionnaire to its local legal advisers to ascertain any particular additions for that specific jurisdiction. A multi-jurisdictional transaction will often require a master questionnaire, along with questionnaires for each country involved. The local counsel should prepare these country questionnaires since they inquire into specific issues relating to the laws of that jurisdiction. The results should be reviewed and co-ordinated by both the home and foreign lawyers.

On a share sale, if any of the selling shareholders are not also directors, they may have little personal knowledge of the matters raised. Consequently, the seller's lawyers will have to obtain much of the information which is requested about the structure of the company and the running of the business from the management of the target company. Whatever the source of the information, the seller has little to gain from giving evasive replies (particularly if the replies are to be attached to the disclosure letter, thus qualifying the warranties). So, provided the seller is satisfied as to the confidentiality of any information passing to the buyer, it should give full and frank replies to the enquiries.

The buyer's lawyers, in conjunction with the client and the rest of the team, should check the replies carefully and follow up any points which remain outstanding. As with the accountants' report, the replies are likely to have a significant bearing on the warranties and indemnities required by the buyer.

3.4.3 Data room

In transactions where information about the target business is highly sensitive, or where the sale is by way of an auction with a number of potential bidders, access to information provided by the seller is usually by way of a secure 'data room'. In the data room the seller, aided by its legal advisers, will make information about the target available to the buyer. The seller's advisers will carefully consider what information should be made available and, in many transactions, a secure website will be created through which the buyer's advisers can gain electronic access to the key documentation.

In setting up a data room, either real or virtual, the seller's advisers must try to ensure that the key documentation a potential buyer would want to review is included, whilst also attempting to protect any commercially sensitive material. Confidentiality of information can be further protected by agreeing a definitive list of who will have access to the data room, and by providing documents in 'read-only' format. When reviewing the information in the data room, the buyer's advisers must focus on the key areas of concern for the buyer; if the information provided seems insufficiently detailed, the buyer may need to make additional enquiries of the seller. For larger transactions, the buyer's advisers may well use artificial intelligence software to categorise and analyse the documents provided, and to extract key information and data. This approach greatly increases the efficiency of the due diligence review, and may minimise the risk of missing key information in contracts.

3.5 COMMON AREAS OF INVESTIGATION

3.5.1 Corporate information

As mentioned at **3.4.1** above, useful information about a target company registered in England and Wales can be obtained by making a search of the company's file at Companies

House. Similar such searches are possible in many other jurisdictions. The buyer's lawyers will usually seek this information at the outset of the due diligence process, and repeat the search for confirmation purposes shortly before the sale and purchase agreement is concluded.

Where a company is selling the assets of a business or shares in a subsidiary, a search should be made against the selling company. Also, a seller is wise to search the file of a corporate buyer to satisfy itself that it is of sufficient substance to effect the acquisition and to fulfil any post-completion obligations, such as the payment of any deferred consideration.

The company search does have serious limitations, however, which means that the information it reveals may not be entirely reliable. For example, the obligation to file information at Companies House is placed on the company itself, and although the company and its officers are liable to fines on default, there is no provision for compensating a third party who suffers loss as a result of this information being incomplete or inaccurate. Indeed, the buyer of shares is not given any statutory assistance in these circumstances. In addition, even if the target has duly filed its returns on time, the information revealed by the search will in many cases be out of date.

3.5.1.1 Constitutional documents

Where the assets of a business are being acquired from a company, the buyer's lawyers should check that the company's constitutional documents give it the power to dispose of its assets, and that the articles enable the directors to exercise that power.

The buyer's lawyers will also study the constitution of the target company to check that the company has power to carry on the business and to discover what steps will need to be taken on completion. The buyer should also check whether the articles contain any restrictions on the transfer of shares. They may, for example, contain pre-emption provisions, obliging shareholders wishing to transfer their shares to offer them pro rata to existing members. In this event, the selling shareholders will usually waive their respective rights as a term of the sale and purchase agreement (although it may be safer to change the article, since pre-emption rights are sometimes triggered by an 'intention' to dispose of the shares). After it has acquired the shares, the buyer may, of course, wish to change provisions of the target company's constitution to suit its own specific needs.

When obtaining constitutional documents, the buyer's lawyers should be aware that the law as to the extent and reliability of publicly available information varies from jurisdiction to jurisdiction.

3.5.1.2 Directors and shareholders

Information provided to Companies House relating to shareholders, directors and company secretary, and the issued share capital should have been updated, or confirmed as correct, when the company delivered its most recent confirmation statement to the Registrar of Companies. This is a useful starting point for the buyer's lawyers in preparing the initial draft of the sale and purchase agreement, but they will need to ask the seller's lawyers to provide details of all changes since the return date because the information revealed may be out of date. The buyer's lawyers require accurate information as to the existing shareholders, in order to ensure that the correct persons enter into the agreement, and as to the current directors, so that the buyer can consider what arrangements should be made with them on completion (the buyer may intend that some directors resign on completion and that others enter into new service contracts with the target company). The buyer's lawyers will also check whether the target's directors hold any other directorships. This may be of interest to the buyer, particularly if it transpires that any of the target's directors are also directors of companies which have been trading with the target.

3.5.1.3   Internal registers and minutes

The buyer's lawyers will wish to inspect the internal registers of a target company registered in England and Wales (statutory books and otherwise). The register of members and the minute books will be of particular interest; the buyer's lawyers should check that allotments and transfers of shares have been carried out in accordance with statute (eg CA 2006, ss 550 and 561 on issues of shares) and with the articles of the company (eg in compliance with any pre-emption provisions). Copies of charges created by the company and copies of directors' service contracts should also be available for inspection.

In the US, companies must maintain a shareholders' register. Smaller companies usually keep these in the minute book with the minutes of meetings of shareholders and directors. Some European jurisdictions may not require an internal register, though a shareholders' register is usually required for larger companies (for example, in Germany for AGs and in the Netherlands for NVs).

Subject to any confidentiality restrictions, the buyer's lawyers may be able to look at any board minutes that are included in the statutory books. These minutes can be a very good source of information, as they will record important decisions made by the company and will evidence whether required company procedures have been followed correctly.

Most jurisdictions have legal restrictions on the disclosure of information. Many jurisdictions impose an additional duty not to disclose confidential company information on the management and employees on top of any contractually agreed limitations. Some jurisdictions require that prior approval is sought before disclosure. The management of a German GmbH, for example, cannot disclose certain corporate information without shareholder approval, and the board of a German AG would need to consider whether the disclosure of information is in the best interests of the company.

3.5.2   Financial information

3.5.2.1   Accounts

Whether or not a full accountants' report is commissioned, the buyer's solicitor should study the target's accounts. In the case of a company, copies of the audited accounts for the last three years should be requested, together with any recently produced management accounts. In conjunction with the accountants, the buyer's solicitor can then consider what warranties or indemnities should be included in the agreement as a result of information revealed in the accounts. For this reason, and for drafting and negotiating other aspects of the sale and purchase agreement, such as the provision of completion accounts, the solicitor must have a clear understanding of business and company accounts (see **4.3.4.1**).

The introduction of International Financial Reporting Standards (IFRS) has removed some of the differences in availability, content and presentation of the financial information between European countries. Despite the harmonisation achieved by IFRS, national accounting standards of European countries are still applied in certain cases; consequently there are differentiations in the use of the 'true and fair view' judgement of company accounts across the European Union.

The IFRS are not mandatory for US companies, and they will usually apply a different set of standards deriving from the US Generally Accepted Accounting Principles (GAAP).

3.5.2.2   Loans

On an asset acquisition, existing banking arrangements in relation to the target will generally cease and the buyer will need to organise its own facilities. The buyer should enquire whether any of the assets which are being transferred are the subject of a charge; any such charge will have to be removed on completion, or the consent of the chargee obtained for the asset to be transferred subject to the charge.

On a share acquisition, the buyer should request copies of all loan documentation in order to ascertain the nature and extent of the target's borrowing commitments and obligations. It should check whether any loans are repayable on demand (this is common with bank overdraft facilities) or entitle the lender to demand immediate repayment of the balance of the loan on a change of control of the target. In either case, unless the buyer can make satisfactory arrangements with the lender directly, it must be confident of securing funds from elsewhere.

A buyer of shares will also be interested in whether the seller has guaranteed any obligations of the target (eg repayment of a fixed-term loan). Although this is the primary concern of the seller, whose liability will continue after completion, the buyer should anticipate that it may be asked to try to procure the release of the seller from such guarantees and to indemnify the seller if the release is not obtained on completion. Whoever has the benefit of the seller's guarantee is likely to require at least equivalent pledges from the buyer before agreeing to release the seller.

Lastly, where the target company is a member of a group, it may have guaranteed various obligations of other members of the group. The buyer will insist that such guarantees do not continue in place after completion.

3.5.2.3 Charges

A search against a company disposing of a business will reveal whether there are any charges over the assets which are being transferred. The buyer will usually insist that these charges are released on completion.

Similarly, the buyer of shares will want to establish the extent to which a target company has charged its assets as security for loans. For a company registered in England and Wales, this information will be held on the Charges Register at Companies House. However, the information held on record may not be up to date, since the company may have recently created charges which have still to be registered within the statutory period of 21 days from creation. Even if such charges are not registered within the statutory period, they are, nevertheless, valid against the company itself, and thus the buyer of shares receives no protection against late registration or non-registration. Indeed, the target company is in a vulnerable position in relation to charges which have not been registered, as the loan becomes repayable immediately.

3.5.2.4 Credit reports

A quick and easy method of obtaining general (and up-to-date) financial information about a target company is for the buyer to request a credit report from a reputable credit rating agency, such as Dun & Bradstreet or Standard & Poor's. As well as commenting on the company's creditworthiness in general, such reports will also deal with specific aspects of its performance and financial position (eg average debt collection and payment periods, and the company's 'liquidity', ie its ability to pay off short-term liabilities out of realisable assets).

3.5.2.5 Checking the solvency of the seller

In England and Wales, bankruptcy searches at the Land Charges Department should be carried out against individual sellers of shares or of a business immediately before completion. Similarly, a search of the file at Companies House of a corporate seller of shares or a business should be made prior to completion to ensure that no notice of insolvency procedures has been entered. As this information may not be up to date, a telephone enquiry should also be made to the Central Registry of winding-up petitions. This is important as any transactions entered into after the commencement of insolvency procedures may be void.

The Recast Insolvency Regulation 2015/848 requires all EU Member States, other than Denmark, to establish and maintain one or more insolvency registers containing specified information relating to insolvency proceedings. The European Commission is currently trialling a system on its e-justice portal to integrate Member States' insolvency registers, to provide a single online access point for registers. Currently, therefore, a search should be made of each of the relevant national registers, until all registers become available through the Commission's e-justice portal.

3.5.3   Key contracts

3.5.3.1   Contracts fundamental to the business

One of the main advantages of a share acquisition is the lack of disruption which it causes to the target's trade, since outstanding contracts generally remain unaffected by the change in ownership of the company. This contrasts with an asset acquisition, where the benefit of existing contracts entered into by the seller will not pass to the buyer unless the contracts are assigned or novated or transferred automatically in accordance with particular jurisdictional requirements (see **8.1.2**). In either case, however, the buyer will require full details (and copies) of all significant contracts into which the target has entered. On an asset sale, the buyer should examine those contracts which the buyer considers vital to the well-being of the business, to see whether they require consent to assignment or contain other restrictions on assignment. The buyer of shares must check that none of these significant contracts will be affected by the change of control of the company.

Contracts which may be fundamental to the business (and which may account for much of its turnover) include long-term contracts for the supply of the target's goods or services, distribution and agency agreements, contracts for the supply of raw materials to the target, intellectual property licences, service contracts for key staff, leases for important plant and machinery, etc. The buyer of shares should check which contracts are due to expire in the near future so that it can investigate the chances of renewal, perhaps by contacting third parties directly (subject to confidentiality). Similarly, some of these contracts may be terminable on short notice, and the buyer will want to be satisfied that this is not likely to happen as a result of the change of control.

The buyer of shares faces a danger in relation even to long-term contracts entered into by the target company. Such contracts may include a term which entitles the other party to terminate the agreement if control of the target changes hands ('change of control' clauses). Such clauses are sometimes included in, for example, distribution agreements, franchise agreements and joint venture agreements.

The buyer of a target should also check that all of these fundamental contracts have been properly executed and that none contains provisions which infringe EU or UK competition laws.

In conducting the review of the target's contracts, it is important that the buyer's advisers bear in mind the buyer's post-completion plans for the business. The buyer must be satisfied that the terms of on-going contracts are appropriate and, where contracts are to be brought to an end after completion, any provisions on early termination, for example, must be closely considered.

3.5.3.2   Rights triggered by a change of control

Some examples of where 'change of control' clauses in contracts may be found have been given in **3.5.3.1** above. Clauses conferring rights on parties where a company changes hands may also be found in employment contracts. For example, directors' service contracts might contain a so-called 'golden parachute clause', which entitles the director to a payment if the company changes hands (usually on the basis that the director can treat themselves as dismissed in such circumstances). Also in the employment context, the right of employees to exercise rights to buy shares at a favourable price under share option schemes are sometimes triggered by a change of control of the company.

3.5.3.3   Non-arm's length trading relationships

It is also possible that individual sellers of a target company may have been supplying goods or services to the target company (or receiving goods or services from the target company) either directly or through other companies in which they have an interest. The buyer's analysis of the profit figures of the target may be very different in the light of these sorts of arrangements. Past profits may be a poor indicator of future performance of the business if these sources of supply (to or from the target) are terminated after completion, or if the terms of supply are changed significantly.

Where the target is a member of a group, the buyer should ask for information on all goods and services which have been supplied by or to other members of the group (including administrative and management services supplied by a parent company). As it is unlikely that such arrangements will continue once the group relationship is broken, the buyer should assess the impact of their ceasing on completion of the acquisition. In circumstances where the sudden cessation of group support services would prove problematic, the buyer and seller may enter into a 'transitional services agreement' whereby the seller agrees to continue to provide specified support services to the target for a defined transitional period (often 12–24 months from completion). The buyer will, of course, pay for the transitional services, which will enable the target business to continue to run smoothly whilst the buyer makes arrangements for the target to become fully independent from the seller.

3.5.4   Intellectual property rights and data

Depending on the type of business, the seller or target may own or use on licence trade marks, patents, registered designs, know-how, service marks or copyrights. These intellectual property rights may be crucial to the business, and a thorough review of this area is essential to ascertain whether rights are adequately protected, what agreements or licences are in place and, on a share purchase, whether a change in control will affect such arrangements. The buyer will also want details of the computer system and software packages used by the target (the buyer may wish to integrate these with the buyer's own systems). On an asset acquisition, the buyer may have to approach third parties with a view to renegotiating licences or agreements entered into with the seller.

In addition to requiring full details of all intellectual property rights from the seller, the buyer should, in appropriate cases, carry out searches at the UK Intellectual Property Office in order to establish not only that the target's intellectual property rights are valid, but also that the target is not infringing any intellectual property rights owned by others. Clearly, equivalent steps should be taken in other jurisdictions to investigate intellectual property rights registered there.

Establishing ownership of intellectual property rights and, if required, ensuring that such rights are appropriately transferred to the seller (or target) so that the buyer can acquire those rights is often key in acquisitions where technology or particular design rights are at the heart of the transaction.

Intellectual property rights may sometimes have been registered in the name of a founder of a company (particularly if it is a 'start-up' or if the company was set up some time after the founder (or founders) started working to develop their business idea). If the intention of the acquisition of the target company is to acquire key intellectual property rights that are assumed to be owned by the target, in such an instance where the rights are in fact registered under the founder, acquiring the target company would be inadequate. Investigating and establishing under whom an intellectual property right has been registered is therefore vital.

Similarly, an intellectual property right might well be registered under the name of a current (or former) consultant to the company or someone that is not an employee of the target company, in which case, again, acquiring the company would not lead to acquiring the desired rights. Additional complexity can arise if, for example, the right might have been acquired by the target (or seller) from another company or following an intra-group transaction or reorganisation. In both such instances, the right might have still remained registered under its original owner's name (a scenario which is not unrealistic – change of ownership can often be overlooked and not recorded). These examples illustrate the need to investigate under whom rights are recorded as it may not always be the case that the target or seller is the registered owner.

Once it has been established under whom rights are recorded, where required and if not already done so, rights should be transferred to the target (or seller) by way of (1) an assignment of the rights to the target, and (2) the recording of such assignment in relevant intellectual property registers. Upon completion of the acquisition, the rights should be transferred from the target (or seller) to the buyer (see **8.2.3** and **9.1.2.7** for related acquisitions of assets and shares, respectively).

It should be noted that if an assignment of a right is not recorded within six months of the date of such assignment, only the beneficial title to the right is transferred while the legal title is not, a situation which substantially weakens the protections of the rights owner in the event of an infringement.

Consideration should also be given to the target's IT systems and its collection and use of data, particularly where the target uses or offers services that involve access to personal data. The due diligence process should establish the extent to which IT systems are secure, where core databases are located, and it should examine the possible impact that data privacy rules may have on the use of the data post-acquisition.

In recent years, cybersecurity and data protection have become areas of significant focus for due diligence. With the introduction of more stringent data protection laws, such as the EU General Data Protection Regulation, presenting the prospect of greater fines being imposed for data breaches, due diligence assessing cybersecurity and data protection compliance has increasingly become a necessity in most acquisitions.

3.5.5 Employees and pensions

3.5.5.1 Terms of employment

The buyer's lawyers will want to obtain full details of the target's workforce, and in particular the contractual terms that apply to its directors and managers. The terms of employment should be checked even if the buyer is only acquiring the assets of the business, because the rights and obligations of the employees working in that business will usually transfer automatically to the buyer (see **8.3** for the application of TUPE 2006 in the UK and similar provisions in other EU Member States pursuant to the Acquired Rights Directive).

In particular, the buyer's lawyers will want to review the current employees' service contracts and acquire details of any discretionary or customary arrangements. Also, any recent disputes, dismissals or changes in the terms and conditions that may result in a potential claim by an employee should be investigated. The buyer should also ask for details of anyone who works in the business but who is not employed by the target. For example, where the target is a subsidiary company, some individuals working in the business may have contracts with the parent company and will not, therefore, be available to work in the target business after the acquisition.

It will be particularly important to obtain full information on the employees if the buyer intends to make major changes to the workforce, such as integration with its existing employees, general reorganisation of the business, or redundancies. In such a case, the target company, or the buyer on an asset acquisition, may be faced with contractual claims from the affected employees, so careful planning, including an assessment of the potential financial consequences of the action, will be required. Additionally, the buyer should scrutinise any gender pay gap report published by the target, together with any work carried out in preparation for its next gender pay gap report, as this may highlight the risk of potential future claims.

It should be noted, however, that not all jurisdictions provide for possible claims by employees if they are dismissed due to the acquisition. In the US, in the absence of an express written agreement or binding oral statement, the employee's contract can be terminated without notice and without cause at any time. Employees may, however, in some circumstances be able to file claims for discrimination under both federal and some state laws in the US, since provisions that are discriminatory as to race, religion, sex, disability, age or national origin are generally illegal.

In the US, if the acquisition will result in significant dismissals (50 or more) then at a federal level the Worker Adjustment and Retraining Notification Act (WARN) requires employers to provide at least 60 days' notice. Many other countries also have specific procedural rules in case of mass lay-offs. For example, in Argentina a notification should be made, which triggers a preventive procedure before the Argentinean Labour Authorities.

3.5.5.2   Collective agreements

The buyer's lawyers should also consider any collective arrangements that may apply to the target, such as trade union recognition agreements or workplace agreements. It is important to check whether there are any consultation requirements to be followed either in relation to the acquisition itself, or in relation to any reorganisation of the workforce that may result from the transaction (see **8.3**). In many European jurisdictions, if the proposed acquisition is likely to result in any changes to the workforce, the workers' representatives must be consulted. In particular, France and Germany have very strict rules about notification to employees of any proposed transfer. Under the German civil code, either the seller or the buyer must inform the employees of the reason for the transfer, the legal, economic and social consequences of the transfer, and any measures to be taken in relation to the employee.

3.5.5.3   Retaining directors and managers

If the buyer is keen to retain certain directors or managers of the target, it should consult with them as early as possible in the acquisition negotiations (subject to considerations of confidentiality). It may be able to negotiate a term in the sale and purchase agreement that certain key personnel enter into new service contracts on completion. However, if a director or manager chooses to leave the target, the rights of the parties will depend on the terms of any existing contract with the target company, or the seller, as appropriate.

3.5.5.4   Restrictive covenants

The buyer should check whether the service contracts of the target's key personnel contain effective restraints on their activities after termination of their contracts. This is, of course, particularly important in relation to senior personnel whose contracts will definitely come to an end on completion of the acquisition. Typical clauses include covenants by the employee not to work in a competing business and not to solicit or entice away customers of the target company. The employee may also be prohibited from using or disclosing confidential information about the business of the target. In the absence of express terms, few post-termination restraints are implied into an employment contract (there is an implied term, however, that the employee will not reveal highly confidential information).

Under English law, restraints of this nature are valid and enforceable at common law only if they protect a legitimate trade interest of the employer (eg they protect the goodwill of the business), are not against the public interest and are reasonable between the parties, as was recently confirmed in *Tillman v Egon Zehnder* [2019] UKSC 32. A non-competition covenant, for example, is likely to be considered void as being in restraint of trade unless its scope is limited in terms of duration and the geographical area which it covers. Similarly, a non-solicitation clause should be limited to customers who have recently dealt with the target (eg within the previous 12 months). It is now well established that clauses preventing the disclosure of information after termination can only be effective in relation to highly confidential information or trade secrets (*Faccenda Chicken Ltd v Fowler* [1986] IRLR 69, CA).

If any of the directors who are leaving are also selling shares in the target, the buyer should ensure that they agree to restrictive covenants in the sale and purchase agreement (see **5.10**). The courts will more readily uphold restraints which have been freely negotiated between parties to an acquisition than those included in employment contracts.

Even if restrictive covenants are prima facie valid, they will not survive a repudiatory breach of contract by the employer. This is on the basis that, by committing such a breach, the employer is indicating that it no longer considers itself to be bound by the contract and cannot, therefore, hold the other party to obligations contained within it. There is a danger here for buyers proposing that the target dismisses some of the management team; if dismissals are carried out in breach of contract, this may discharge the former employees from compliance with restrictive covenants (*General Billposting Co Ltd v Atkinson* [1909] AC 118, HL). Even if the covenant purports to enable the employer to enforce the covenant whatever the reason for the termination of the contract, this will not be effective (*Briggs v Oates* [1991] 1 All ER 411). Some directors' service contracts, however, permit the company to pay them salary in lieu of notice. Since, in this event, the company is not in breach of contract in terminating the contract without notice, it should be able to rely on post-termination covenants.

3.5.5.5 Pensions

The parties will need to give careful consideration to the pension aspects of the acquisition, including whether the target has satisfied its obligations to enrol workers in a pension scheme, and to make contributions on their behalf, under the auto-enrolment regime, which came fully into force in April 2017 as regards existing firms and in February 2018 for new employers. This is a complex area and one where the potential costs may be very high. It will often be necessary to refer issues regarding the pension fund to specialist pensions lawyers and actuaries. Therefore, in undertaking the due diligence review it is important to obtain as much information as possible about the pension provisions made by the target and any pension scheme operated by it.

The buyer's lawyers will require full details of any pension scheme, including copies of the trust deed and rules under which the pension fund is administered, a list of the members of the scheme and confirmation that the scheme enjoys a privileged tax position.

The buyer should ascertain the type of pension scheme operated; in the UK the two main possibilities are a final salary scheme and a money purchase scheme. In a final salary scheme, the members are guaranteed a particular level of benefit on retirement, whereas the benefit received by the members in a money purchase scheme is entirely dependent on the return on the fund invested. Unlike a money purchase scheme, there is no direct correlation between the contributions made to the final salary fund (by employer and employee) and the benefits received by the employee. A final salary scheme may therefore be in surplus or deficit at the time of the acquisition, depending on the prevailing economic conditions and the amount of the claims. In recent years, final salary schemes have become increasingly difficult to manage, leading many companies to close them to new employees who are instead offered participation in a money purchase scheme. It is therefore possible that the target may operate both types of pension schemes.

The buyer will also want to establish whether the pension scheme is a stand-alone, discrete scheme that can be transferred at completion, or whether the target's employees are members of a larger scheme involving other employees. In the latter case, arrangements must be put in place to transfer out, at completion, appropriate funds for those employees transferring to the buyer. Whether the buyer adopts the pension scheme or takes a transfer payment, it must ensure that the fund is sufficient for the trustees to fulfil their obligations. Accordingly, the value of the fund will be assessed by actuaries and any deficit or surplus will be dealt with by, for example, an appropriate adjustment to the purchase price of the target.

Comparative position in the United States

In the US, pension schemes that have a privileged tax status are referred to as 'tax qualified' retirement plans. There are basically two types: a defined contribution plan (with fixed contributions to an individual account for each participant), and a defined benefit pension plan (with contributions by an employer to a fund benefiting all participants). The issues surrounding such funds are similar to those in relation to a money purchase or a final salary scheme in the UK. The funding of a defined benefits plan is likely to be an issue, with similar concerns as to whether it may be under- or over-funded.

3.5.6 Property

The buyer's lawyers will not always carry out comprehensive searches and enquiries in relation to all the properties owned and occupied by the target. The timetable agreed by the parties for the acquisition often rules out a full investigation of all the conveyancing aspects. It may also prove impractical for full structural surveys to be carried out, particularly when the seller is keen not to alert its workforce to the proposed sale. The risk to the buyer in these circumstances depends on the importance of the properties. If they are relatively insignificant in the context of the deal as a whole, limiting the scope of the investigation may be justified. Also, the buyer may be able to rely on other means of protection against title or other property-related problems. Apart from a full title investigation by the buyer's lawyers, the two main means of protection for the buyer under English law are as follows:

(a) *A certificate of title given by the seller's solicitor.* The chief certification sought by the buyer is that the properties have good and marketable title. Although the precise wording and format of the certificate may be the subject of negotiation between the parties, a standard form of certificate, settled by the Land Law Committee of the City of London Law Society, is in use and is generally accepted in commercial transactions. The certificate is addressed to the buyer, who can sue the seller's lawyers if it has been prepared negligently. However, if a false statement or an omission in the certificate is a result of incorrect information supplied by the client, the seller's solicitor will not generally be liable, provided the certificate makes it clear that that statement or omission was based on information given by the client. In these circumstances, the buyer will be left without a remedy, unless it has obtained a warranty direct from the seller that the information on which the certificate is based is true and accurate.

In many civil law jurisdictions, a search as to ownership and encumbrances attached to the seller's immovable assets should be carried out in the land register of that jurisdiction. In France and the Netherlands, a *notaire* or *notaris* will conduct such investigations. In Germany, all real property has to be registered in the land register (*Grundbuch*), and although an exception applies for property owned by the state and local authorities, churches, rivers and railways, which can be registered on application of the owner, in practice most of this real property has also been registered.

(b) *Property warranties given by the seller in the sale and purchase agreement.* The buyer will usually seek warranty statements, including that the target company (or seller) has good title to all the properties, that they are free from any charge or encumbrance, that all relevant planning legislation has been complied with, that any restrictions, conditions and covenants affecting the properties have been observed and performed, that there are no outstanding disputes, and that the properties are in good repair and fit for their current use.

Where a full investigation is to be carried out, the buyer's lawyers will need to make all the usual conveyancing searches and enquiries in relation to the properties being transferred (asset acquisition) or owned or occupied by the target company (share acquisition). It is not intended to explore these in detail; however, a number of points may be of particular concern to the buyer.

3.5.6.1 Inspection/valuation/survey

The practical difficulties of the buyer and its representatives carrying out inspections and surveys of the target's premises have already been discussed. However, physical inspection of properties which are important to the target is advisable, as this may disclose obvious problems which ought to be addressed prior to completion or may prompt further enquiry of the seller (eg whether certain uses have planning permission). In the case of leasehold premises, one of the main purposes of making an inspection is to ascertain whether the repairing obligations under the lease have been complied with. Also, by requisitioning a valuation of the properties concerned, the buyer will be able to compare their actual values with the values which appear in the accounts of the target business or company, although this may not be necessary if the buyer has access to a recent valuation carried out on behalf of the seller.

A full structural survey (of all the properties) is the ideal, but is often not feasible in the circumstances.

3.5.6.2 Landlord's consents

On an asset acquisition, the consent of the landlord will frequently be required for the assignment of any leasehold premises included in the sale, as a term of the lease. Even on a share transfer, where the properties do not change hands, the buyer's lawyers should check the terms of leases carefully. It is not unusual for the landlord's consent to be required on a share acquisition (the lease may, for example, define assignment as including a change in control of the tenant company).

The buyer's lawyers should also ascertain whether the seller has guaranteed the lease obligations. The seller is likely to ask for an undertaking from the buyer (as a term of the main agreement) that the buyer will use its best endeavours to obtain the release of the seller from such guarantees and, in the meantime, to indemnify the seller against any liability. The buyer's lawyers should ask the landlord (subject to confidentiality) whether it will agree to release the seller and, if so, on what terms. (The landlord is likely to insist that the buyer enters into a similar guarantee.)

3.5.6.3 Original tenants of leasehold property in the UK

For UK leases granted before 1 January 1996, the original tenant of leasehold premises is in an invidious position because it remains liable to the landlord for breaches of the terms of the lease even after it has assigned the lease to a third party. Although there is an implied indemnity by the assignee in favour of the original tenant, this will be of little use if the assignee becomes insolvent. Indeed, the present tenant's insolvency is likely to be the reason why the landlord is pursuing the original tenant for breach of covenant.

On an asset sale, the seller may, therefore, have a contingent liability after completing the assignment to the buyer of leasehold premises of which it was the original tenant. On a share sale, the buyer's lawyers should ask whether the target company has been granted a lease at any time. Since the target company will remain liable on any such lease, they should ask for a copy of the lease to establish the extent of the potential liability.

For leases granted on or after 1 January 1996, the concept of continuing original tenant liability has been abolished. An original tenant who lawfully assigns its lease is generally released from liability as from the date of assignment, but could be required by the terms of the lease to guarantee performance of the lease obligations by its immediate assignee under an 'authorised guarantee agreement'.

Considerable differences exist between the lease of a property in common law jurisdictions and in civil law jurisdictions. Generally speaking, at common law a lease of a property is an interest in the land, whereas a lease in civil law is considered to be a contractual right, which usually does not need to be registered.

3.5.6.4   Problems of investigation on a share purchase

A buyer of shares will not obtain protection from searches of official registers in the same way as a buyer of the assets of a business. This is because protection is usually afforded to, inter alia, a buyer of an interest in land, whereas on a share acquisition there is no change in ownership of the target company's properties. It has already been seen that, under English law, failure to register a charge at the Companies Registry does not render it void against the company itself. The position is similar with searches at HM Land Registry, including searches of the Land Charges Department registers and the Local Land Charges Register. Although pre-completion searches at HM Land Registry will reveal most registered charges, etc, the buyer of shares does not have the benefit of any priority period within which it can safely complete the acquisition without further matters appearing on the register (this follows from the fact that unregistered charges are valid against the company in any case). In addition, the buyer of shares is not entitled to receive compensation from a local authority which fails to register a local land charge. (The Local Land Charges Act 1975 provides for the payment of compensation to a person who acquires an interest in the land.)

3.5.7   Environmental matters

3.5.7.1   The environmental problem in acquisitions

With both an asset acquisition and a share acquisition, the buyer does not know the nature and extent of the environmental liabilities. If the deal is to be undertaken by a share acquisition then the buyer would be directly liable for the past actions of the company as it is, in effect, taking over the identity of the target company. This situation is of greater concern than the alternative, an asset acquisition, but there are still significant concerns even in that situation – the state of the site(s) being the most obvious.

To illustrate the problems, consider the operations of a typical factory. In this case, the environmental problems for a buyer fall into three categories:

(a)   First, there is the buyer's requirement that the factory should continue to operate after completion of the deal, and in order that the factory continues to operate, all relevant environmental permits must be in place and must be transferred to the buyer if necessary.

(b)   Secondly, the buyer will be concerned to know whether the operations of the factory have resulted in pollution of the site, or of anywhere else. The buyer will also need to consider the historical use of the site and whether this may have caused pollution. If the site owned by the target company is polluted then the target and/or its new owner could be liable for the costs of cleaning it up, whether the pollution was caused by the operations of the factory or by, for example, previous owners of the site.

(c)   Thirdly, any pollution caused by the factory may give or have given rise to third party claims against the target, for example claims for nuisance, negligence or trespass, and breaches of environmental legislation may result in criminal sanctions.

3.5.7.2   Legislation relating to environmental permits

A detailed explanation of the system of environmental regulation is beyond the scope of this book. However, a number of points of particular relevance to a potential buyer of a target business or company are made below.

The Environmental Permitting (England and Wales) Regulations 2016 (SI 2016/1154), as amended by the Environmental Permitting (England and Wales) (Amendment) Regulations

2018 (SI 2018/110), require an environmental permit to be obtained by any person operating a regulated facility. Regulated facilities include those carrying out certain activities relating to waste, water discharge, groundwater, radioactive substances, solvent emissions or flood risk. Licences issued under previous legislation relating to such activities automatically became environmental permits when the current regulations came into force.

If an environmental permit is required, it will be issued subject to certain conditions. These will often include specific restrictions on the operation of the relevant process and requirements to use best available techniques, both of which may entail considerable expense.

Depending on the particular activity being carried out, responsibility for the issue and review of environmental permits lies with the relevant local authority or, in England, the Environment Agency (in Wales, the Natural Resources Body for Wales).

3.5.7.3 Penalties, directors' liability and clean-up costs

Breach of various provisions of the environmental legislation, such as operating a regulated facility without an environmental permit, will give rise to criminal liability involving stiff penalties. An offence is also committed by any person who knowingly caused or knowingly permitted the offence. This could lead, for example, to an individual such as a director or manager being found guilty of an offence for knowingly permitting a company to operate without an environmental permit. The provision of false or misleading information to a regulator may also constitute a criminal offence.

A court may order steps to be taken to remedy the matter that gave rise to the offence, and an individual or a company could also face liability in tort for any damage done to other property. Clean-up costs and any damages resulting from civil liability can prove to be extremely substantial.

3.5.7.4 Public information

Information on environmental matters is available to the public through registers, each of which is compiled and maintained by the relevant regulator. The buyer of a business or company is, therefore, able to obtain useful information on the environmental background of the target. Publicly available information includes details of the grant and variation of environmental permits, any enforcement notices served and any environmental permitting convictions. The register will also include any information obtained by the relevant regulator as a result of its monitoring, including any information provided by the target in compliance with the conditions of an environmental permit. However, information may be excluded from the public register in the interests of national security or on the grounds that it is confidential.

3.5.7.5 Investigation and transfer of environmental permits

When acting for the buyer, it is important to ask the seller's lawyers for copies of all relevant environmental permits. An environmental lawyer or consultant can advise on the types of environmental permit which a particular target business should have. They will need to be checked to make sure that they:

(a) cover all the operations of the business;

(b) are still in force;

(c) do not contain any requirements regarding future upgrading of pollution control equipment; and

(d) are not due to be reviewed in the near future, as further upgrading requirements could be imposed as a result of the review.

A transfer of an environmental permit to a new operator, such as the buyer of a business, is only possible if the regulator is satisfied that the transferee is competent to operate the regulated facility in accordance with the terms of the permit. The proposed transferee will therefore need to provide the regulator with details of its proposed policies and procedures for running the regulated facility and minimising the risk of pollution from the activities covered by the permit. If any enforcement notice is outstanding in respect of the environmental permit, the transferee will need to ensure that this is complied with.

Another possible issue is that the seller should have an environmental permit but does not. It is likely that considerable expenditure on pollution control equipment would be needed before such an authorisation could be obtained.

In cross-border transactions, it will be important to investigate the environmental regulation that applies in all the relevant jurisdictions. Most countries have a similar system of licensing processes, with equivalent provisions imposing penalties and clean-up liability. The Environmental Permitting (England and Wales) Regulations 2016 themselves transpose the provisions of 15 EU Directives.

3.5.7.6   Other searches and enquiries

The extent of the buyer's enquiries of the seller will depend on the nature of the target business. However, even the most environmentally friendly business may be occupying a site which has a contamination history. The seller should be asked to provide details of any applications for authorisation, any statutory notices served on it or the target, and any complaints made by third parties. The seller should also be asked whether an environmental audit has been carried out in relation to the target and, if so, to provide a copy, together with the details of any environmental insurance that may be in place for the target.

Although in many transactions the buyer will be content with a site visit, or a 'desk-top survey' (ie a review of available information), where a target business or company is involved in environmentally sensitive operations, or where land sites may have a history of contamination, the buyer should also consider commissioning a full environmental audit prior to entering into the agreement. This is likely to prove expensive and will require the full co-operation of the seller. However, the extent of the buyer's potential liability in these circumstances will often make it a worthwhile investment.

3.5.7.7   Climate change related investigations

In recent years, with the benefit of greater understanding of the climate change related risks presented by businesses, investigation of a business's activities increasingly extend to how their activities impact the climate. Proposals to introduce mandatory reporting and disclosure obligations on companies of their climate risks mean that climate related investigations are likely to be an increasingly common feature of target due diligence.

3.5.8   The Bribery Act 2010 and the Modern Slavery Act 2015

The Bribery Act 2010 (BA 2010) came into force on 1 July 2011 and is enforced chiefly by the Serious Fraud Office (SFO). The Act creates four offences – broadly, those of offering a bribe, accepting a bribe, bribing a foreign public official and, for commercial organisations, failing to prevent bribery – and covers all transactions, whether they be in the public or private sector. It has wide-reaching territorial effect, covering all acts or omissions occurring in the UK and also those which take place outside the UK if the particular corruption would be an offence had it taken place within the UK. The legislation touches not only UK incorporated companies, but also non-UK companies which carry on a business or part of a business in the UK.

Breach of the BA 2010 carries stiff criminal penalties – for individuals, up to 10 years' imprisonment and/or an unlimited fine, and unlimited fines for companies. Early indications were that fines imposed on companies would be substantial (R v Innospec [2010] EW Misc 7 (EWCC)). Guidelines from the Sentencing Council, on Fraud, Bribery and Money Laundering Offences, in force from 1 October 2014, identify the harm caused by an offence committed by a corporate body as a financial sum. This sum is described as the gross profit from the contract obtained, retained or sought as a result of the offence, or the costs avoided by failing to put in place appropriate measures to prevent bribery. When imposing a fine, this sum will often be a starting point for the court, with uplifts of up to four times that figure possible where the corporate offender is found to be highly culpable and/or there are other factors increasing the seriousness of the offence (such as previous convictions, cross-border offences, or substantial harm caused to the integrity or confidence of markets). In appropriate cases, the SFO may use its powers to make a civil recovery order or confiscation order, either as an alternative or in addition to a criminal prosecution.

The offence of failing to prevent bribery, amongst others, poses an additional compliance burden for commercial bodies, the main defence lying in the organisation being able to show that it has in place 'adequate procedures' for the prevention of corruption.

Clearly, the effect of this legislation must be considered by a buyer, who should explore potential liabilities through the due diligence process and obtain warranty protection against hidden risks in the usual way. Although the BA 2010 does not have retrospective effect, and a buyer will not personally be liable for the acts of the target which took place prior to completion of the acquisition, there may nonetheless be serious risks for the buyer. The target company and/or its senior officers could be prosecuted, leading to fines, confiscation of assets or revenue acquired through corrupt practices, loss of key employees, and damage to the reputation of the target and associated businesses. Additionally, conviction of an offence under the BA 2010 could lead to the target company being debarred from procurement, preventing it from tendering for public sector work and thus losing revenue that it otherwise might have earned. A buyer should therefore take into account the risks of such a breach.

Similar anti-corruption systems also operate in other jurisdictions, notably in the US under the Foreign Corrupt Practices Act 1977. As part of the due diligence process, therefore, the potential corruption risk inherent in the target business should be assessed, bearing in mind that certain jurisdictions or industries may pose a higher risk than others, and particular attention should be paid to any major public sector contracts. In addition, the buyer's solicitor should obtain details of the target's compliance policies in this area and should investigate the involvement of senior management in securing compliance with anti-corruption procedures. The SFO has published guidance which may be helpful in determining whether the target's approach to reducing corruption is adequate.

Specific corruption risks identified during the due diligence process can be dealt with by the buyer in the usual ways, for example by reducing the purchase price, excluding relevant assets, requiring the seller to provide an indemnity or, where the perceived anticipated liability is too damaging, withdrawing from the transaction. However, since most corrupt practices will, evidently, not be documented, the buyer should also seek warranty protection, with the seller at least warranting that anti-corruption procedures are in place and have been enforced.

Transparency International UK (a non-government body and a widely recognised anti-corruption organisation) provides useful practical guidance for anti-bribery due diligence in the acquisitions context. The recommendations include investigating whether the target company has an adequate anti-bribery programme in place, and what commitment the board has to countering bribery, as well as considering what might be the likely impact if bribery were discovered after completion of the acquisition transaction.

On a related compliance point, any organisation which has a turnover of £36 million or more is obliged to publish a transparency statement under the Modern Slavery Act 2015. The statement must confirm either the steps the company has taken during the previous financial year to ensure that slavery and human trafficking are not taking place in its supply chain, or that the company has taken no such steps. Although legal sanctions in relation to this obligation are few, the buyer should nonetheless take into account the negative market attention likely to be consequent on a missing or unsatisfactory statement on the part of the target.

In some countries, legislation is being introduced that imposes mandatory human rights due diligence obligations on companies, which go further than the obligations seen in the UK's Modern Slavery Act 2015. In 2017, France (through its Law No 2017-399 on Duty of Care of Parent Companies and Ordering Companies) introduced a duty of vigilance on companies above a certain size to detect and prevent human rights risks arising in their operations. In the United States, similar legislation was proposed in the form of the Corporate Human Rights Risk Assessment, Prevention and Mitigation Act, the Slave-Free Business Certification Act and the Business Supply Chain Transparency on Trafficking and Slavery Act. It seems likely that, in future, a buyer of a target may need to assess compliance with such emerging legislation as part of the due diligence exercise it conducts.

3.6 DUE DILIGENCE REPORTS

In large transactions, the legal advisers may be expected to produce a legal due diligence report, either on an on-going basis during the investigation process or as a final report once the investigation of the target is complete. The information revealed in the report will then be used in negotiation of the acquisition documentation and, in particular, will have a significant bearing on the warranties and indemnities required by the buyer.

A number of specialist lawyers or other professional advisers may have been involved, exploring different aspects of the target business. In addition, if the target has overseas subsidiaries, due diligence investigations may also have been undertaken by lawyers in the relevant overseas jurisdictions. The results of all these investigations must be co-ordinated and the key points brought to the buyer's attention in the report. The type of report that is required will depend on the particular circumstances of the transaction.

3.6.1 Types of report

3.6.1.1 Interim

On very large transactions the due diligence process may be very lengthy and the buyer may require interim reports summarising any issues of key importance. This is intended to provide an early warning mechanism in relation to matters that may be so serious that the buyer will consider withdrawing from the deal, or at least renegotiating the main contract terms.

3.6.1.2 Full audit

A full audit is a complete audit of the target business, including an in-depth summary of all the target's legal obligations. This type of report is very rare because it is very expensive to produce, and is required only if the buyer is particularly concerned about the risks associated with proceeding with the acquisition.

3.6.1.3 By exception

The usual form of report is a 'by exception', or 'exceptions only' report. This report focuses only on matters that are material to the proposed acquisition, or on matters that are unusual or unexpected. This type of report is probably the most difficult to write, as the buyer's solicitor must make an assessment of what is material or unusual, and they must therefore have a good understanding of the type of business being reviewed.

3.6.2 Format of report

3.6.2.1 Executive report

The due diligence report will usually start with an executive summary which sets out the key findings of the report. It may also include key proposals either in terms of consents or conditions that must be fulfilled before the acquisition can proceed, or in terms of key contractual protections that should be included on the buyer's behalf in the acquisition documentation.

3.6.2.2   Scope of investigation and statement on liability

As with the accountants' report, the buyer will have claims under English law against the reporting legal advisers if the report is negligently prepared (both in contract for breach of the implied duty of reasonable skill and care, and in tort for negligent misstatement).

Statements by third parties

The buyer of shares or the assets of a business may have relied on statements, forecasts and opinions (in relation to financial matters, in particular) made by parties other than the seller. Where the buyer has relied on such statements, it will have a remedy against these third parties if the information turns out to be false or misleading. The scope of negligent misstatement generally and its application to acquisitions in particular have been considered in several important English court decisions.

Caparo Industries plc v Dickman [1990] 2 WLR 358

Caparo, which was a shareholder in Fidelity plc, acquired control of the company relying on the audited accounts. Caparo claimed that the accounts were inaccurate and misleading in showing a pre-tax profit, when in fact the company had made a loss. It sued the company's auditors for negligence in auditing the accounts (and certifying them as 'true and accurate'). Caparo alleged that the auditors owed it a duty of care either as a potential investor, or as an existing shareholder. The Court of Appeal held that the auditors owed Caparo a duty of care as a shareholder but not as a potential investor.

The House of Lords emphasised that the imposition of a duty of care in economic loss cases required 'proximity' of relationship as well as foreseeability of loss (a third criterion being that it must not be unreasonable to impose a duty of care). In determining the question of proximity, there was no single general principle, and the court should be guided by established categories of negligence. A review of previous cases in this area led the House of Lords to identify three conditions for proximity to exist. It must be shown that the maker of the statement knew the following:

(a)   that the statement would be communicated to the person relying on it or to a clearly defined class of person to whom that person belonged; and

(b)   this would be done specifically in connection with a particular transaction or a particular type of transaction; and

(c)   the person would be very likely to rely on it in deciding whether to enter into the transaction.

The House of Lords decided that the auditors owed no duty of care to Caparo as an investor or a shareholder; their Lordships were not prepared to find a duty of care on auditors to members of the public at large as potential investors (or bidders). As for shareholders, they considered that the auditor's duty in relation to the accounts was owed to the shareholders as a body to enable them to exercise collective control of the company, and not to individual shareholders to assist in their decision whether to buy more shares.

Morgan Crucible plc v Hill Samuel and Co Ltd [1991] 2 WLR 665

Caparo was distinguished in the *Morgan Crucible* case. Following a takeover bid for a listed company by the plaintiffs (claimants), the chairman of the listed company incorporated various statements and profit forecasts in documents issued to shareholders and to the press as a defence to the bid. The plaintiffs increased their bid and successfully acquired control of the company. Some of the financial statements and forecasts were misleading and the company was not as valuable as this information had led the plaintiffs to believe. They sued the chairman, the auditors and the merchant bank advising the board in negligence.

On an application to amend the statement of claim after the decision in *Caparo* (the original claim had also been based on financial statements made prior to the bid and the plaintiffs wished to restrict it to statements, etc made after the bid), the Court of Appeal granted leave on the grounds that the amended claim disclosed a reasonable cause of action. The Court was of the view that it was arguable that there was a sufficient degree of proximity since the defendants intended the plaintiffs to rely on the representations in deciding whether to make an increased bid. (The case settled before reaching trial.)

To limit any possible exposure to such claims, the due diligence report will usually include a section that sets out the agreed scope of the investigation and any limitations on the liability of the advisors who have prepared it.

3.6.2.3 Main report

The main report is usually divided into sections covering each area of the target business. Each issue investigated is identified, together with the results of that investigation and any possible impact there may be for the proposed acquisition. Lastly, wherever possible, the report will indicate how particular issues may be practically resolved, for example by measures such as an adjustment of the purchase price of the target or by acquiring an appropriate consent from a third party.

PART II

THE TERMS OF THE ACQUISITION

THE SALE AND PURCHASE AGREEMENT

LEARNING OUTCOMES

After reading this chapter you will be able to:

- understand the structure of a sale and purchase agreement
- explain the uses of completion accounts and how their preparation can be controlled
- describe the main forms of consideration.

4.1 STRUCTURE OF THE AGREEMENT

This chapter sets out the main elements of a typical agreement governing the terms of a share acquisition or an asset acquisition (where a business is acquired as a going concern).

The order of the agreement will usually be as follows:

(a) parties and date;

(b) operative provisions;

(c) schedules;

(d) execution by the parties.

Although English is often the chosen language for cross-border acquisitions, language can be a concern in an international context. Local law may require specific documents to be in the relevant local language or to be made up in a specific form. In a French *fonds de commerce* acquisition, for example, French law requires that the sale and purchase agreement is in French. However, the laws of many jurisdictions allow a certain amount of flexibility as to the form and content of sale and purchase documents.

An international acquisition with multiple jurisdictions will often involve a main agreement (a framework or 'umbrella' agreement) and additional agreements related to the transaction in each relevant jurisdiction. The framework agreement is in general drafted in English and, especially if one of the parties is based in the UK or the US, often governed by English or New York law. In each specific jurisdiction the relevant documents are often prepared in the local language and may be governed by the local law. If documents are prepared in multiple languages, the framework agreement and the local agreements should clearly state which version prevails in the event of a conflict. Local lawyers should review the framework agreement to make sure that it does not conflict with the relevant local law. Moreover, a lawyer should make sure that an accurate explanation of any documents that are in an unfamiliar language will be forthcoming.

4.2 PARTIES

The parties to the agreement will usually be the buyer and the seller. Where there is more than one seller, the details of all the sellers will usually be set out in a schedule to the agreement.

Usually, all of the sellers will give the warranties to the buyer. However, in some circumstances some of the sellers, such as trustee shareholders or private equity sellers, may be unwilling to give warranties (see **5.8**). In this case, the parties will be described in the agreement as the seller(s), the warrantor(s) and the buyer(s).

The parties may also include guarantors of the seller's or buyer's obligations. For example, the seller may be required to provide a guarantor in relation to its potential liability under the warranties (see **5.9.1**). Similarly, if some part of the purchase price is to be left outstanding on completion, the seller may require that the buyer's obligation to pay that amount is guaranteed.

When the parties execute the agreement it will be dated, so creating a binding contractual agreement to buy and sell either the shares of the target company or the assets of the business.

In international acquisitions, there is a predominance of documents in English governed by English or US law. Although many Continental European and Latin American countries are influenced by the large influx of acquisition agreements drawn up by common law lawyers, the UK or US style of documenting an acquisition differs considerably from civil law countries. It is often said that common law contracts are far longer than civil law contracts, and one of the reasons is that common law does not have any code provisions so that it is the contract itself that governs the relationship between the parties. The structure and the content of the contract, as well as the form of the words chosen, are very important in common law contracts. Contracts in civil code jurisdictions rely on the underlying code, which includes a number of statutory contractual provisions, as well as an interpretation of the intentions of the parties according to the underlying principle of good faith. In general, therefore, civil law contracts tend to be shorter than common law contracts.

4.3 OPERATIVE PROVISIONS

The operative provisions set out the basis on which the buyer agrees to purchase the shares or assets of the business, and on which the seller agrees to sell. This can cover a wide variety of issues, including a description of the assets to be acquired, the price and payment terms, and any contractual reassurances being provided with the sale. The precise details are often set out in the schedules to the agreement.

4.3.1 Definitions and interpretation

As a matter of good drafting, the operative provisions should commence with a definitions and interpretations clause. This defines terms which are used throughout the agreement (including the schedules) and, consequently, avoids repetition and the need for cumbersome cross-references.

An aspect of interpretation clauses which sometimes proves controversial concerns references to statutory provisions. The buyer will usually want it to be provided expressly that references to statutory provisions are to be interpreted as including subsequent amendments to those provisions. This is dangerous for the seller, particularly in relation to its potential liability under the warranties, because, by agreeing to such a clause, it would take the risk of those liabilities increasing as a result of legislation enacted after completion which has retrospective effect. For example, this could be a significant factor in the context of environmental protection legislation which may well become more strict in the future.

4.3.2 Conditions precedent

Completion of an acquisition, whether of shares or of assets, is normally simultaneous with exchange of contracts. The parties usually try to avoid any gap between exchange and completion and the consequent problems connected with running a business during this period. However, this is not always possible. Sometimes the sale and purchase agreement may be entered into on the basis that it will be completed when a certain condition is fulfilled. If the agreement is conditional it is usual to include an obligation on the parties to seek fulfilment of the condition, a longstop date by which the condition must be fulfilled or waived, and a time frame within which the acquisition must complete once the condition has been fulfilled (see **7.1** and **7.2**).

4.3.3 Agreement to purchase

The agreement will set out exactly what is being bought and sold, by reference to a schedule detailing either the shareholdings (share purchase) or the assets (asset purchase) being acquired.

The agreement will also provide that the parties agree to sell and purchase the specified shares or assets, and will usually provide that the buyer is not obliged to buy any of the shares or assets unless it can purchase all of them simultaneously.

4.3.4 Consideration

The sale and purchase agreement will stipulate the agreed price, the form that it will take, and the timing of payment.

Where there are multiple sellers, the amount of the purchase price payable to each seller will usually be stated in a schedule to the agreement.

On an asset sale, the amount of the consideration which is attributable to each separate asset will be specified in the agreement (the agreed apportionment is usually set out in a schedule). In the UK, the parties have some flexibility in making this apportionment, and are usually influenced heavily by taxation and stamp duty implications (see **8.4.4.5**).

The purchase price may be fixed, or provisions may be included in the agreement allowing for adjustments to the price, for example as a result of the preparation of completion accounts or the operation of an earn-out agreement (see **4.3.4.2** below).

4.3.4.1 Completion accounts

Reasons for use, and form

When negotiating the price, the parties may have based their valuation of the target on dated information, such as the last audited accounts or estimates in unaudited management accounts. The buyer may want confirmation that the figures on which the valuation was based have not altered significantly since the date to which the original accounts were made up. This may be of particular concern if the target experiences significant fluctuations in its net assets, or if its supposed current earnings were an important factor in the price negotiations. In these circumstances, the parties may agree that the purchase price should be adjusted to reflect the actual net assets or earnings of the target on the completion date, as determined by a set of agreed accounts drawn up after completion. An additional advantage of this method is that detailed negotiations on the value of the target are delayed, thereby saving time in the run-up to completion.

The completion accounts can take a variety of forms depending upon their purpose and the nature of the particular transaction. They may consist of a full profit and loss account and balance sheet, a balance sheet alone, or a simple statement of net assets. Where the purpose of the completion accounts is to investigate very specific concerns of the buyer, the accounts may take the form of a valuation of particular assets which may be difficult or impossible to value accurately before completion, such as cash, debt, working capital, or stock.

Control of the completion accounts

The seller's accountant, who is likely to be the target company's auditor up until completion, is often nominated to prepare the first draft of the completion accounts since it will already be familiar with the business. However, as the buyer will be in control of the target after completion, it may make more practical sense for its advisers to deal with the task and, in any event, the buyer may prefer the greater opportunity for financial scrutiny that this provides. The final decision as to who will control preparation of the completion accounts is ultimately a matter for negotiation between the parties.

Typical provisions in the sale and purchase agreement

The sale and purchase agreement will usually provide for a maximum amount of the purchase price to be paid on completion, with a further adjustment payment or repayment to be made once the completion accounts have been prepared. Any adjustment to the purchase price is usually made in cash and on a pound for pound basis according to the results of the completion accounts (see **4.3.5.1** for tax consequences). The actual adjustment made and how it is to be paid will depend upon what the parties have agreed. For example, the parties may agree that the buyer will be entitled to a repayment if the net assets fall short of amounts on which the valuation was based, but that the seller is not entitled to any further payment if the figure exceeds the original figure. Similarly, if the valuation consisted of applying a multiplier to the earnings of the target, the agreement may provide for the purchase price to be adjusted by applying the same multiplier to any shortfall in earnings identified by the completion accounts. There are many variations on this theme and, in all cases, the legal advisers must ensure that the relevant contractual provisions are drafted carefully so as to implement precisely what the parties have agreed. It is also important that the sale and purchase agreement contains clear provisions guarding against possible double recovery that could occur where, for example, a reduction in net assets at completion also constitutes evidence of breach of warranty. The buyer should not be able to recover under an action for breach of warranty whilst also benefitting from paying a smaller purchase price as a result of the completion accounts.

An agreed mechanism for drawing up the completion accounts will be included in the sale and purchase agreement, usually within a schedule. As the results of completion accounts will determine any necessary price adjustment, the agreed mechanism must be drafted with care.

A typical provision on completion accounts will provide for the following:

(a)   the completion accounts to be drawn up within a specified period after completion (eg 30 business days). The accountant preparing the accounts is often instructed to do so on a basis which is consistent with the latest set of audited accounts but, in any case, the specific accounting policies and methods to be applied should be clearly stated in the schedule to the sale and purchase agreement;

(b)   the buyer (or the seller if the buyer's accountant has prepared the first draft of the accounts) and its accountant to have the right to review the completion accounts within a specified time period;

(c)   in the absence of agreement as to the accounts, a limited period during which the parties will attempt to resolve any disputes;

(d)   in the case of continued dispute, the matter to be referred to an independent firm of accountants acting as experts, such firm to be as agreed between the parties or as nominated by the President of the Institute of Chartered Accountants in England and Wales.

Specific accounting policies and narrowing the scope for dispute

The accounting policies to be used in the preparation of the completion accounts, and their priority, should be clearly set out in the sale and purchase agreement. These may include a mixture of specific policies agreed by the parties for the purpose of drawing up the accounts, the policies used in the last audited accounts of the target, and standard accounting policies such as GAAP, UK GAAP, or the IFRS.

It is also vital to document the method by which these policies will be applied to avoid grey areas which could give rise to disputes. For example, the valuation of stock tends to be on the basis of 'the lower of cost and net realisable value', and it is usual to provide for a level of 'slow-moving or obsolete' stock. Although these descriptions are standard, they are nevertheless subjective and, as such, open to different interpretation. It is appropriate, then, to provide guidance in the sale and purchase agreement as to how these terms should be applied. 'Net realisable value' could be the actual selling price of the stock or its market price at completion. Similarly, the parties must consider what will constitute slow-moving stock – it is common to provide a sliding scale for valuation, for example that stock which is more than three months old will be valued at 50% of cost, and stock over six months old at 25% of cost.

In valuing the target's debtors there is also great scope for disagreement, particularly in assessing the level of bad and doubtful debts and whether adequate provision has been made in the accounts. Again, disputes can be avoided if the parties can agree to apply a specific schedule of timings to identify bad debts, such as that, say, 50% of debts over six months old and 100% of debts over 12 months old will be considered to be bad debts.

The valuation of fixed assets can also be somewhat subjective – the sale and purchase agreement should clearly state whether the assets will be included in the completion accounts at historic cost, recent market valuation, or a valuation on some other basis. In addition, it is important to define the applicable depreciation policy clearly, including the period over which the various assets will be depreciated.

Obviously the parties and their advisers must take great care in negotiating the contractual provisions that will apply to the preparation of the completion accounts to try to avoid lengthy disputes once the target has changed hands. In the event that there will be a period between signing the sale and purchase agreement and completion, it is advisable for the parties to consider the imposition of restrictive covenants to prevent either of them trying to improve the results of the accounts by making unnecessary changes within the business. The seller, for example, should be bound in the pre-completion period preventing it from, say, overstocking the business.

Fixed price or 'locked box' transactions

It is clear from the above paragraphs that, although completion accounts can be a useful device, there is also great scope for time-consuming disputes in their preparation and finalisation. This has resulted in a recent trend towards fixed price, or so-called 'locked box', transactions where the parties agree a price for the target company (it is most commonly used in share acquisitions) which is fixed before the sale and purchase agreement is signed. This method is attractive for the seller but riskier for the buyer whose only opportunity for a price adjustment after completion is by bringing a valid warranty claim. A deal that proceeds as a locked box transaction will nonetheless see careful negotiations of the agreed accounts that are used for setting the price (the 'locked box balance sheet') and the buyer is likely to seek warranty cover in relation to them, such as that the balance sheet has been prepared with all reasonable care.

In a locked box transaction, the economic interest in the target passes to the buyer at a pre-signing date (the 'locked box date'), and the buyer therefore has the benefit of the cash profits generated by the business from that date. The seller, however, does not receive the sale proceeds until completion, and to compensate the seller for this, the buyer will typically pay interest on the purchase price for the period between the locked box date and closing.

For its part, the buyer is wise to include provisions in the sale and purchase agreement to protect against 'leakage' – that is, the seller extracting value from the target between the date of the agreed accounts and the completion date, other than as permitted by the sale and purchase agreement. 'Leakage' could include payment of a dividend, unsanctioned transfer of assets to target shareholders, or inappropriate payment of expenses by the target. The seller will usually be obliged to undertake to repay such 'leakage' to the buyer on a pound for pound basis. 'Permitted leakage', that is leakage that is agreed between the parties, will be clearly specified in the sale and purchase agreement, together with details of whether such leakage will result in a reduction in price. Leakage claims should be carved out of the de minimis and maximum thresholds applied to the general warranties and indemnities.

Although the advantages for a seller in using a locked box mechanism are clearer, this type of transaction has pros and cons for both parties. For both buyer and seller, there is certainty of price at an early stage, and both benefit from the simplicity of the process and the lower costs that it entails – management time will not be tied up in post-closing matters.

The seller enjoys increased control over the setting of the price and, in an auction sale, the price adjustments are likely to be less aggressive, making it easier to compare bids. However, the seller must have a suitable balance sheet available (ie recent, audited, and separately identifiable) to be able to use a locked box process, and must ensure that the interest charged between the locked box date and closing is not too low.

The buyer must set the practical advantages of the mechanism against the possible downsides – such as the need to negotiate price adjustments earlier in the process, and with less knowledge of the target, no possibility of clawing back value after closing, and the risk that the business may deteriorate between the locked box date and closing. The buyer must ensure that the sale and purchase agreement clearly defines who is a 'seller' (or 'related person') for the purposes of identifying leakage, that systems are in place to identify all transactions between those parties and the target between the locked box date and closing, and that the leakage warranty is carefully drawn.

4.3.4.2 Earn outs

The term 'earn out' is used to describe an arrangement whereby at least part of the consideration is determined by reference to the future profitability of the target for a specified period after completion (eg for the three accounting periods following completion). Earn outs are often considered appropriate where the sellers continue to manage the target company after completion. Typically part of the purchase price will be paid at completion, followed by a further payment or series of payments made depending on the profits made by the target within the period specified.

Determining part of the purchase price on the basis of future profits not only avoids the buyer having to pay too much for a target which fails to perform as expected, but also acts as a motivating factor for the sellers/managers of the target who are staying on post-acquisition and on whom the business (particularly one that is 'employee-orientated') may be heavily reliant.

The earn-out provisions will usually provide for accounts to be prepared for the relevant periods by the buyer's accountant (ie the target's auditor after completion), with the adjustment to the purchase price dependent either on a certain level of profitability being achieved. This price will usually be based on a multiple of the profits achieved. As with completion accounts, the parties will specify how the accounts determining those profits will be calculated and will also agree the precise definitions of those items which will determine the amount of the deferred consideration, such as 'net profit' or 'earnings'. In addition, the parties will agree a clear timetable for review of the accounts, agreement of the earn-out profit and payment of it, together with provisions on how any dispute as to profit will be resolved.

In some civil law jurisdictions, provisions regarding the determination of the price need to be drafted carefully. For example, French law requires that the price is defined, or can be defined; if it is not then the contract is void. When the price is not fixed (as is the case on an earn out), the parties need to specify all the calculation data as well as a dispute resolution procedure. The provisions within the sale and purchase agreement should enable the price to be determined without any further involvement from the parties. In addition, under French law, the concept of '*leonine clauses*' (that is, clauses where one party has rights which are disproportionate to its obligations) should be borne in mind, since such clauses can be held to be void. Applying this principle, French law has held that a minimum price on an earn out would be void as a '*leonine clause*', and similarly the contract should not provide that a party be allotted the whole of any future profit, nor be released from the whole of any losses.

A difficulty with an earn-out arrangement is that the sellers who continue to manage the target after completion and the buyer may be pulling in different directions. The former will be keen to maximise profitability in the earn-out period, whereas the latter will often be more concerned that decisions are taken which will benefit the target in the long term, at the expense, perhaps, of short-term profits. The parties may try to limit this tension by defining the objectives of the company during the earn-out period and agreeing to certain limitations on the conduct of the business post-completion. The buyer may, for example, undertake not to dispose of the whole or part of the business, or not to permit any non-arm's length trading between the target and the buyer (or other members of an acquiring company's group) during this period.

4.3.5 Payment terms

Payment on an acquisition will often be by way of a fixed amount paid in cash on the completion date, but the parties are free to agree other payment terms. For example, it may be agreed that part of the purchase price is paid at a later date (known as 'deferred consideration'), or that some or all of the purchase price is satisfied by a corporate buyer issuing shares or debentures to the seller.

4.3.5.1 Deferred consideration

In certain circumstances, the seller may be prepared to allow part of the purchase price to remain outstanding on completion.

The seller may simply agree to receive payment by instalments, for example to assist the buyer in financing the acquisition, but in these circumstances the seller will usually demand interest on the outstanding amount and will insist on some form of security for the payment.

In addition, the purchase price is often subject to an adjustment dependent on completion accounts, so the final payment may be delayed and, where an earn-out arrangement has been agreed, a part of the purchase price will necessarily be deferred until the earn-out accounts have been prepared, as detailed at **4.3.4.2** above.

Alternatively, the buyer may insist on a retention of part of the purchase price as security in case a warranty claim arises in relation to the target (see **5.9.2**). Although such a retention will usually be resisted strongly by the seller, it may be appropriate where the parties are aware of a potential liability, or where the buyer expects a particular benefit to accrue from the sale, such as the continuance of trade with a valued customer, or because there is an identified but unqualified liability (for example an environmental claim or pending litigation).

In most Continental European countries, retention of the purchase price as security may be possible but is uncommon. Where the buyer requires this, it may be a difficult point of negotiation with the local counsel.

Tax treatment of deferred consideration in the UK

The general rule is that the seller will be charged to tax as at the date of sale on the total amount of the consideration, regardless of whether that consideration has actually been received. If the consideration is certain, the fact that some of it is deferred will not affect the seller's tax position.

However, where the consideration cannot be ascertained at completion because it is dependent on future events, such as the profitability of the target after the sale (as with an earn-out arrangement), the rule set out in *Marren (Inspector of Taxes) v Ingles* [1980] 3 All ER 95 applies and tax is charged on the disposal of two separate capital assets. The first disposal is of the shares of the target company or assets of the target business. On this initial disposal, the seller is treated as having received as consideration both the consideration actually received at completion plus a valuable 'chose in action' – that is, the right to receive a further payment if future profits are attained. This right to receive further payment is given a value by HMRC. When the earn-out payment is actually received, this is treated as a second disposal by the seller – in this case, the disposal of the contractual right to receive the payment. If the payment exceeds the original valuation by HMRC, the seller is treated as having made a capital gain and charged to CGT or corporation tax accordingly. A loss in these circumstances will be an allowable loss for the seller's capital tax purposes (see **9.4.3**).

The buyer's tax position for stamp duty purposes is similarly dependent upon whether the deferred consideration is ascertainable or not at completion. Where the consideration is certain but deferred, stamp duty is payable within 30 days of the completion date – no allowance for the deferral is made.

Where the amount of the deferred consideration has not yet been determined but is ascertainable at completion, for example because it is dependent on the preparation of completion accounts, the Stamp Office applies the 'wait and see' principle. In other words, stamp duty will be charged once the consideration has been finally determined. The buyer should nonetheless submit the stock transfer forms for stamping within 30 days of completion, and make a payment on account of stamp duty, to avoid penalties and reduce interest charges (which run from 30 days after the completion date even if the consideration has yet to be ascertained).

Where the deferred consideration is unascertainable at completion, as with an earn-out arrangement, no stamp duty is payable on it unless the 'contingency' principle applies. Under the contingency principle, if the consideration is stated to be subject to a minimum or a maximum amount, or is to be calculated by reference to a basic or 'benchmark' figure, then stamp duty is chargeable on that minimum, maximum or benchmark sum. Where both a minimum and a maximum are specified, stamp duty is charged on the maximum amount.

4.3.5.2 Security

Whatever the reason for the deferred consideration, where part of the purchase price does remain outstanding on completion, the seller may seek security for the outstanding sums in one of the following ways:

(a) by taking a charge over some or all of the assets transferred to the buyer;

(b) by requiring a guarantee of the buyer's obligation to pay the balance of the price from, for example, individual shareholders, directors or the parent company of a corporate buyer;

(c) by providing in the agreement that title to specified assets is to remain with the seller until the purchase price is paid in full;

(d) by obliging the buyer to place a specified sum in a joint deposit account (or escrow account) on completion and defining the circumstances in which this (and accrued interest) can be released to the parties (though this will not be appropriate if the seller is simply allowing the buyer time to finance the acquisition).

4.3.5.3 Form

The most common form of consideration is cash. The buyer will rarely have sufficient cash reserves to pay for the acquisition, so will usually borrow at least part of the purchase money. The buyer's lawyers must ensure that all necessary financial arrangements for this borrowing are properly in place before the buyer enters into any commitment to pay the purchase price.

Where the buyer is a company, all or part of the consideration may be satisfied by the company issuing equity securities (shares) or debt securities (loan notes) to the seller. This is a very attractive option for a corporate buyer as it avoids the need to increase borrowing commitments or to make disposals of assets to fund the acquisition. In the UK, the seller on a share sale may be attracted by the tax treatment of a securities exchange: if certain conditions are fulfilled, the seller is able to roll over any capital gain made on the disposal of shares in the target, thus deferring the capital tax which it would otherwise pay at this time until disposal of the securities in the acquiring company received in exchange (see **9.4.2.3**).

In other jurisdictions the buyer or seller might not benefit from similar tax treatment, and local tax counsel should be consulted as to the tax position of the parties.

Shares

The seller will accept consideration in the form of shares only if the shares are readily marketable, ie they can in the future be realised for cash. This rules out shares in most private companies, which will rarely have a ready market and will often, in practice, be subject to restrictions on transfer. Shares in companies listed on an investment market, such as the London Stock Exchange, may, on the other hand, be virtually equivalent to cash for the seller.

Where shares are issued as consideration, the agreement should specify how they rank with the other shares of the acquiring company and what rights the seller will have to any dividend declared in relation to a period in which completion falls.

If the buyer is worried that the market for its shares may be adversely affected by the seller disposing of all the consideration shares at once, it may insist on a clause in the agreement restricting the seller from, for example, disposing of more than a certain percentage of its allocation within a specified period after completion.

Where the acquiring company wishes to issue shares as consideration but the seller is only really interested in receiving cash for the target company, this can be achieved, albeit in a roundabout way, by what is called a 'vendor placing'. This is an arrangement whereby the acquiring company issues shares to the seller but arranges (through its financial advisers) for the shares to be sold on immediately to institutional investors. The acquiring company undertakes in the sale and purchase agreement that the sale of the consideration shares will yield a specified sum.

If the seller obtains shares in a foreign company, the value of those shares may be influenced by currency fluctuations. In many jurisdictions the issue of shares by a foreign company in consideration for the transfer of shares in the target company triggers a prospectus requirement unless an exemption applies (for example the company has less than a certain number of employees).

Debt securities (loan notes)

An acquiring company may issue debt securities such as loan notes to the seller for the purchase price or part of it. These loan notes will usually be issued on terms that the seller can demand repayment of all or part at six-monthly intervals after a certain period from completion (eg 12 months). It may suit the seller to receive staggered payments in this way with interest on the balance outstanding, particularly as roll-over relief from capital tax is available in the UK on the same basis as for shares under a securities exchange (see **9.4.2.3**).

The loan note itself is usually a fairly straightforward document recording the grantor's indebtedness to the holder, the interest payable and the terms of the repayment. The form of the loan note will usually be agreed between the parties and set out in a schedule to the sale and purchase agreement (see **4.4**). A loan note may or may not be secured, and will usually be an acceptable form of payment for the seller only if the creditworthiness of the buyer can be assured. Accordingly, loan notes generally form part of the consideration only where the buyer is a substantial company.

It is uncommon for parties in an international acquisition to choose loan notes as consideration. Most jurisdictions do not have similar tax relief opportunities as in the UK, where the seller may choose to defer tax on any gains on the disposal of its shares if it receives loan notes in exchange.

4.3.6   Contractual protections

The remaining section of the operative provisions in the sale and purchase agreement will set out the basis on which the seller will provide any contractual reassurances, or warranties, about the target business or company. The actual warranty statements will appear in a (usually lengthy) schedule to the agreement. However, the operative provisions will set out the basis on which the warranties are given and will usually include some agreed limitations on the seller's liability for breach of warranty.

Similarly, the agreement may provide for certain specific indemnities in relation to identified problems (see **5.6**). On a share purchase this will include tax indemnities, whereby the seller agrees to indemnify the buyer in respect of any tax liability which arises in the target in relation to activities occurring before the sale. Although these tax indemnities (or 'covenants') may be drafted as a separate deed, they are more usually incorporated into the body of the main agreement (see **9.3**).

In addition to the comfort provided by the warranties and indemnities, the buyer will seek to protect the goodwill of the business by including restrictive covenants restricting the activities of the seller after completion.

4.3.7   Dispute resolution and governing law

Disputes between the parties may arise following the acquisition (for example where a claim under one of the warranties is made), and the sale and purchase agreement should address the manner in which these disputes will be adjudicated. The parties may choose to resort to an alternative dispute resolution method or to litigate, in which latter case they should insert a forum selection provision and a governing law provision. If multiple agreements are implemented in connection with each other, any choice as to the forum and governing law should be consistent among the various documents.

By specifying the jurisdiction or law that will apply, a party may be protected against a particular forum's mandatory arduous law, such as a short statute of limitations for example. Additionally, a party may benefit from the protection of a particular jurisdiction's laws that may not exist or be enforceable in the jurisdiction that would otherwise be the default selection. Given the complex nature of international acquisitions, there will be multiple bases for jurisdiction and equally as many possibilities for governing law. By agreeing beforehand in which forum a dispute will be adjudicated, and which law will govern its resolution, the parties have clarity and certainty and will save the time and expense of litigating these issues in the event of a dispute.

Most sale and purchase agreements will contain a notice clause providing a mechanism for the service of notices from one party to the other as a way of exercising contractual rights or demanding compliance with certain obligations under the contract. The laws vary between jurisdictions as to the way these clauses should be drafted and as to their effectiveness. Generally speaking, a notice clause specifies the place where the notice is to be served, the method of service and when service is deemed to take place. Deemed service is extremely important where the end of a limitation period is approaching or where performance has to be made before a certain time.

In an international acquisition agreement, special attention needs to be paid to the interplay of international time zones, different business days and national holidays in the relevant jurisdictions.

4.4 SCHEDULES

Usually, much of the bulk of the sale and purchase agreement is attributable to the schedules. The issues covered by the schedules will be determined by the terms of the transaction and whether it is an asset or a share acquisition. In civil jurisdictions, however, all matters may well be dealt with in the main text of the sale and purchase agreement.

Although a totally comprehensive list of possible schedules would be very long indeed, in broad terms a sale and purchase agreement may include schedules detailing some of the following matters:

(a) details of the assets or shareholdings to be transferred with appropriate price allocations;

(b) details of any price adjustment mechanism, such as completion accounts or earn-out arrangements, together with provisions governing subsequent payment terms and the resolution of disputes;

(c) warranty statements about the condition of the target business and its assets;

(d) limitations on the seller's liability in relation to warranty claims (although this is sometimes placed within the body of the agreement);

(e) specific indemnities agreed between the parties in relation to identified risks, eg the tax covenant on a share sale (see **9.3**);

(f) agreed forms of documentation governing associated transactions, such as the transfer of a pension fund;

(g) if the agreement is to be exchanged conditionally (ie there will be a gap between exchange and completion), agreed restrictions on running the target business or company pending completion and details of the documentation required to complete the transaction (see **7.2**);

(h) details of the completion procedure, specifically the documents which each party must deliver to the other and the steps each party must take on completion. Agreed forms of minutes of board and general meetings of the target company to be held on completion may also be included.

The advantage of consigning much of the fine detail of the sale and purchase agreement to schedules is that the main body of the agreement is not broken up with long lists of detailed information, which makes the agreement as a whole easier to follow.

4.5 EXECUTION

The agreement will provide for its execution by the respective parties, usually the buyer and the seller, though on occasion a third party may be a party to the agreement.

The sale and purchase agreement is purely a contract setting out the terms on which the acquisition will be undertaken, so it can simply be signed by the parties. However, to avoid any question about whether appropriate consideration has been given in relation to specific indemnities and restrictive covenants included in the agreement, the buyer may prefer the agreement to be executed as a deed.

In most jurisdictions, a distinction is made between simple contracts, which can be signed by the parties without any further formalities or requirements as to the execution, and contracts which require certain formalities for proper execution, such as the signing by witnesses or the execution of a notarial deed before a (civil law) notary. Some European countries and Latin American countries require the sale and purchase agreement, as well as the actual transfer, to be executed by notarial deed. Some countries, such as Germany and the Netherlands, require the notary formalities only in respect of the actual transfer.

As with any major contract, prior to exchange and completion the legal advisers will confirm the parties' capability to enter into the agreement (see 7.3).

ALLOCATION OF RISK: BUYER'S PROTECTION

LEARNING OUTCOMES

After reading this chapter you will be able to:

- appreciate the purpose of warranties and indemnities, and the circumstances in which each is appropriate
- explain the nature of damages available in the event of a breach of warranty or indemnity
- understand how the law of misrepresentation may apply in the acquisitions context
- understand who may be prepared to give warranties on a particular transaction
- describe how a buyer can further protect its position by restricting the seller's post-completion activities.

5.1 INTRODUCTION

The buyer will want some reassurances about the nature and state of the company or business it is acquiring, and some possibility of recompense if the acquisition turns out to be other than expected. In the context of a share or asset acquisition, warranties and indemnities included in the sale and purchase agreement go some way towards providing the buyer with this comfort.

5.2 PROTECTIONS IMPLIED INTO THE CONTRACT

5.2.1 Shares

On a share acquisition under English law, neither common law nor statute protects the buyer by implying terms into the contract; the principle that applies is *caveat emptor*. It was noted in **Chapter 1** that there is indeed every reason for a buyer of shares to beware, because it will be inheriting indirectly all the liabilities of the target company, whether it knows about them or not. In the absence of express provisions, an aggrieved buyer has very little comeback on the seller unless a misrepresentation can be established (discussed at **5.5.1**). In order to protect itself from the many risks involved, the buyer must therefore make express provision in the acquisition documentation.

5.2.2 Assets

Under English law, the buyer of the assets of a business is not in such an exposed position, as it does not assume automatically all the liabilities of the business. The buyer may also get the benefit of some limited warranties under the Sale of Goods Act 1979 for some of the assets being transferred. However, as on a share acquisition, there will be many safeguards which the buyer will wish to incorporate expressly into the sale and purchase agreement.

5.2.3 Comparison with civil code jurisdictions

Most civil code jurisdictions provide statutory provisions that are implied into the terms of the acquisition in order to protect the buyer, who is seen as the party most at risk in an acquisition. Each national code provides that statutory warranties are implied into the terms of the acquisition. Although the provisions vary in each jurisdiction, these statutory warranties will usually outline the minimum protection to be provided to any buyer. The statutory warranties are often expressed as a guarantee by the seller that the individual warranty statements are true.

Civil code jurisdictions also impose a duty of good faith between the parties throughout the negotiations for the proposed acquisition. Such a duty does not generally apply under English law. The exact scope of the duty of good faith varies from country to country but will usually include an obligation on each party to inform the other of all important or material facts that the other party could not discover on its own, and to observe moral and ethical standards of behaviour. Where this duty is breached, the injured party may claim damages arising from that breach.

Despite these statutory protections and an obligation of good faith, the buyer will usually seek additional contractual warranties, although the underlying system of protection often means than these additional warranties can be drafted in wider terms than would be expected in common law jurisdictions, such as the UK and the US. The parties will often include a repetition of any statutory warranties, as well as deal-specific warranties, in the sale and purchase agreement

5.3   FULL OR LIMITED TITLE GUARANTEE

Whether a transaction takes place as an asset or a share acquisition, there are two bases on which the agreement for sale can be made which will attract the benefit of covenants implied by English law. The covenants are implied by the Law of Property (Miscellaneous Provisions) Act 1994, and the alternative dispositions are sale with full title guarantee and sale with limited title guarantee.

Where the sale is expressed to be made with full title guarantee, this implies that:

(a)   the seller has the right to dispose of the property;

(b)   the seller will do all it reasonably can, at its own expense, to pass to the buyer the title it purports to give; and

(c)   the property is free from all charges, encumbrances and third party rights, other than those of which the seller is unaware and could not reasonably be expected to be aware.

If the sale is said to be made with limited title guarantee, this implies the covenants mentioned at (a) and (b) above, and also that, since the last sale for value, the seller has neither created nor allowed to be created any subsisting charge or encumbrance, and is not aware that anyone else has done so.

Of course, the type of guarantee to be given, if any, is a matter for negotiation. The implied covenants can be, and often are, modified by express provisions in the sale and purchase agreement relating to the nature and perfection of title to the assets. In general, although a receiver or trustee selling assets may be prepared to offer no more comfort than limited title guarantee, in the context of most other acquisitions full title guarantee will be appropriate.

By contrast, in some civil code jurisdictions the national code will provide a number of statutory warranties (expressed as guarantees) about the title of the object of the purchase. For example, in Germany, the civil code will imply a statutory warranty, regardless of what is stated in the sale and purchase agreement, that the shares are sold free from any restrictions and from any defects in title.

5.4 WARRANTIES

In common law jurisdictions, much of the acquisition agreement is usually taken up with specific warranties by the seller in favour of the buyer, covering a whole range of aspects of the target business or company, including the accounts, subsisting contracts, employees, pensions, intellectual property rights, etc (see **Chapters 8** and **9** for details of typical warranties in asset and share acquisitions respectively).

A party from a civil law country may not expect such lengthy documentation. Although influenced by the practice of extensive warranties, in civil code jurisdictions warranties are generally shorter and may be more general because of the underlying protection that the civil code will provide to the buyer (see **5.2.3**).

The warranties are contractual statements about what is to be acquired. On a share acquisition the warranties will include statements about the shares to be acquired, for example that the shares are not subject to any charges, as well as about the company which is being transferred.

As the warranties are terms of the contract, if they prove to be untrue, the buyer will have a claim for damages against the warrantor(s) for breach of contract. This provides a clear means of redress for the buyer after completion of the acquisition. However, during negotiation of the sale and purchase agreement, one of the purposes of including warranties is to elicit information about the business from the seller. The seller will try to avoid later liability for breach of warranty by disclosing relevant information (that is, information that, undisclosed, would put the seller in breach of warranty) before the acquisition is completed (see **6.3.1**).

The warranties are made about the state of the target as at a specified point. Where exchange and completion are simultaneous, the warranties will be statements given at the moment of completion, ie statements about what is being acquired at the moment that it is acquired. Where there is a gap between exchange and completion, warranties are made at exchange when the parties become contractually bound, and may then be confirmed at completion. This can be problematic, as any changes in the condition of the target between exchange and completion must be addressed. The parties will negotiate specific terms in the sale and purchase agreement as to how they will deal with such changes (see **7.2.3**).

5.4.1 What damages are recoverable under English law?

Under English case law set out in *Hadley v Baxendale* (1854) 9 Exch 341, loss will be recoverable if it is not too remote. It must fall within one of the two following categories:

(a)　loss which flows naturally from the breach – in other words, it is a natural consequence of the breach, the type and extent of which a reasonable person would expect in the circumstances;

(b)　loss which was fairly and reasonably in the contemplation of both parties, at the time they entered into the contract, as the probable result of the breach. This might cover a more unusual type of loss due to special circumstances which were known or should have been known to the parties at the date of the contract.

The aim of contractual damages is to put the buyer in the position it would have been in if the contract had not been breached, subject to the duty to mitigate. This measure of damages allows recovery for loss of bargain.

5.4.2 Application of general principles

How are these general principles applied to breach of warranty on a share acquisition?

The buyer's loss in these circumstances is the difference between the value of shares if the warranty had been true and their actual value, ie the difference in the value of the shares with and without the breach. The basis used for valuing the shares will therefore be relevant in assessing the loss.

For example, the shares may have been valued on an earnings basis, perhaps by applying a multiplier to a warranted level of profit. If this profit has been overstated, the buyer's loss should be calculated by applying the same multiplier to the deficiency. On the other hand, where there is a breach of warranty which results in the assets of the target being less than expected, this may not have a direct effect on the value of the shares, unless they were valued on an assets-related basis.

5.4.3 Pre-estimate of damages

The parties will often seek to reduce the uncertainty involved in assessing loss in this way by specifying in the agreement how the loss should be quantified if certain warranties are broken. For example, where profit levels have been warranted, the parties may agree a formula which specifies an appropriate multiplier to apply to any shortfall. It is also quite common for a clause to be included which obliges the seller to pay for any deficiency in assets or any undisclosed liability arising from a breach of warranty, thus avoiding the need to prove an equivalent diminution in the value of the shares (the seller may resist what is essentially an indemnity basis for breach of warranty).

Under English law, the parties to a contract are free to agree in advance a sum payable in damages in the event of a breach of contract; however, there are limits to this freedom. Where the contractually agreed consequences of a breach are oppressive, the penalty rule applies, as clarified in *Cavendish Square Holding BV v Talal El Makdessi* [2015] UKSC 67, and the courts may refuse to uphold the provision. In *Makdessi*, the Supreme Court said that determining whether a provision is a penalty does not just involve a narrow assessment of whether it is a genuine pre-estimate of loss suffered as a result of the breach, but should include a broader consideration of the innocent party's wider interests. The true test for a penalty is therefore now 'whether the impugned provision is a secondary obligation which imposes a detriment on the contract-breaker out of all proportion to any legitimate interest of the innocent party in the enforcement of the primary obligation'.

In the US, it is common practice to provide for an agreed basis of damages. The seller may be required to pay for any deficiency in assets or any undisclosed liability arising from a breach of warranty, thus avoiding the need to prove an equivalent diminution in the value of the object of the acquisition.

In many civil code jurisdictions, warranties are likely to be structured as guarantees, whereby the seller guarantees that the individual warranties are correct. In the event that the object of the purchase does not meet the standards set out in the warranties, the buyer will be entitled to the remedies as set out in the sale and purchase agreement. The provision of such express remedies could include the obligation to pay for any deficiency in the object of the purchase.

5.5 REPRESENTATIONS

Typically, the signing of the sale and purchase agreement will be the culmination of extensive contact and correspondence between the parties and their advisers. The buyer and its advisers will have sought replies to a whole range of questions affecting the target and its business. If any statements which have been made by or on behalf of the seller prove to be untrue, the buyer may under common law have a claim for misrepresentation.

5.5.1 General principles under English common law

A misrepresentation is a false statement of fact made by one party to the contract to the other, which induces the other party to enter into the contract. Accordingly, where a buyer has relied on a representation of past or existing fact about the target which turns out to be untrue, it will, prima facie, have a claim for misrepresentation, the remedies for which are rescission or damages.

5.5.1.1 Rescission

Whether the misrepresentation is fraudulent, negligent or innocent, the buyer has the right to rescind the sale and purchase agreement. Rescission is a remedy aimed at putting the parties back into the pre-contract position. However, under English law, the right to rescind is subject to two important qualifications.

First, s 2(2) of the Misrepresentation Act 1967 enables the court to award damages instead of rescission for innocent or negligent misrepresentation, that is, a representation which is made 'otherwise than fraudulently'. The court may exercise this discretion if it feels that rescission is too drastic a remedy in the circumstances (see **5.5.1.2** below for further discussion of the discretion to award damages under s 2(2)).

Secondly, rescission is an equitable remedy and will not be available if, for example:

(a)   it is impossible to restore the parties to their pre-contract position; or

(b)   bona fide third party rights have been acquired; or

(c)   the innocent party, knowing of the misrepresentation, takes some action affirming the agreement; or

(d)   there is undue delay in seeking relief.

These 'bars' to rescission may mean that the remedy will not be available once a share or asset acquisition has been completed, because of the difficulties in restoring the parties to their pre-contract position. On the other hand, where exchange and completion are not contemporaneous, rescission should be available if a misrepresentation is discovered between exchange and completion.

5.5.1.2 Damages

If the misrepresentation is innocent or negligent, s 2(2) of the Misrepresentation Act 1967 provides that the court 'may declare the contract subsisting and award damages in lieu of rescission'. It should be noted that, under s 2(2), the court only has a discretion to award damages; there is no right to damages.

The question arises as to whether the court can still award damages in lieu of rescission if rescission itself has been lost due to one of the equitable bars. In *Salt v Stratstone Specialist Ltd* [2015] EWCA Civ 745, the Court of Appeal held that, in order for the court to award damages in lieu of rescission, the right to rescind must not have, in fact, been lost.

Where the misrepresentation is negligent, ie the maker is unable to show that they had reasonable grounds for believing, and did believe, that the statement was true, the innocent party is entitled to damages under s 2(1) of the 1967 Act. As s 2(1) provides a right to damages for negligent misrepresentation, the innocent party in such a case will generally bring a claim for damages under s 2(1) rather than rely on the court's discretion under s 2(2).

Under s 2(1), damages are measured on the tortious basis, which aims to put the innocent party in the position it would have been in if the tort had not been committed. In the context of an acquisition, this involves restoring the innocent party to the position it would have been in if it had not entered into the acquisition agreement; in other words, the court must try to assess to what extent the innocent party has lost out by entering into the agreement.

In the US, a misrepresentation as to the character or essential terms of a proposed contract prevents the formation of the contract. Generally, if a party is induced to enter into the contract by a material or fraudulent misrepresentation, then the contract is voidable at the misled party's option.

Misrepresentation as such does not exist in most civil code jurisdictions, but similar concepts can give rise to causes of action, although these vary between jurisdictions. In civil code jurisdictions, contract and tort are considered as part of a wider concept of 'obligations'. An action, carrying a right to rescission, can be brought for breach of an obligation. For example, in France the seller and its advisers can incur liability for wilful deceit or for a failure to disclose information, and a party may be liable to pay damages if it has acted in bad faith. In Germany, a seller may be liable for incorrect statements or an omission to disclose material information.

5.5.2   Representations and warranties under English law

The nature of a sale and purchase agreement renders it likely that any representations made by the seller in pre-contract discussions and negotiations, which induce the buyer to enter into the agreement, will be included as warranties in the agreement. It is rare, therefore, for a claim for misrepresentation to be founded on a matter which is not included in the contract. Indeed, it is common for the agreement to incorporate an acknowledgement by the buyer that it has not relied on any representations which are not contained in the contract (a 'non-reliance' provision; see **5.5.2.2**), and that the contract sets out the entire agreement and understanding between the parties (known as an 'entire agreement clause'; see **5.5.2.1**). Under English law, such a clause will usually attempt to exclude liability for misrepresentation, though the exclusions must be reasonable in order to be effective (Misrepresentation Act 1967, s 3, as substituted by the Unfair Contract Terms Act 1977 (UCTA 1977), s 8).

5.5.2.1   Entire agreement clause

An entire agreement clause was considered in the English case of *Thomas Witter Ltd v TBP Industries Ltd* [1996] 2 All ER 573. The judge ruled that a contractual term purporting to confine the parties' agreement to the terms of the contract will not, per se, exclude liability for misrepresentation. In order to exclude liability for misrepresentation, an express exclusion provision in clear terms must be included in the contract, as confirmed in a number of cases, including *Axa Sun Life Services plc v Campbell Martin Ltd and others* [2011] EWCA Civ 133. As a result of this, and to reinforce the entire agreement provision, the sale and purchase agreement will usually also include a non-reliance provision covering all pre-contractual statements whether or not they have made their way into the written contract.

5.5.2.2   Non-reliance provision

A non-reliance statement estops the buyer from claiming that it entered into an agreement in reliance on pre-contractual statements made by the seller. This gave rise to the suggestion, discussed in cases such as *EA Grimstead & Son Ltd v McGarrigan* [1999] All ER (D) 1163, that non-reliance statements were not subject to the reasonableness test in s 3 of the Misrepresentation Act 1967, on the basis that they prevented liability for misrepresentation from arising rather than excluding such liability. However, in *Springwell Navigation Corp v JP Morgan Chase Bank* [2010] EWCA Civ 1221, the Court of Appeal rejected this argument and made clear that, where a pre-contractual representation has been made and relied upon, the practical reality of a subsequent non-reliance clause is that it attempts to exclude or restrict liability. Such a non-reliance clause is therefore subject to the s 3 reasonableness test. This approach was confirmed by the Court of Appeal in *First Tower Trustees Ltd v CDS (Superstores International) Ltd* [2018] EWCA Civ 1396.

The non-reliance provision in *Witter* (**5.5.2.1** above) did not distinguish between different types of misrepresentation, and the judge suggested that it would therefore fail the reasonableness test since it would never be reasonable to exclude liability for fraudulent misrepresentation. It is therefore still common for the seller to ensure that the buyer confirms its non-reliance only in relation to non-fraudulent misrepresentation, with an express exclusion in relation to fraudulent misrepresentation. However, the House of Lords decision in *HIH Casualty and General Insurance Ltd v Chase Manhattan Bank* [2003] UKHL 6 suggests that this is not necessary. The court in that case recognised that 'in the absence of words which expressly refer to dishonesty, it goes without saying that underlying the contractual arrangements of the parties will be a common assumption that the persons involved will behave honestly'.

5.5.2.3   Right of rescission

Even where an entire agreement clause and a non-reliance provision are included in the agreement, this does not render misrepresentation redundant. Many of the representations which the seller makes to the buyer in the lead-up to the signing of the agreement will be included as express warranties in the agreement itself. If any of these warranties are broken, the buyer will be able to claim damages for breach of contract as explained at **5.5.1.2** above. Section 1 of the Misrepresentation Act 1967 makes it clear, however, that where a misrepresentation has become a term of the contract, this will not affect the innocent party's right to rescind (provided none of the equitable bars operates). In contrast, a breach of warranty does not enable the buyer to discharge the contract. This may not be significant where the misrepresentation is discovered only after completion, if by then it is too late to rescind. However, it will be important if the buyer becomes aware of the falsity of the representation after exchange but before completion.

Where there is an interval between exchange and completion, the buyer will usually seek to negotiate a contractual right to withdraw from the contract if it becomes aware of any breach of warranty. This will often be backed up by obliging the seller to inform the buyer if the seller becomes aware of anything which is inconsistent with the warranties or makes them inaccurate.

Such a provision is of advantage to the buyer, as it will enable it to 'rescind' the agreement whether or not the breach of warranty is also a misrepresentation (avoiding argument as to whether the warranty is a repeated non-contractual statement which the buyer has relied upon).

In the US, the same basic principles apply, but the right to rescind based on misrepresentation is a matter of general contract law and is typically not codified in statute.

5.5.2.4   Measure of damages under English law

Where the remedy sought is damages, the difference in the measure of damages for breach of contract and misrepresentation may also be significant. It has been seen that the contractual measure allows for loss of bargain and, on a share purchase, involves assessing the difference between the actual value of the shares and their value if the warranty had been true. On the other hand, the aim of tortious damages is to put the buyer in the position it would have been in if it had not entered into the agreement; this will involve calculating the difference between the price paid for the shares and their actual market value. The contractual measure will often lead to higher damages because of the ability to recover for loss of bargain. However, this will not always be the result, particularly where the bargain is not a good one (eg in a share acquisition, where a buyer has paid more than market value for the shares). In these circumstances, the buyer may be better off with the restitutionary approach.

5.6 INDEMNITIES

The buyer may seek further contractual protection in the form of indemnities included in the sale and purchase agreement or, occasionally, incorporated in a separate deed.

5.6.1 What is the difference between a warranty and an indemnity?

Under English law, a warranty is an undertaking by the seller that a particular state of affairs exists. On a breach of warranty, the buyer must establish its loss under normal contractual principles. For example, on a share sale, it will have to establish the reduction (if any) in the value of the shares (see **5.4.2**).

An indemnity, on the other hand, is essentially a promise to reimburse the buyer in respect of a designated type of liability which may arise in the future. On a share sale, there is no need to assess any reduction in the value of the shares; the recipient of the indemnity simply receives an amount equal to the actual liability (the indemnity clause will usually provide for costs and expenses relating to it to be recovered as well). For example, if the buyer is worried about an outstanding debt owed to the target, it could seek an indemnity against the possibility of the debt becoming bad. If this happens, the buyer will receive the amount of the outstanding debt and, possibly, incidental costs in seeking to recover it.

Another difference between a warranty and an indemnity is that, in the case of the latter, there is no duty to mitigate the loss; such a duty may, however, be incorporated in the contract.

In the US, it is common practice to provide how the loss for a breach of warranty should be quantified. The effect of such provisions can mean that payment for a breach of warranty can be ascertained on an indemnity basis (see **5.4.3**).

Other jurisdictions do not recognise the same distinction between warranties and indemnities. Many civil code jurisdictions have a system of statutory warranties and will also provide for additional contractual warranties. These warranties are usually structured as guarantees by the seller that these individual statements are true, and if they are not, this will entitle the buyer to specified remedies. This means that there is not always a clear distinction between the remedies available for a breach of the seller's guarantee and the provision of an indemnity. Indeed, the practice of combining warranties with specific rights of recovery has become widespread practice in France in particular.

Another important distinction is that in some jurisdictions it is possible to rescind an agreement for a breach of a contractual obligation. In Germany, for example, the right to rescind may arise in the event of non-performance or deficient performance of the agreed contractual obligations.

5.6.2 Taxation indemnities

It is common for buyers of shares to seek protection from tax liabilities in the form of both warranties and indemnities. On an asset acquisition, extensive safeguards are unnecessary in the UK because almost all tax liabilities remain with the seller.

The warranties usually deal with the target's compliance with tax and VAT requirements, such as the proper submission of returns and the correct implementation of the pay as you earn (PAYE) system, etc, as well as other areas where the buyer is mainly concerned with prompting disclosures from the seller (eg whether there are any existing disputes with HMRC). The indemnities, on the other hand, will cover specific tax charges which may arise over and above those provided for in the accounts, and which are referable to the seller's period of ownership.

Dealing with most tax matters by way of indemnity has the advantage to the buyer that there is no need to prove the link between the unexpected tax liability and the value of the shares. However, warranties are often appropriate for many matters in respect of which buyers seek indemnities, and the seller should consider arguing this point.

5.7 TAX CONSEQUENCES IN THE UK OF PAYMENTS UNDER WARRANTIES AND INDEMNITIES

The following discussion applies to payments made by the seller under any warranty or indemnity brought by the buyer following completion of the acquisition, not merely to payments in respect of taxation warranties and indemnities.

5.7.1 Warranties

Warranties are always given in favour of the buyer.

On the sale of the assets of a business or shares, the seller may have made a chargeable capital gain on the disposal, based on the consideration received. Let us assume that, later, the seller has to make a payment to the buyer under a warranty contained in the sale and purchase agreement. What are the tax consequences for the seller and the buyer of such a payment?

Section 49 of the TCGA 1992 provides that no tax allowance will be made in the first instance for any contingent liability in respect of a warranty or representation. However, if the liability crystallises, an adjustment will be made to the price of the target for capital gains purposes. If, therefore, the seller makes a payment under a warranty to the buyer, the capital tax computation would be adjusted as follows:

(a) The consideration which the seller is treated as having received on completion will be reduced by the amount paid out under the warranty claim, thus reducing any gain. If the seller has already paid the tax, it will be entitled to a refund.

(b) The buyer's acquisition cost is reduced by the same amount: its potential gain on a subsequent disposal of the target is therefore increased because its acquisition cost has reduced.

5.7.2 Indemnities

The position is not as straightforward when it comes to payments under indemnities. Consider the example of a standard tax indemnity in a sale of shares. The buyer will be keen to ensure that the target company has accounted for all outstanding taxes and has no hidden tax liability. The sale agreement will contain an indemnity in the event of the target company being called upon to pay additional tax. It used to be the practice that indemnities were often given in favour of the target company itself, not the buyer, as it is the target company on which the tax liability would fall. However, under English case law, this right to claim under the indemnity was deemed a chargeable asset for tax purposes and so subject to taxation.

The application of this rule was clarified by HMRC, by Extra Statutory Concession D33, which made it clear that payments made to the buyer under warranties would not be considered a chargeable payment. The Concession also states that indemnity payments by the seller to the buyer will be treated the same way as warranties, ie the seller's sale proceeds are adjusted and the buyer's cost of acquisition in the event of a further disposal is reduced by the sum received. The Concession does not deal with payments made to the target company itself. Therefore, the safe approach is that indemnities should be expressed to be in *favour of the buyer*, not in favour of the target company.

The practice of providing that payments under indemnities are made to the buyer has been widely adopted in the UK, and relevant provisions are now normally contained in the main sale and purchase agreement. As the payment should be expressed as being in favour of the buyer, tax indemnities are usually drafted in the form of a covenant by the seller to pay the buyer an amount equal to the tax liability that has arisen in the target. The practice of using a covenant to pay the buyer reflects its principal function as a means of adjusting the price where the target proves to be worth less than the buyer thought.

5.8   WHO GIVES WARRANTIES AND INDEMNITIES?

The sellers of the target and those giving the warranties and indemnities are not always one and the same. Some sellers may be unwilling to accept any liability, or at least may try to limit their share of liability. The buyer, on the other hand, will usually want all the sellers to give the warranties and indemnities, and to do so on the basis that they are jointly and severally liable for any breaches.

5.8.1   Joint and several liability

Where there is more than one warrantor the buyer will invariably insist that they accept joint and several liability; this will enable it to sue any one of the warrantors for the full amount of the liability. Under English law, s 1 of the Civil Liability (Contribution) Act 1978 gives the party called upon to discharge the liability the right to recover a contribution from the other warrantors who are liable in respect of the same damage.

In proceedings under s 1, the court determines the amount of the contribution recoverable from the others on the basis of what it considers just and equitable having regard to the extent of their responsibility for the particular damage (s 2). It is likely that these contributions would reflect the amount of the purchase price which each warrantor received, although there is nothing to prevent the court from also taking into account other factors connected with the acquisition. As a result of this uncertainty, it is common practice in the UK for the warrantors to agree how any liability should be borne between them. This is permitted by the 1978 Act, and will usually be on the basis that liability is shared in proportion to the allocation of the purchase consideration. Such an agreement may be in a separate document ('a deed of contribution'), or it may be incorporated in the sale and purchase agreement. In the latter case, the clause allocating liability will usually be expressed to be 'as between the warrantors'. It is important to appreciate that the buyer will not be affected by an agreement in these terms and will still be able to sue any warrantor for the full amount. In other words, the risk of a warrantor being unable or unwilling to pay their share falls on their fellow warrantors and not on the buyer, whose concern is simply that it should be able to recover compensation from someone.

5.8.2   Who may be unwilling to give warranties?

On a share sale involving a large number of shareholders, the buyer will not always insist that all of them give the warranties and indemnities. This is particularly so in relation to minor shareholders who may, often justifiably, not wish to be exposed to the risk which joint and several liability entails.

Problems often arise where some of the shares of a company are held in trust. Trustees will wish to avoid personal liability and may refuse to give any warranties or undertakings, other than that they have unencumbered title to the shares. If the trust holds a significant number of shares, this puts both the buyer and the other shareholders in a dilemma; the buyer has less security in the event of a breach and the other shareholders may feel aggrieved at undertaking a contingent liability disproportionate to the benefit they are receiving.

A solution which may be acceptable to all concerned is for the buyer to acknowledge in the sale and purchase agreement that the trustees' liability is limited to the net value (ie after tax) for the time being of the capital of the trust. The danger to the buyer of the capital being distributed shortly after completion may be met by obliging the trustees to require any beneficiary receiving capital to give appropriate warranties to the buyer. However, the terms of the particular trust may preclude the trustees from committing themselves to doing this.

Lastly, even relatively substantial shareholders, and institutional investors such as private equity funds, may try to avoid giving warranties and indemnities, on the grounds that they have had no involvement with the management of the target company and therefore cannot be expected to give promises in relation to matters about which they know nothing. It is true that one of the purposes of warranties is to extract information about the target and that this information will generally come from the target's management. Nevertheless, the other (and probably more important) role of warranties is to allocate risk between seller and buyer. The price will be negotiated on the assumption that the warranties are true, and this is the basis on which all the shareholders (whether executive directors or not) receive their share of the consideration. If a breach of warranty means that the shares are not as valuable as the parties envisaged when entering into the deal, then it seems reasonable that there is an adjustment to the amount received by each shareholder; otherwise those shareholders who are not also warrantors effectively receive a windfall benefit.

5.8.3 Seller's rights against the management of the target

On a share sale, where the shareholders of the target company are not also directors, it will be the latter who will provide much of the information about the business which is requested by the buyer. Where this information is inaccurate or incomplete, this may lead to the selling shareholders becoming liable to the buyer for breach of warranty or misrepresentation; they may in turn be inclined to shift responsibility to the directors of the target by bringing a claim against them.

The buyer will wish to avoid the sellers' responsibility for breach of warranty effectively being shifted back onto the directors of the target who may well still be employed by the target. This is usually achieved by the selling shareholders waiving any right they may have to bring a claim against the management or the target itself in these circumstances (except in the case of any directors of the target who are also sellers).

5.8.4 Assignment of warranties and indemnities

If the buyer decides to sell the target soon after acquiring it, will it be able to assign the benefit of the warranties and indemnities which it received from the seller to the 'new' buyer? The general position under English law is that, unless the contracting parties agree otherwise, the benefit of an agreement can be assigned to a third party without the consent of the other party to the contract. The seller is therefore likely to insist on an express provision stating that no assignment is permitted, or that it is permitted only in certain limited circumstances.

If the buyer foresees the possibility of selling the target, it may try to negotiate with the seller an express right to assign the benefit of the warranties and indemnities. Its own buyer will certainly want the benefit of the usual protections, and an assignment of the existing warranties is a more attractive proposition than providing these warranties itself.

A seller is likely to demand at least some express restrictions on assignment, as it would otherwise potentially have no control over the identity of the assignee of the warranties. This is particularly the case where a buyer is an individual. In the case of a corporate buyer, the seller may agree to the buyer assigning the benefit of the warranties to members of the buyer's group.

5.9 BUYER'S SECURITY FOR BREACH

The potential liability of the seller in relation to the warranties and indemnities is usually substantial, and may not come to light until some time after completion. The buyer is in an exposed position in relation to contingent liabilities which are the subject of warranties and indemnities. It, or the target itself, may be directly liable to third parties, but may be unable to recover the loss if the seller is in financial difficulties. The buyer should consider reducing the risk by insisting on some form of security from the seller.

5.9.1 Guarantees

Where the sellers of a business or shares are individuals, the buyer will want to be satisfied as to the sellers' financial status and ability to cover any claims, so may insist on taking a charge over their assets or receiving a guarantee from a third party.

Where the seller of a business or shares is a company which is part of a group, the seller's parent company may be prepared to guarantee the seller's obligations. However, where a company owned by individuals is selling its business, it is likely to be a mere shell after completion which may be wound up shortly afterwards as a way of remitting the proceeds to the shareholders. In these circumstances, the financial security of the seller is clearly in doubt, and the buyer should seek guarantees from its shareholders at the very least.

5.9.2   Retentions from the purchase price

Another method of securing the buyer's position is for the sale and purchase agreement to provide for the buyer to retain part of the purchase price of the target for a certain period after completion and for this sum to be used to pay any successful claims under the warranties or indemnities. Such provision may be made in the following terms:

(a)   payment of the retention into a joint account in the names of the seller's and buyer's solicitors;

(b)   the retention to be remitted to the seller on a certain date after completion (eg 12 months after completion) unless the buyer makes a claim under the warranties or indemnities before that date;

(c)   where the buyer does make such a claim, only the balance of the retention, after deducting the amount of the claim, to be paid to the seller on the specified date;

(d)   the buyer to be paid the amount of the claim within a short period (eg 14 days) of this being determined and any balance remitted to the seller;

(e)   payment of accrued interest on the fund to the parties in the same proportion that they receive the retention;

(f)   an obligation on the buyer to pursue any claims against the seller which may delay the remittance of the fund promptly and diligently.

The seller may also insist that any claim which delays payment of the retention must be made properly. For example, the buyer may be obliged to provide full details of the claim, perhaps backed up with an opinion of counsel.

The retention will not affect the capital tax position of the parties. Only if it is used to pay warranty claims will there be an adjustment to the consideration for capital tax purposes, as explained at **5.7.1**.

5.10   RESTRICTIONS ON THE SELLER

Whether it is an asset acquisition or a share acquisition, the value of the buyer's investment could be reduced substantially by the post-completion activities of the seller, whose detailed knowledge of the target would enable the seller to cause it considerable harm. It is in the buyer's interests to protect its investment by making express provision in the sale and purchase agreement to curtail any such activities of the seller. This section deals with the position where no express agreement is made, the type of restrictions which the buyer may seek to impose and whether the validity of such provisions can be challenged.

5.10.1   What can the buyer do if there are no express restraints?

Under English case law, *Trego v Hunt* [1896] AC 7 established that on the sale of the goodwill of a business, the courts will refuse to imply a covenant by the seller not to set up in competition. In the absence of express provision, very limited protections for the buyer of goodwill (the position of a buyer of shares was not considered) will be implied into the sale and purchase agreement. The only implied undertakings of the seller are as follows:

(a)   not to use or disclose confidential information relating to the business;

(b)   not to represent itself as successor to the business, or as carrying on the same business;

(c)   not to solicit customers of the business (ie those who were customers prior to the sale).

5.10.2   Express restrictions

The buyer of the assets of a business or shares will usually value the target on the assumption that its goodwill will be preserved. Indeed, on the acquisition of the assets of a business, a specific value will be attributed to the asset of goodwill. The buyer is, in effect, paying for the benefit of the good name of the target and the expectation that existing customers (and suppliers) will continue to deal with it (and, indeed, that new customers will be attracted to it).

As the seller is being paid for goodwill, the buyer is justified in seeking ways of preventing the seller from damaging it by, for example, taking away customers of the business. The buyer does not, however, have unlimited scope to restrain the activities of the seller after completion, since the law is reluctant, on public policy grounds, to restrict competition in general and a person's ability to earn their livelihood in particular. The buyer must go no further than is reasonably necessary to protect the goodwill of the target.

The buyer commonly seeks to include in the agreement some or all of the following undertakings by the seller:

(a)   a covenant not to be engaged or concerned in any competing business for a specified period after completion;

(b)   a covenant not to try to solicit or entice away from the target customers or suppliers who have recently dealt with the target for a specified period after completion;

(c)   a covenant not to try to solicit or entice away from the target employees of the target for a specified period after completion;

(d)   an undertaking not to use or disclose any confidential information about the target or its customers;

(e)   a covenant not to use the name of the target (where a business is acquired from a company, the selling company may be required to change its corporate name).

5.10.3   Will these restrictions be valid at common law?

Under English law, all covenants in restraint of trade are prima facie void at common law. However, the court will not strike down restrictive covenants which it considers to be reasonable to protect a legitimate interest of the buyer. The preservation of goodwill, which is reflected in the value of the business or shares, and the protection of business secrets are the interests which the buyer is concerned to protect; the restraints must therefore go no further than is strictly necessary to achieve this. The factors which the court considers relevant are the same on an asset sale as on a share sale, namely:

(a)   the duration of the restraint;

(b)   the geographical area of the restraint;

(c)   the activities restricted.

5.10.3.1   Duration

The buyer will usually seek to prevent the seller from competing and soliciting customers, etc for between one year and five years after completion. Where the seller is prevented from using or disclosing confidential information, it will not generally be necessary to stipulate a time limit on this restriction.

5.10.3.2   Area

The geographical area in which a covenant preventing the seller from setting up a business of the same type is intended to operate must be closely related to the area in which the target operates. What is permissible, therefore, varies considerably and depends on whether the business is based locally or nationally. If the covenant is appropriately worded, it may not be necessary to stipulate a geographical limit. For example, if the clause disallows the seller from setting up a 'competing business', this has the effect of limiting the restraint to the area in which the target carries on business (otherwise it would not be competing for the same clientele). If, on the other hand, the clause restricts the seller from carrying on a defined business, it will be necessary to specify a reasonable area of restriction to prevent it from being considered too wide.

5.10.3.3 Activities

Any attempt to extend the restrictions to activities which are not carried on by the target itself will fail, on the grounds that they are excessive in order to protect the goodwill of the target. Accordingly, the buyer will not be able to prevent the seller from competing with other businesses that the buyer owns or intends to acquire in the future. Indeed, in *Ronbar Enterprises Ltd v Green* [1954] 2 All ER 266, the court considered a clause preventing the seller carrying on a business 'similar to' that of the target to be too wide.

Another relevant factor is the extent to which the parties being asked to give the covenants have been actively involved in the business. It may be difficult, for example, to enforce a non-competition covenant against a minority shareholder who has taken no part in managing a target company and has never been involved in the same industry.

A non-solicitation clause should not be so wide as to include those who have had no recent dealings with the target prior to completion. It may, for example, be unreasonable to restrict the seller from contacting 'customers' or 'suppliers' who have not dealt with the target for more than one year before completion.

5.10.4 Enforcement

If the restrictive covenants are reasonable, the buyer will be able to claim damages for breach of contract and may be granted an injunction. But what if only some of the restrictions are reasonable?

If each restraint is contained in a different clause or sub-clause, and they are expressed to be separate and independent restrictions, even if the court considers one restraint to be too wide, the others will remain enforceable. Also, the court will not always strike out the whole of a clause or sub-clause. It is sometimes prepared to 'blue pencil' certain parts of a clause (ie to draw a line through certain words), leaving the remaining parts enforceable, as was recently confirmed in *Tillman v Egon Zehnder* [2019] UKSC 32, although the court will not rewrite a clause to make it reasonable. It is quite common to find a clause in the sale and purchase agreement where the parties agree that, if any of the restrictions is found to be invalid, but would be valid if, for example, the period or area of the restriction were reduced, such restriction shall apply with such amendments as are required to make it valid. Such a clause is unlikely to be effective.

5.10.5 The Competition Act 1998

The Competition Act 1998 introduced provisions into English law that are very similar to the regime that applies under Arts 101 and 102 of the Treaty on the Functioning of the European Union (TFEU). These articles replaced, without significant amendment, Arts 81 and 82 of the EC Treaty from 1 December 2009 following ratification of the Treaty of Lisbon. Section 60 sets out the governing principle, directing that questions relating to competition are to be

> so far as is possible ... dealt with in a manner which is consistent with the treatment of corresponding questions arising in EU law in relation to competition within the European Union.

However, following Brexit, the UK is no longer bound by these requirements. Nevertheless, the EU and UK regimes remain closely aligned. It is thought that the UK competition authorities and courts will be reluctant to introduce inconsistencies between the two competition law regimes, particularly when this adds to the burden of UK businesses that must comply with both EU and UK competition law.

For the time being, there remains a general prohibition of anti-competitive agreements and a prohibition of abuse of a dominant position.

If an agreement is found to breach s 2 or s 18 of the Competition Act 1998 (see **5.10.5.1** and **5.10.5.2**), the agreement or (subject to severance) the anti-competitive terms will be unenforceable.

5.10.5.1 Anti-competitive agreements

The wording of s 2 of the 1998 Act follows closely that of Art 101 TFEU. There is a prohibition on agreements and other business arrangements between two or more undertakings which may affect trade in the UK and which have as their object or effect the prevention, restriction or distortion of competition within the UK. Section 2(2) provides a non-exhaustive list of agreements which infringe the prohibition, similar to that found in Art 101 TFEU.

As with Art 101, there are block and general exemptions. The exemptions cover similar ground to that covered by the Art 101 exemptions, with block exemptions dealing with common agreements such as exclusive distribution agreements, franchise agreements and distribution agreements. In any event, parallel exemptions apply to agreements that are covered by a European Commission exemption, or would be covered if the agreement had an effect on trade between Member States. There are also *de minimis* provisions similar to those contained in the Notice on Agreements of Minor Importance. Significantly, any agreement that is exempt under EU law will also be exempt under UK legislation.

5.10.5.2 Abuse of a dominant position

The wording of s 18 of the 1998 Act concerning abuse of a dominant position is similar to that of Art 102 TFEU. There is a prohibition on the activities of one or more undertakings which amount to the abuse of a dominant position within the UK or a substantial part of it.

In the context of a sale and purchase agreement, a buyer should be aware that, in particular, restrictive covenants could fall foul of UK competition law.

5.10.5.3 Consequences of infringement

Restrictions in breach of the 1998 Act will be void. The CMA is empowered to impose fines of up to 10% of an undertaking's turnover. The parties may be ordered to cease or modify the agreement. The CMA has substantial investigative powers, including the right to raid premises unannounced (the so-called 'dawn raid'), provided a search warrant has been obtained from a High Court judge. There is the possibility of an appeal from the decisions of the CMA to the Competition Appeal Tribunal.

5.10.6 EU v UK competition law

Restrictive covenants in the sale and purchase agreement may breach Arts 101 and 102 TFEU (particularly Art 101) if trade between Member States is affected.

In relation to restrictive covenants, useful guidance is provided by the European Commission's Notice of March 2005 (OJ 2005/C56/03) on restrictions directly related and necessary to concentrations. In issuing the Notice, the Commission recognises that certain restrictions are necessary to guarantee the stated value of the shares transferred to the buyer. Restrictions falling within this Notice are automatically covered by any EU Merger Regulation clearance decision. The Notice confirms that, on a transfer of goodwill, a non-compete period of up to two years will be appropriate, whereas a period of three years is justified where the buyer acquires know-how and goodwill. Non-solicitation clauses should be considered in the same way as non-compete provisions.

5.10.7   United States competition law

Under US law, as under English law, when advising on the enforceability of a restrictive covenant ancillary to the sale of a business, it is necessary to consider both restraint of trade and US competition law. The restraint of trade doctrine forms part of the law of contract in each state. The applicable state laws will therefore determine whether the covenant is enforceable, and federal or state competition laws may impact on the enforceability of the covenant.

5.10.7.1   Restraint of trade

The US law on restraint of trade varies from state to state but is essentially similar to English law in that a covenant must protect the buyer's legitimate interest in the goodwill acquired and must be reasonable in scope. However, unlike English law, the fact that a covenant is too broad in scope is not necessarily fatal to its enforceability. Under the laws of certain states, courts are willing to enforce a covenant to the extent it is considered reasonable rather than holding that the entire provision is invalid.

5.10.7.2   Competition law

Section 1 of the Sherman Act 1890, a federal statute, states that 'every contract, combination … or conspiracy in restraint of trade or commerce … is declared to be illegal'. Certain agreements are considered so harmful that they are *per se* illegal. Price fixing and market sharing cartels are examples of *per se* illegal agreements. Other agreements are not so obviously illegal and are subject to the rule of reason analysis, which considers whether an agreement has an anti-competitive effect and, if so, whether any pro-competitive effects of the agreement outweigh this anti-competitive harm.

Restrictive covenants fall under this latter category and are therefore analysed under the rule of reason. Generally, they are found to be lawful if they are ancillary to the sale of a business and limited in scope to protecting the goodwill of the target. Reasonableness is determined on a case by case basis depending on the specific facts of the proposed acquisition and the terms of the covenant, although covenants not to compete for up to five years are presumed lawful and the courts have even upheld covenants for up to 10 years.

Almost all US states have state-level counterparts to s 1 of the Sherman Act. While generally modelled on and construed in accordance with the Sherman Act, the impact of state competition laws on the enforceability of the covenant should also be considered.

ALLOCATION OF RISK: SELLER'S LIMITATIONS

LEARNING OUTCOMES

After reading this chapter you will be able to:

- explain how the seller can limit its exposure under the warranties and indemnities
- describe the general limits on contractual claims that the seller may negotiate
- explain how disclosure can help the seller to limit its exposure to claims.

6.1 LIMITING THE SCOPE OF WARRANTIES, REPRESENTATIONS AND INDEMNITIES

As seen in **Chapter 5,** the buyer will seek to include warranties and indemnities in the sale and purchase agreement to provide contractual reassurances about what is being acquired. For its part, the seller will seek to limit its potential exposure to liability by negotiating specific provisions in the sale and purchase agreement, and by making appropriate disclosures in the disclosure letter or disclosure schedule.

The first draft of the sale and purchase agreement prepared by the buyer will often include extensive warranties and indemnities with few specific limitations on the seller's liability. In most cases, there is considerable scope for negotiating the agreement, and it is the warranties and indemnities which usually take up most of the time and energies of the parties' solicitors. Indeed, the final agreed version often bears little resemblance to the original draft.

The seller may be able to limit its liability by arguing successfully for the deletion of certain of the warranties and indemnities. Even if it is unable to achieve this, negotiating changes to the wording of a clause which effectively 'water it down' may make a significant difference to the seller's exposure. There is considerable merit in analysing carefully the wording of each warranty and indemnity. For example, the initial draft of a warranty may state: 'No customer of the company will cease to deal with it as a result of the acquisition.' The seller's solicitor may try to amend this by requiring knowledge of the seller and restricting the warranty to substantial customers; thus the agreed version may read: 'The seller has no knowledge, information or belief that any substantial customer of the company will cease to deal with it as a result of the acquisition.' Similarly, the seller may be asked to warrant that the company is not in breach of a particular agreement. The seller's solicitor may be able to limit the scope of the warranty by again requiring knowledge of the seller and by restricting it to breach of 'material terms' of the agreement.

Where warranties are given by reference to the 'knowledge, information or belief' of the seller in this way, the buyer will usually insist on the seller acknowledging that in giving the warranties it has made all due enquiries and taken all reasonable steps to ensure their accuracy.

6.2 LIMITATIONS ON CLAIMS

In addition to negotiating the terms of each warranty, the seller will also seek to restrict its liability in relation to the warranties and indemnities generally by including a set of standard limitation clauses in the agreement. Such limitations on the seller's liability for breach of warranty contained in a share sale agreement are not controlled by UCTA 1977 since Sch 1, para 1(e) precludes the application of its relevant provisions to any contract so far as it relates to the 'creation or transfer of securities or of any right or interest in securities'. Asset sale agreements, though, are not the subject of a similar specific exclusion.

Section 3 of UCTA 1977, which invalidates attempts to exclude liability unless they satisfy the requirement of reasonableness, applies only where one party deals on the other's written standard terms of business, although the reasonableness test will, of course, be relevant in connection with any exclusion of liability for misrepresentation (see **5.5.2**). In any event, freely negotiated warranty limitations contained in an acquisition agreement are unlikely to be the subject of a successful challenge.

6.2.1 Limits on the amount of claims

The concept of joint and several liability and attempts by sellers to limit their share of liability have already been discussed (see **5.8.1**). In addition, it is usual to include maximum and minimum limitations.

6.2.1.1 Maximum limits

The seller will negotiate for a maximum liability under the warranties and indemnities. The limit will be below the price that the buyer paid for the target. Few sellers are prepared to risk being sued for more than they receive for the shares or assets, and most buyers will accept this limitation. The buyer must take care in agreeing to such a clause, however, if the actual purchase price is relatively low but it is obliged as part of the deal to inject money into the target to discharge certain liabilities, such as outstanding loans owed by the target to the sellers. The amount of such liabilities should be treated as part of the consideration for this purpose.

In some circumstances, damages claimed for warranty or indemnity breaches can exceed the purchase price. This could arise, for example, when a target company has been sold at undervalue, ie less than market value. Even in circumstances where damages may exceed the purchase price, it is possible that a properly drafted maximum liability clause may protect a seller and limit its liability to the maximum liability it has contractually agreed with a buyer, as was seen in 116 *Cardamon Ltd v MacAlister* [2019] EWHC 1200 (Comm). Care should be taken to ensure any maximum liability agreed captures ancillary liabilities such as litigation costs. In *Equitix Eeef Biomass 2 Ltd v Fox & Ors* [2021] EWHC 2781 (TCC), it was held that the contractual cap on liability for breach of warranty claims did not capture ancillary liabilities such as costs in relation to litigation.

6.2.1.2 Minimum limits

The parties will often agree a minimum threshold for claims. In the UK, this threshold will typically be from 0.5% to 1% of the consideration. In other words, the buyer is prevented from making any claim unless the aggregate of all claims exceeds the threshold. This is really on the basis that it is virtually impossible to gauge precisely the value of a business or a company and the parties accept that there is margin for error. The effect of warranty claims is to adjust retrospectively the purchase price, and it seems reasonable for the parties to take the view that relatively minor adjustments do not justify the expense and inconvenience involved in pursuing warranty claims. The buyer is, however, wise to insist that once the threshold is exceeded, it can recover the full amount, rather than just the amount by which the threshold is exceeded. So, for example, on a £5 million sale, where the threshold is £50,000 and the loss suffered is £60,000, the buyer will be entitled to recover £60,000 rather than £10,000.

The seller may also seek to set a *de minimis* limit on individual claims, to apply even where the aggregate threshold has been exceeded. For example, the buyer may be prevented from bringing any claim worth less than £5,000. Difficulties can arise, however, in respect of continuing breaches and claims which are similar in nature or arise from the same default. Where, for example, the seller has warranted that all book debts will be fully recoverable, claims relating to debts from different sources should not be treated as separate for this purpose. As so often with acquisition documentation, careful attention to detail in drafting such a clause is necessary.

6.2.2   Time limits

Under English law, the limitation period for bringing a claim for breach of contract is normally six years from the date of the breach. For a breach of warranty, this would be the date on which the warranty statement was given, which on simultaneous exchange and completion would be the date of the sale and purchase agreement. Where the share or asset sale is by deed, the limitation period is 12 years (or if there is a separate deed of tax indemnity, the period will be 12 years in relation to the tax matters covered). In the US, time limits applicable to the commencement of a claim are set out in the laws of each state, but are typically six years for a contract or four years for contracts involving the sale of goods. In many European jurisdictions, such as Germany, the limitation period may vary depending on the type of contractual provision. Under German statutory law, the standard limitation period for breaches of contract is three years. However, certain warranties and representations will be implied into contracts, and in relation to some of these implied provisions a shorter limitation period of two years will apply.

Most sellers will wish to be 'off the hook' well before the limitation periods expire. In the UK, it is common to link the period in which the buyer can make claims relating to tax matters to HMRC's time limit for making an assessment to tax (four years (previously six years) from the end of the relevant tax year except to recover tax lost through fraudulent or negligent conduct). The buyer may therefore legitimately insist on this limitation period being as long as four or, to be on the safe side, five years; and a buyer in a strong negotiating position may even try to insist on the period being as long as seven years, since the limit of four years may be extended to six years if the tax has been lost as a result of carelessness on the part of the taxpayer or its agent.

For non-tax matters, the period negotiated is usually much shorter and, on a share sale, tends to be linked to the target company's audit (on the basis that the audit may 'flush out' breaches of warranty). A period allowing for two full audits to be carried out and their results digested is commonly agreed. In jurisdictions other than the UK, similar time limits on claims are usually agreed. For example, in Germany, statutory warranties are usually replaced by individually negotiated warranties, and a time limit of between 18 months and two years is common for claims under these.

The agreement may allow the buyer to bring claims outside these time limits provided it has notified the details to the seller within the period (ie sufficient information to identify the nature and substance of the claim). In these circumstances, there should be a long-stop time limit for instituting proceedings, so that the buyer is not able to extend the limitation period 'by the back door'.

6.2.3 Insurance cover

The seller will invariably seek to prevent the buyer from bringing a claim where the loss is covered by insurance taken out in relation to the target. The main argument between the parties often centres around whether this should extend to insurance cover that the buyer could reasonably be expected to take out (perhaps related to the level of cover in place before the acquisition).

6.2.4 Recovery from third parties

The buyer may also be required to give credit for any sums received from third parties in relation to the subject matter of the claim. This will usually be expressed widely enough to cover tax reductions (eg an undisclosed liability may be a deductible expense for tax purposes, resulting in a saving of tax).

6.2.5 Assets understated in the accounts

The seller may want to include a provision that any claim will be reduced by the amount by which the seller can show that the net assets of the target were understated in the accounts drawn up before completion, for example, by demonstrating either of the following:

(a)   that assets have been realised for more than their value in the accounts; or

(b)   that liabilities have been satisfied for less than is specified in the accounts.

The buyer should be wary of accepting this, particularly where the valuation of the target was not assets-based.

6.2.6 Conduct of claims

Claims made by third parties against the target may result in the seller becoming liable to the buyer under a warranty. The seller may, for example, have warranted that the target company has not manufactured any products which are faulty in any material respect. A successful action against the target in respect of damage caused by a defect in a product manufactured by the target prior to completion would amount to a breach of this warranty. The buyer will seek to reclaim the amount of any judgment entered against the target and costs incurred in connection with the claim.

The seller may argue that since it will ultimately bear the liability, it should have the right to have conduct of the claim. It may be worried that if the buyer has control over the dispute, the buyer may be less than vigorous in defending a claim when it knows that it will be able to sue under a warranty if it succeeds. The buyer is under a duty to mitigate its loss, but it may be difficult for the seller to prove a failure to mitigate in these circumstances.

The buyer, on the other hand, may have reservations about allowing the seller to have control, on the basis of the possible damage to the reputation and goodwill of the target which may ensue as a consequence. For example, it may feel that the seller's main concern will be to protract the matter rather than come to a settlement which leaves the target's reputation intact.

Whichever party it is decided should have control of claims, the agreement will often provide for the other party to have some influence over its conduct (eg requiring consent to settle the claim). If the seller is given control, the buyer may reserve the right to require the provision of security and/or an indemnity in respect of costs and expenses which the target or buyer may incur in relation to the claim. The buyer, for its part, will be obliged to notify the seller promptly of any circumstances which may give rise to a claim.

6.2.7 Notification of claim provisions

Although not a limitation per se, a seller may attempt to (or may be able to) restrict its liability by negotiating and demanding specific requirements that should be met following a breach of warranty or indemnity claim. Following a breach, a buyer should therefore ensure that its notice of claim to the seller complies with any agreed notification obligations, contains all requisite information, including the grounds of the buyer's claim, and identifies the applicable clause or paragraph to which the claim relates.

The importance of following agreed notification obligations was highlighted in *Teoco UK Ltd v Aircom Jersey 4 Ltd* [2018] EWCA Civ 23, in which claims for warranty breaches were struck out on grounds of failing to comply with notification requirements agreed between the parties. In *Stobart Group Ltd v William Stobart* [2019] EWCA Civ 1376, the court took a similarly objective view of the construction of notice claims, leading to tax warranties claims being struck out for not complying with notification obligations agreed between the parties. A similar approach was taken in *Dodika Ltd & Others v United Luck Group Holdings Ltd* [2020] EWHC 2101 (Comm) and more recently in *Drax Smart Generation Holdco Ltd v Scottish Power Retail Holdings Ltd* [2023] EWHC 412 (Comm). And in *Towergate Financial (Group) Ltd & Ors v Hopkinson & Ors* [2020] EWHC 984 (Comm), a notice in respect of claims was held to be invalid as it was not served 'as soon as possible' because the buyer had knowledge of the claims for at least a year prior to serving notice. Albeit in relation to an earn-out, the importance of complying with notification obligations and agreed procedures was further highlighted in *Asher & Ors v Jaywing plc* [2022] EWHC 893 (Ch).

6.3 DISCLOSURE

6.3.1 Nature and purpose of the disclosure letter (or schedule)

One of the aims of including a long list of warranties in the sale and purchase agreement is to elicit information about the target from the seller. Warranties can be seen as providing a checklist for the buyer of all the matters which may be of concern to it in relation to the acquisition. Much of the information requested by the buyer is produced in the form of disclosures by the seller, which have the effect of qualifying the warranties. The incentive for the seller in making disclosures is that they avoid it being in breach of warranty in relation to those matters disclosed. This can be illustrated by considering a few examples in the context of some standard warranties.

EXAMPLE 1

The agreement includes a warranty that the target is not engaged in any litigation as claimant or defendant. The target is, however, being sued for breach of copyright.

The seller can avoid liability for breach of warranty by disclosing full details of the copyright action. This is easier than negotiating an alteration to the terms of the warranty to exclude the copyright action from its scope (the buyer would not agree to the deletion of the warranty as it would be left without any protection against undisclosed claims). The buyer must take a view on the significance of the disclosure to the deal which has been negotiated. It may prompt it to withdraw from the acquisition, renegotiate the price, or ask the seller for an indemnity for any damages awarded against the target and any costs incurred in relation to the claim.

EXAMPLE 2

The agreement includes a warranty that the target company is not party to any contract or agreement which cannot be terminated by the company on three months' notice or less. The company is, however, party to a distribution agreement which either party can bring to an end by giving 12 months' notice, and two of the directors have nine months of their fixed-term service contracts to run.

Once again, the simplest way for the seller to avoid liability is to disclose the existence and main terms of the three agreements, and attach copies to the disclosure letter.

> **EXAMPLE 3**
>
> The agreement includes a warranty that the disclosure letter contains full particulars of the pension scheme for the target's employees.
>
> This is a different type of warranty which obliges the seller to give full and accurate details of the pension scheme (the seller will normally provide copies of the trust deed and rules).

The disclosure letter has such an important role in determining the potential liability of the seller and, correspondingly, the risk undertaken by the buyer, that it will be the subject of the same careful scrutiny by the parties as the sale and purchase agreement itself. Indeed, the practice in many jurisdictions is to make the disclosures part of the sale and purchase agreement by including the disclosures within a schedule to the agreement. Several drafts will pass between the parties, and the buyer may ask for further information on any issues included within the disclosure letter so as to perfect its knowledge of the target well ahead of the completion date. The seller is advised to make full and early disclosure of potential issues – late disclosures carry the risk that the buyer will either refuse to accept the disclosure as fully limiting the seller's liability in the relevant area, or even that the buyer will withdraw from the deal at a stage when significant professional costs have been incurred.

In civil code jurisdictions, the disclosure process is informed by the obligations of the parties in relation to the duty of good faith. In negotiations for the acquisition, each party is under an obligation to inform the other of any material information that the other party could not discover on its own. The extent of this obligation may vary between jurisdictions, but in general terms it will usually mean that the seller is expected to inform the buyer if there are any major problems with the object of the purchase. There may also be a moral obligation on the seller to clarify exactly what is being sold and to disclose any potential issues that may affect its value.

6.3.2   Format of the disclosure letter

In the UK, the disclosures will usually be in the form of a letter from the seller to the buyer. A bundle of documents (referred to as the disclosure bundle) will be attached to the letter, comprising all the documents referred to in the letter as providing information which qualifies the warranties (such as the distribution agreement referred to in Example 2 and the pension details in Example 3 in **6.3.1** above).

In many other jurisdictions, including Germany and the US, it is customary to include the disclosures in a schedule to the sale and purchase agreement.

The parties' legal advisers will negotiate the disclosure letter or schedule and bundle until it is in an agreed final form ready for completion of the acquisition. Disclosure is a means by which the seller can negate its liability under a warranty, and therefore it is in the seller's interests to disclose as much information as possible. However, the buyer must consider whether it is prepared to accept every disclosure without further information or contractual protection. If the disclosure relates to a matter of significance to the buyer, it may decide to require an indemnity from the seller to cover any identified potential liability, to reduce the purchase price it is prepared to pay or, if the matter is very significant, to withdraw from the purchase.

In the UK, on exchange of contracts, two copies of the agreed form of disclosure letter and bundle will be available; one to be given to the buyer and one to be retained by the seller. The letters and associated bundles will be initialled by the parties as evidence that they are identical. Thus in the event of a claim that there may have been a breach of warranty, each party will be able to refer to the agreed disclosure documentation. If the disclosures are contained within a schedule to the sale and purchase agreement, the parties will have evidence of the disclosures made within the body of the agreement itself.

The disclosure letter or schedule will generally be divided into two sections. First, general matters of which the buyer will be deemed to be aware, and secondly, details of specific disclosures.

6.3.2.1 Deemed disclosures

The disclosure letter or schedule will state that a number of matters are deemed to have been disclosed to the buyer. These deemed disclosures are often referred to as 'general disclosures'. These general disclosures relate to publicly available information which the buyer can be expected to find out for itself and, occasionally, to information that has been made available to the buyer during the due diligence investigation. The effect of deemed or general disclosure is to pass to the buyer the risk that elements of this information will qualify the warranties and therefore limit the seller's liability post-acquisition. The deemed disclosures will usually include the following types of information:

(a)   information on a target company's file at the Companies Registry or jurisdictional equivalent;

(b)   matters apparent from the deeds of properties owned or occupied by the target and any information available from Land Registry or the Land Charges Department, or which would be revealed by appropriate searches and enquiries of local authorities or jurisdictional equivalent. This extensive disclosure is likely to qualify a number of property warranties (eg that the target has good title to the properties, that they are free from mortgages and charges, and that the use of each property is a permitted use for planning purposes);

(c)   matters which would be disclosed by physical inspection of each property. The buyer should be prepared to accept this only if it has commissioned a survey of all the target's properties (time constraints will often prevent this);

(d)   matters which are in the public domain. This is very wide-ranging and the buyer may try to restrict its scope to matters of which the buyer could reasonably be expected to be aware as affecting the target;

(e)   matters disclosed or referred to in the audited accounts of the target company (eg for the last three years);

(f)   matters included or referred to in the accountants' report prepared on behalf of the buyer. The nature and purpose of the accountants' report is discussed in **Chapter 3**. There is often considerable disagreement between the parties as to how the report should be treated for this purpose. Reports are often very comprehensive, covering a great deal of ground; accordingly, a disclosure in these terms may considerably reduce the buyer's scope for suing for breach of warranty (eg where the inaccuracy of certain warranties could have been ascertained from the contents of the report). The buyer may, however, be prepared to accept this deemed disclosure in return for the seller warranting the accuracy of the report;

(g)   matters disclosed or referred to in the replies to the preliminary enquiries and the documents enclosed within those replies (or supplied in a data room). There is often some dispute between the parties as to whether these replies to enquiries should be deemed to be disclosed. The buyer will argue that this information is provided to assist in its assessment of the proposed acquisition and should not be used by the seller as a means of limiting its potential liability under the warranties. The relative bargaining strengths of the parties will determine whether this general disclosure is included in the final form disclosure letter;

(h)   information and documentation passed to the buyer and its advisers in the pre-contract period. If the buyer accepts this disclosure in principle, then it will usually prefer that copies of all that information and documentation which it or its advisers have received in this way during this time are attached to the disclosure letter. This will mean that the buyer's advisers will have the task of working through the attached bundle of documents to check that the buyer knows and understands what is being disclosed.

It should be noted that it is not customary in the US to accept general or deemed disclosure. US practice is to set out specific exceptions to the warranties which are cross-referenced to the warranty that they qualify. In particular, a US buyer will not usually accept as disclosed any material that had been supplied by it as part of its due diligence investigations.

6.3.2.2   Specific disclosure

Specific disclosures draw to the buyer's attention specific information about the target which is inconsistent with one or more warranties given by the seller. For ease of reference, the disclosures made will usually refer to specific warranty statements in the sale and purchase agreement. However, there is often a significant degree of overlap between the warranties, and so the disclosure letter or schedule invariably provides that each disclosure is deemed to be in respect of all the warranties and not merely the warranty referred to in it (although note US practice outlined above).

6.3.3   Standard of disclosure

It is in the interests of the buyer and the seller that all disclosures are fairly made. The buyer will want as accurate a picture as possible of the target at a time when the terms of the acquisition are still in the course of negotiations, and the seller will want to negate the possibility of any later warranty claim.

The sale and purchase agreement will usually specify the standard of disclosure required for a disclosure effectively to negate a liability under the warranties.

6.3.3.1   Adequate disclosure

The sale and purchase agreement will provide that the warranties are given subject to matters disclosed in the disclosure letter. The buyer may insist that the disclosures are properly made, ie that they are accurate and fully disclose the matters to which they relate. It is understandable that the buyer will not want to accept limitations on the seller's potential liability under the warranties unless it has full details of the relevant circumstances. From the seller's point of view it will also be advisable to make any disclosures to the buyer as detailed as possible to avoid any doubt as to whether the disclosure has been properly made.

In the case of *Levison v Farin* [1978] 2 All ER 1149, the buyers were generally aware of the run-down condition of the business, but this did not preclude them from successfully claiming for breach of a warranty which said 'there will have been no material adverse change in the overall value of the net assets of the Company'. On the facts of this case, the warranty had been given subject to the phrase 'save as disclosed' but there had been no formal disclosure letter. In his judgment Gibson LJ held that 'a clause in this form is primarily designed and intended to require a party who wishes by disclosure to avoid a breach of warranty to give specific notice for the purpose of the agreement, and protection by disclosure will not normally be achieved by merely making known the means of knowledge which may or do enable the other party to work out certain facts and conclusions'.

The issue of what constitutes effective disclosure has been further considered in the case of *Infiniteland Ltd v Artisan Contracting Ltd* [2005] EWCA Civ 758, which concerned the acquisition by share purchase of a group of companies. The Court of Appeal held that the sufficiency of disclosure must be measured by reference to the agreed contractual provisions and to the context of the acquisition. The disclosure that is made must match the standard agreed in the contract in order to negate a warranty claim. In this case, the warranties were given 'save as disclosed', and the contents of the disclosure letter were warranted as having been made 'fully, clearly, and accurately'. The agreement included a warranty that the accounts gave a true and fair view of the group's financial position. Specific disclosures against that warranty had not been made, but the disclosure letter provided for a general disclosure of all matters contained in documents provided to the buyer's reporting accountants for the purpose of their due diligence review. The accounts for one of the group companies contained an exceptional item affecting that company's profit and loss account which resulted in the buyer bringing an action for breach of warranty. The Court held that, based on the contractual terms and the context of the transaction, the disclosure requirement was whether it could fairly be expected that reporting accountants would become aware of the issue from an examination of the documents in the ordinary course of carrying out a due diligence review. In this particular case, the disclosure of the accounts documents was held to be effective disclosure because, based on the evidence provided, this was an exceptional item that the reporting accountants could have identified.

This case raised some concerns about the risk for the buyer of accepting general disclosures of information supplied in the course of a due diligence exercise. However, it is some comfort that in the first instance decision in *MAN Nutzfahrzeuge AG v Freightliner Ltd* [2005] EWHC 2347 the judge considered (obiter) 'the disclosure of all matters revealed by an inspection of specified documents' would not extend so far as to include inferences which might be drawn from the documents inspected, although it should be noted that the judge did not rule out the possibility that an appropriately drafted disclosure could extend to such inferences.

6.3.3.2 Buyer's knowledge

The buyer will usually insist on limiting disclosure specifically to matters revealed in the disclosure letter and bundle, and there will often be a clause in the sale and purchase agreement saying that the warranties are only qualified by matters contained in those documents and not by the buyer's own knowledge. The advantage of such a provision is that it limits the relevant information to be considered on a warranty claim to the agreed documentation of the transaction. However, such a clause may not achieve the buyer's objective. In the case of *Eurocopy plc v Teesdale* [1992] BCLC 1067, the buyer inserted the following clause into the sale and purchase agreement:

> The Warranties are given subject to matters set out in the Disclosure Letter ... but no other information relating to the Company of which the Purchaser has knowledge (actual constructive or imputed) shall preclude or affect any claim made by the Purchaser for breach of any of the Warranties or reduce any amount recoverable.

The sellers had warranted that all material facts had been disclosed to the buyer. The buyer brought a breach of warranty claim on the grounds that the sellers had failed to disclose certain material facts (relating to maintenance contracts for photocopiers). The sellers claimed that the buyer had actual knowledge of those facts from their due diligence and that this knowledge must have affected the price they were willing to pay. The buyer moved to strike out this aspect of the defence, on the basis that the agreement stated that the warranties were subject only to the disclosure letter. The Court of Appeal refused to strike out this aspect of the defence on the basis that the point was arguable and so the action should be allowed to proceed.

Whilst this case was only an interlocutory application, it must still be borne in mind when advising a buyer who has information on the target which may lead to a warranty claim. You may come across similar clauses in practice, but the client should be advised that it may not prevent the seller from raising the defence that the buyer knew of the actual problem and therefore cannot sue for the breach. It will therefore always be preferable for a buyer to acknowledge full disclosure of a breach and seek an indemnity or reduction in the purchase price before completion.

The issue of the buyer's knowledge was also addressed in obiter comments in *Infiniteland Ltd v Artisan Contracting Ltd* [2005] EWCA Civ 758. The agreement contained the following clause 7.4:

> The rights and remedies of the Purchaser in respect of any breach of the Warranties shall not be affected ... by any investigation made by it or on its behalf into the affairs of any Group Company (except to the extent that such investigation gives the Purchaser actual knowledge of the relevant facts and circumstances).

The buyer did not have actual knowledge of an exceptional item in the accounts that was revealed post-completion even though it had been included in the documentation provided to the buyer's accountants. The buyer sued for breach of warranty.

Since the buyer did not have actual knowledge, the Court considered whether the wording of the clause would affect the rights and remedies of a buyer who had constructive or imputed knowledge. The Court confirmed that it would give effect to an express provision in the sale agreement prohibiting warranty claims of which the buyer had constructive knowledge (ie matters of which the buyer should have been aware) but the clause in question did not expressly deal with constructive knowledge.

The issue, then, was whether the imputed knowledge of the buyer should be considered the same as its actual knowledge and therefore fall within the exception outlined in the clause. On a 2:1 majority it was held that 'actual' and 'imputed' knowledge are different. The knowledge of the professional adviser was not the buyer's knowledge, and the seller was therefore prevented from raising the buyer's knowledge as a defence to the warranty claim.

The judges' comments in *Infiniteland* make it clear that the parties need to stipulate in the agreement what type of knowledge will or will not affect a buyer's rights and remedies for a claim for breach of warranty.

Where a buyer may have partial knowledge or knowledge of only some matters which may indicate the possibility of a future claim, it is unlikely to constitute actual knowledge nor is it likely to preclude a claim, as was seen in the recent case of *MDW Holdings Ltd v Norvill* [2022] EWCA Civ 883.

In civil codes, a clause excluding the buyer's knowledge would be considered as contrary to the obligation of good faith. Under German statutory law, for example, the buyer cannot sue for a breach of warranty in relation to a matter of which it was aware at the time it concluded the contract unless the parties have contracted out of such provision (which would be rare).

6.3.3.3   Liability for information from third parties

A further disclosure issue for the parties (and in particular the seller) to consider is the impact of statements made by employees or agents of the seller or the target company during negotiations or the due diligence process. In the Court of Appeal decision in *MAN Nutzfahrzeuge AG v Freightliner Ltd* [2007] EWCA Civ 910, the seller was held to be vicariously liable for the fraudulent pre-contractual statements of its agent, who had been put forward as having authority to speak on its behalf. A prudent seller should exercise some caution when putting together its negotiating team and, to a lesser extent, when allowing employees of the target company to provide information during the transaction. (There is less risk that the seller would be vicariously liable for statements made by target employees during due diligence, but care should be taken if target employees are to be involved in the negotiation of terms.)

6.3.4   Deliberate non-disclosure

A practical problem can arise where the seller deliberately fails to disclose the existence of particular facts, such as a pending dispute, which may later lead to a warranty claim. The seller may prefer to compensate the buyer in due course after completion rather than raise the issue during negotiations, for fear that the buyer may withdraw from the purchase. However, in these circumstances the buyer will have been induced to enter into the sale and purchase agreement by way of a deliberate concealment and this would constitute fraud.

Deliberate non-disclosure will also give rise to a right to damages in those jurisdictions that impose a duty of good faith on the parties during the negotiations. Under the duty of good faith, each party is under an obligation to inform the other party of all material information and to follow moral and ethical standards. A deliberate non-disclosure is likely to be viewed as a breach of that duty.

In addition, under English law, in the context of a share acquisition, ss 89 and 90 of the Financial Services Act 2012 make it a criminal offence for a person knowingly or recklessly to make a statement, promise or forecast which is misleading, false or deceptive. It is also an offence under the section for a person with the requisite intent to conceal dishonestly any material facts. The person will be guilty of the offence if they make the statement, etc or conceal the facts for the purpose of inducing, or are reckless as to whether it may induce, another person, inter alia, to enter into an investment agreement (which includes a share sale agreement, though not an asset sale agreement). A person guilty of an offence is liable to a fine, or imprisonment for a maximum term of seven years for conviction on indictment, or to both.

6.4   INSURING AGAINST LIABILITY

Increasingly, buyers and sellers are seeking to cover the risk of potential warranty claims by taking out warranty and indemnity insurance (sometimes referred to as a 'W&I policy'). This trend is likely to accelerate – not least because following the economic downturn brought about by the Covid-19 pandemic, distressed sales as well as quick sales of businesses are likely to increase, and such transactions tend to pose the greatest risks for warranty breaches. Two main types of policy exist – buyer's side (more popular) and seller's side. Increases in the number of underwriters offering insurance, and consequent reduction in prices, have led to increasing numbers of buyers viewing warranty insurance as a credible deal protection measure.

Premiums are typically between 0.80% and 1.50% of the insured limit of liability in the London market, and between 2% and 3% in the New York market, and will often involve the insurers in picking through the acquisition documentation (usually via their own lawyers and at the insured party's expense). The insurers will not agree cover until they have analysed the scope of each warranty, the effect of the disclosures and the extent of the general limitations on the seller's liability. Any policy is likely to contain a number of general exclusions (eg excluding liability in respect of matters within the knowledge of the buyer at the date of the contract) and there will be an agreed excess, often equal to the agreed minimum claims threshold in the sale and purchase agreement.

An emerging trend in the W&I policy market has been the use of 'synthetic' policies. In such policies, the terms of any insurance are negotiated between the buyer and the underwriter/ insurer, with no involvement in the negotiations by the seller. The terms agreed need not fully match the terms of the underlying transaction. The benefit of such a policy is that it affords the buyer what is arguably bespoke protection. In short, the market for warranty insurance is evolving.

In addition to the set premium, it should be remembered that insurance premium tax will be due – in the UK, this represents an additional 12% tax on the value of the premium.

COMPLETING THE ACQUISITION

LEARNING OUTCOMES

After reading this chapter you will be able to:

- discuss the reasons for a conditional contract
- explain how risk can be managed where exchange and completion of the contract are not simultaneous
- describe preparations for completion and the mechanics of the completion meeting
- explain what tasks may be necessary after completion.

The sale and purchase agreement is a contractual agreement that sets out the terms on which the acquisition will take place. On the exchange of the duly executed sale and purchase agreement, the parties undertake to perform the agreed steps required to transfer the legal interest in the shares or assets to the buyer. This is known as completion. In most acquisition transactions, the actual transfer of the assets or shares occurs as soon as the parties have become contractually bound to do so, ie exchange and completion are simultaneous. However, it is not always possible to achieve this. In this chapter, the reasons why a sale and purchase agreement may be entered into on a conditional basis are discussed. Provisions dealing with the possible risks that may arise while the conditions are being fulfilled, and the mechanics of completing the transfer of the shares or the assets of the business are also considered.

7.1 REASONS FOR CONDITIONALITY

Before completing an acquisition various approvals, consents and clearances may be required, and ideally should be obtained before the sale and purchase agreement is signed. However, obtaining the necessary consents and approvals can take some time, and the parties may prefer not to delay exchange of contracts until all such matters have been resolved.

The sale and purchase agreement may, therefore, be made conditional on one or more matters, for example:

(a) in the UK, HMRC issuing a clearance, say, on a share acquisition in relation to roll-over relief from capital tax on a securities exchange (see **9.4.2.3**);

(b) the CMA, or the jurisdictional equivalent competition authority, notifying the buyer that the acquisition will not be subject to a Phase 2 investigation (see **2.2.1**);

(c) the provision or transfer of a regulatory licence for the particular industry, for example environmental licences for regulated industrial processes;

(d)   a substantial customer or landlord providing its consent to an assignment, or confirming that it will not exercise a contractual right to terminate an agreement with the target company on the change in control of the target company;

(e)   the shareholders of a corporate buyer passing a resolution, for example for the issue of shares to the seller in consideration for the target and, if required, making arrangements for such shares to be listed on a market;

(f)   clearance being received in respect of any voluntary or mandatory notification made under the National Security and Investment Act 2021 (see **2.2.1.4**).

In some of these situations, the parties will not want to make the required applications, so making the proposed acquisition public knowledge, until both parties are contractually committed to the acquisition. In other circumstances, the conditions may simply be those required to complete the agreed terms of the purchase. Whatever the reason for the conditional exchange of contracts, both parties will be concerned to agree terms covering satisfaction of the conditions, how and when completion will finally take place, and how the target business will be conducted during the period between signing the sale and purchase agreement and completing the acquisition.

7.2   RISK ALLOCATION ON CONDITIONAL CONTRACTS

If completion of the sale and purchase agreement is to be made conditional, the agreement must clearly state each party's obligations in respect of each condition, the date by which each condition must be met, and any right to terminate the agreement prior to completion. Express provisions will also be included to try to provide for unexpected events that may occur between signing the contract and completion of the acquisition.

The buyer will usually seek to include a contractual right to withdraw from the purchase if a major problem occurs prior to completion. However, the amount of protection given to the buyer often depends on the original reason for imposing the condition. If the condition is a requirement of the buyer, such as the need for shareholder approval, then the seller may justifiably argue that the buyer should assume the risk of any delay.

7.2.1   Conditions precedent

The sale and purchase agreement will set out the conditions to be fulfilled and specific terms relating to their fulfilment.

It is usual to include the following provisions:

(a)   an obligation on one party to take all reasonable steps to try to procure the satisfaction of the condition as early as possible, although this may be implied in some jurisdictions such as France and Italy (or, where appropriate, an undertaking by both parties to co-operate in taking such steps);

(b)   a long-stop date by which the conditions have to be satisfied (or, possibly, waived by the party for whose benefit they were included) and, in default, provision for the agreement to terminate automatically without any liability attaching to either party; and

(c)   if the conditions are satisfied prior to the long-stop date, provision for completion to take place within a specified period of this happening.

The above provisions outline the basis on which the parties are bound to proceed if the conditions are fulfilled, and on which they will be released from the agreement if the conditions are not fulfilled within the required time.

In some civil law jurisdictions, such as France and Germany, a condition precedent may be unenforceable if its fulfilment depends solely on one party, and a condition which is impossible from the outset, illegal or immoral will render the contract void. By contrast, in the Netherlands, it is possible to include conditions that depend on the actions of a sole party for their fulfilment, such as board approval. In this case, the relevant party will normally be required by the contract to use reasonable endeavours to fulfil the condition, though in any event it will also be obliged, under the duty of good faith, to perform any agreed obligations.

7.2.2 Management restrictions

After exchange of a conditional sale and purchase agreement, the buyer is contractually committed to proceed with the acquisition but will not actually take control of the target business or company until completion occurs. The buyer runs the risk that the seller may neglect the business, knowing that the buyer must go ahead with the purchase. The buyer will therefore require undertakings from the seller about how the target company or business will be run in the period between signing the sale and purchase agreement and completion.

The buyer may insist that the seller supplies it with any information concerning the business and that it (or, in the case of a corporate buyer, an authorised representative) is allowed to attend all board meetings relating to the business or, on a share sale, the target company. The buyer may also seek undertakings from the seller in relation to the carrying on of the business, for example, that the seller will procure that the company does not do any of the following (unless the buyer gives prior consent):

(a) lend or borrow money except in relation to routine matters in the ordinary course of business, or grant any mortgage, charge or debenture over its assets;

(b) settle any claim or dispute;

(c) acquire or agree to acquire any property, commit itself to any capital expenditure, or enter into any hire-purchase or leasing arrangements;

(d) enter into any agreement, or dispose of all or part of its business or assets, except in relation to routine matters in the ordinary course of its business;

(e) alter the terms of employment of any employee or director;

(f) in the case of a share acquisition, appoint any additional directors of the target.

7.2.3 Repetition of warranties

A buyer often seeks to protect its position by requiring that the representations and warranties made in the sale and purchase agreement are repeated as at the date of completion.

A buyer in a strong bargaining position may seek to include this as an additional condition precedent, giving the buyer the right to withdraw from the purchase in the event that there is a breach. This provision should be strongly resisted by the seller; and if eventually accepted, the right should be limited to instances of material breach.

If the buyer is given a substantial degree of control over the target business in the period between signing and completion, the seller is unlikely also to agree to a right to withdraw for a breach of warranty (in particular where it may be argued that the breach arises as a result of the buyer's exercise of control).

Consideration should also be given to the effect of any disclosure against such repeated warranties. Generally, disclosure will negate liability under the warranties (see **6.3.1**). However, the buyer is at risk in relation to disclosures made between exchange of contracts and completion because, regardless of the breach disclosed, it is still bound to complete the purchase. To address this issue, the agreement usually provides an obligation to disclose which is subject to the buyer's right to claim damages or exercise any right to terminate for breaches occurring in the gap between exchange and completion.

7.2.4 Material adverse change

In addition to the repetition of warranties, a buyer in a strong negotiating position may also seek to include a right to terminate the agreement in the event of a material adverse change in the business, assets or profits of the target. This provision (known as a MAC clause) is intended to protect the buyer against the general risk of adverse events that may occur in the period between signing the agreement and completion of the acquisition. As with the repetition of warranties, it may be included as a further condition precedent. Such a condition should be strongly resisted by the seller on the basis that any general risk should pass to the buyer on the signing of the agreement. If the seller is forced to agree to such a term, it should limit the provision to specified events such as the loss of a particular customer.

MAC clauses have long been a standard term in many US transactions, but despite an upward trend in buyer requests for such provisions in the UK, they remain relatively unusual in UK private acquisitions. The little English jurisprudence that exists in the area suggests that MAC clauses will generally be interpreted by UK courts, as in the US, in a narrow way that tends to favour the seller.

7.3 COMPLETING AN ACQUISITION

Successful completion of an acquisition (or 'closing') requires a great deal of organisation and project management, usually co-ordinated by the solicitors of both the buyer and seller. This is particularly true on a cross-border acquisition where additional issues such as local formalities and different time zones all need to be taken into account. The lawyers need to determine who should be present at the completion meeting, whether any authorisations are required, what documents must be produced and by whom. Much of this process is managed through the use of an agreed checklist known as the 'completion agenda'. The completion agenda sets out the steps and documentation required, and who is responsible for them at completion. It will be circulated and regularly updated to ensure that completion of the transaction runs as smoothly as possible. The detail of the completion agenda and the documentation to be provided at the completion meeting will be determined largely by the nature of the transaction itself. For example, where the existing management will continue to run the target after completion, there may be less need for a formal handover of company records, customer lists, etc than there would be in a transaction which provides for a new management team to take over from completion.

If there is to be a delay between signing the sale and purchase agreement and completing the acquisition, the completion agenda will be an agreed document referred to in the sale and purchase agreement or set out in a schedule to it. Where exchange and completion are simultaneous, the completion agenda will also detail the documentation required to enter into the sale and purchase agreement. This will include the appropriate number of copies of the sale and purchase agreement and the disclosure letter, in the agreed form, together with any separate indemnities to be provided.

7.3.1 Preparing for completion

One of the first steps in organising a completion meeting is making sure that the appropriate personnel are available and that the correct authorities have been given to enable the execution of any required documentation.

If an individual is unable to attend the completion meeting in person, they may execute a power of attorney giving another person the power to sign the completion documents on their behalf. The terms of the power of attorney will usually be agreed between the parties, and will often be drafted in very broad terms to include a power to sign any additional documentation that may be required in order to effect completion.

7.3.1.1 Seller's preparations

If there is a corporate seller, a board meeting of the seller company should be held to approve the terms of the draft sale and purchase agreement, and to appoint an authorised signatory to execute it. The board may appoint a single director or a committee to attend to completion arrangements on behalf of the company. A certified copy of the minutes of this meeting must be given to the buyer on completion as evidence of the seller's representatives' authority to act (and sign documents) on its behalf. As a third party acting in good faith, the buyer will be able to rely on this certified copy of the board meeting minute as evidence of the corporate seller's authority. However, the parties' lawyers will nonetheless check the seller's articles of association together with any relevant banking security documentation to ensure that all appropriate steps have been taken to authorise the sale.

Approvals may also be required under English company law – the legal advisers should confirm that the sale is in accordance with the directors' duties and, if the sale is to a director or person connected to a director of the target company or its holding company, approval of the shareholders (as a substantial property transaction (CA 2006, s 190)) may be required.

On a share sale, the buyer will also require that a board meeting of the target company is held at completion in order to approve registration of the transfer of the shares (see **7.3.3**). The seller must ensure that the completion board meeting of the target company is quorate and that there is a sufficient majority present to pass the requisite resolutions. If provided for in the target's articles, any director of the target company who is unable to be present at this meeting may appoint an alternate director to attend and vote on their behalf. The precise legal requirements will depend on the particular local laws and constitution of the corporate entities involved.

7.3.1.2 Buyer's preparations

A corporate buyer must also hold a meeting to approve the terms of the draft sale and purchase agreement, and to authorise the signing and completion of it. Under English company law, the board may appoint a single director or a committee to attend to completion arrangements on behalf of the company. A certified copy of the minutes of this meeting will be handed to the seller on completion as evidence of the authority of the buyer's representatives to act (and sign documents) on its behalf.

If the consideration for the acquisition includes shares in the buyer company, shareholders' resolutions may be necessary to authorise the issue of those consideration shares. On the other hand, where the consideration is to be raised by borrowing, the buyer's lawyers must confirm that the requirements necessary for the provision of the finance have been complied with and that the funds will therefore be available at completion.

As a last-minute check before completion, the buyer usually repeats some of the searches made in the early, information-gathering stages of the transaction. In particular, for a company registered in England and Wales, it should repeat searches at the Companies Registry and undertake bankruptcy searches against individual sellers. On a share acquisition, searches should also be made against the target company itself (and any of its subsidiaries). If intellectual property rights are an important aspect of the acquisition, the buyer is well-advised to repeat patent and trademark searches.

On a share purchase, the buyer may also wish to make an appointment with the seller to inspect the statutory books of the target company prior to completion to check compliance with all relevant formalities.

7.3.2 Completion of asset acquisition

Although the general preparations and mechanics of the completion process are the same for all acquisitions, the assets being transferred do, of course, vary. On an asset purchase in the UK, all the assets of the business must be transferred individually as discussed below. The sale and purchase agreement will usually provide that such transfers take place simultaneously, so the seller's solicitor must make all necessary preparations to ensure that this happens. In some jurisdictions, where the transfer relates to the purchase of an ongoing business some assets will be transferred automatically, and this will be reflected in the sale and purchase agreement. In certain jurisdictions, such as Italy and Argentina, a transfer of the ongoing business involving the automatic transfer of assets will be executed as a notarised deed. However, different jurisdictions may have different obligations; for example, under French law, the '*acte de cession*' for the transfer of a '*fonds de commerce*' can be executed as a private deed but will be subject to certain publication formalities.

7.3.2.1 Transferring title

The following formalities are required in the UK to transfer the legal interest in the assets of a business to the buyer:

(a)   conveyances, transfers or assignments of land and premises;

(b)   assignments of goodwill, certain intellectual property rights (including copyrights, patents and trade marks) and the benefit of contracts.

Stock and movable assets, such as loose plant and machinery, are transferable by delivery; it is sufficient if the sale and purchase agreement requires delivery to be given on completion.

If assets are held in other jurisdictions then the local laws relating to the transfer of that asset must be followed. For example, in Germany, land must be transferred by notarised deed, and the transfer of physical assets will usually be subject to formal documentation which will list each asset.

The requirement for a document to be notarised can add a considerable time to the acquisition process, and this should be taken into account when planning for the completion of an acquisition.

7.3.2.2 Documents to be handed over at completion

As indicated above, the parties will agree a detailed completion agenda, setting out the responsibilities of the respective parties with regard to matters to be dealt with and documents to be handed over at completion.

The detail of the completion agenda will vary with the terms of each transaction, but in general, whilst the buyer will make the sale and purchase agreement available, the seller is usually required to hand over or make the following available to the buyer on completion of an asset acquisition:

(a)   where there is no delay between exchange and completion, the agreed form of disclosure letter or schedule;

(b)   where the seller is a company, a certified copy of a board resolution authorising a representative to attend to completion arrangements on behalf of the company and to sign the documentation, or the jurisdictional equivalent;

(c)   documents transferring title to the assets (drafts should have been agreed by the parties prior to completion, and the agreed form may be annexed to the sale and purchase agreement), or the jurisdictional equivalent;

(d)   deeds and documents of title to the assets, including freehold and leasehold properties (or confirmation of title from the bank if the properties remain subject to a charge);

(e)   duly executed releases of charges over the assets and confirmation of non-crystallisation of floating charges, or the jurisdictional equivalent;

(f)   financial records and books of account, customer lists, computer programs, designs, drawings, plans, sales and promotional materials, National Insurance, PAYE and VAT records or the jurisdictional equivalent, employee records, and other documents required by the buyer to run the business. The seller is advised to reserve the right for a certain period after completion to inspect and take copies of the records, etc which are handed to the buyer, in case these are needed in relation to the seller's affairs (eg by the tax authorities);

(g)   originals, counterparts or certified copies as appropriate of licences to assign leasehold property, novation agreements and consents from third parties to assignment of contracts, or the jurisdictional equivalent;

(h)   a certified copy of a special resolution of the selling company resolving to change its name if it has been agreed that the buyer will acquire the right to use the seller's corporate name, or the jurisdictional equivalent (see **5.10.2**).

The buyer will be required to pay the amount of the purchase price due on completion, usually by banker's draft or telegraphic transfer to the seller's bank account. A corporate buyer will also be required to produce an appropriate form of authorisation for a representative to sign the transaction documentation. Under English law this could be a certified copy of a board resolution of the company.

7.3.3   Completion of share acquisition

As with an asset acquisition, the parties will agree a completion agenda, setting out steps to be taken and documents to be provided to complete the acquisition. However, on a share acquisition only one asset, the shares, will be transferred, and the remaining documentation will deal with steps required to transfer control of the target company effectively.

7.3.3.1   Transferring shares

Under English law, the following documents are required to transfer the legal interest in the shares:

(a)   stock transfer form; and

(b)   share certificate.

Although a duly executed stock transfer form will transfer the shares, the buyer is not entitled to exercise its shareholders' rights (including voting at general meeting) until the transfer is registered by the target company. Alternatively, if the company has elected not to keep its own register of members in accordance with CA 2006, s 128B, the buyer will not be entitled to exercise its shareholders' rights until the transfer has been registered at the central registry at Companies House.

The buyer will therefore require the seller to procure registration of the transferred shares, usually (in a private company) by procuring a board meeting of the target company to consider the transferred shares for registration. The existing shareholders may also be required to waive any rights of pre-emption on the transfer of shares that may exist under the constitution of the company. This waiver will usually be contained within the sale and purchase agreement.

In other jurisdictions, the steps required to transfer ownership may vary, and in many jurisdictions some forms of corporate entities do not have shares or share certificates but ownership is held through 'quotas' which are transferable by assignment (see **9.1.1**). Quotas operate in a similar way to shares and are usually referred to in international acquisitions as shares. However, when transferring ownership care must be taken to ensure that the correct form of transfer is used for that particular type of corporate entity. For example, in Germany, only AGs may have share certificates evidencing title to the shares, and title in those shares can be transferred either by handing over the share certificates or by assignment. By contrast, GmbH quotas are transferred by assigning the quota in a notarised sale and purchase agreement or in a separate transfer agreement. Similar provisions apply in relation to the transfer of a limited liability 'quota' company in Portugal or Brazil, where the transfer must be executed before a notary public by means of a notarial deed of assignment of quotas, which must then be registered with the commercial registry.

In the US, shares are transferred by a stock transfer form, which is printed on the back of a share certificate, although a separate form of assignment can be used instead. The particular rules of the state of incorporation of the company should be checked.

7.3.3.2   Completion board meeting

As part of the completion process on a share acquisition of a company registered in England and Wales, the seller will be required to procure a board meeting of the target company to implement any decisions that the buyer requires in order to take immediate control of the target. To ensure the meeting takes place in accordance with the buyer's wishes, the minutes of this required meeting will be prepared in advance by the buyer's lawyers and circulated for approval.

The matters to be covered in a completion board meeting of a target company registered in England and Wales will depend on the extent to which the buyer wishes to make immediate changes to the way the target company is run.

The matters a buyer will usually require to be dealt with at a completion board meeting of the target are set out below:

(a)   approval of the transfer of shares (subject to payment of stamp duty);

(b)   appointment of new directors and company secretary (including obtaining consents to act, any required disclosure of interests, and approval and authorisation of service contracts);

(c)   acceptance of resignations of directors and company secretary (including agreeing any severance payments);

(d)   acceptance of the resignation of the company's auditors and appointment of new auditors;

(e)   change of accounting reference date;

(f)   change of registered office;

(g)   alteration of existing bank mandates and the completion of new finance arrangements.

If the target company also has subsidiaries, the buyer will usually require each subsidiary company to hold a board meeting implementing any required changes to personnel, finance arrangements and administrative matters.

The extent to which such a meeting is required in other jurisdictions will depend on the particular constitution of that company and the local laws.

7.3.3.3   Completion general meeting under English law

Under English company law, the buyer may also require a completion shareholders' meeting to grant any necessary approvals or make any required changes to the constitution of the company.

Matters that may require shareholder approval include:

(a)   giving consent to a substantial property transaction under s 190 of the CA 2006, if the sale of the shares is to a director of the target's holding company, or to a person connected with such a director;

(b)   consenting to a term in a director's service contract whereby the employment is for a term in excess of two years (CA 2006, s 188);

(c)   altering the articles of association of the target company. A corporate buyer may, for example, want to amend the articles so that they are suitable for a wholly-owned subsidiary, or so that they conform with those of other companies within its group.

In practice, changes or approvals to be effected by the shareholders will usually be dealt with by written resolution presented at the completion board meeting of the target company. The buyer does not become a member of the target company until its name is entered into the register of members (CA 2006, s 112). As registration cannot take place until the stock transfer form has been properly stamped, the buyer will not be able to exercise its voting rights until after completion of the acquisition. Consequently, the written resolution (drafted by the buyer's lawyers) must be passed by the sellers as the registered holders of the shares.

7.3.3.4 Documents to be handed over at completion

As with an asset acquisition, the parties will agree a detailed completion agenda, setting out the responsibilities of the respective parties with regard to matters to be dealt with and documents to be provided at completion.

Although the detail of the completion agenda will vary from transaction to transaction and in accordance with relevant local laws, the buyer will usually take responsibility for producing the final form sale and purchase agreement, the seller is usually required to hand over the following documents or procure the following events on completion of a share acquisition:

(a) where there is no delay between exchange and completion, the agreed form of disclosure letter or schedule;

(b) if the seller is a company, a certified copy of a board resolution authorising its representative to attend to completion arrangements on behalf of the company and to sign the documentation;

(c) a stock transfer form duly executed and delivered by each seller together with the relative share certificates (or appropriate form of transfer of ownership for that jurisdiction and type of corporate entity);

(d) a completion board meeting of the target company to implement any specified board decisions if required in that jurisdiction (see **7.3.3.2**);

(e) any written resolutions that may be required, duly executed by the sellers as the registered holders of the shares if required in that jurisdiction (see **7.3.3.3**);

(f) the discharge of outstanding loans made by the seller(s) to the company or vice versa (existing banking arrangements may also be replaced with the buyer's arrangements);

(g) the delivery by the seller's lawyers of the statutory books of the target company if required in that jurisdiction, the title deeds to its properties (or confirmation of title from the bank for properties remaining subject to a charge), any certificates of title given by the seller's lawyers, documents of title relating to other assets, financial records, agreements to which the target is a party and insurance policies.

The buyer will be required to pay the amount of the purchase price due on completion, usually by banker's draft or telegraphic transfer to the seller's bank account. A corporate buyer will also be required to produce an appropriate form of authorisation, such as a board resolution, authorising a representative to sign the transaction documentation.

7.3.4 Virtual completion

It is increasingly common for a completion meeting to be 'virtual', where the parties and their lawyers do not meet face to face. This is particularly the case with international transactions.

Care needs to be taken when conducting a virtual completion to ensure that it is legally valid. Problems can occur due to the need to exchange signed documentation; solutions include using pre-signed signature pages or exchanging signature pages (alone) by email. Completing the transaction in this way can cast doubt upon the validity of the overall documentation, especially if the lawyers negotiate changes after signature. Lawyers conducting completion should ensure that the final versions of all documentation are sent to signatories before completion occurs (for example, as a pdf email attachment), so that the signatories subsequently can give authority for signature pages to be attached to a hard copy of the documentation, and a legally valid completion can then occur. In many jurisdictions, electronic signature is now a legally valid method of executing most forms of legal document and can be particularly convenient for larger commercial transactions. In most instances, advanced electronic signature will be required, whereby the parties access documents uploaded to a third party platform, and complete authentication by means of a password/PIN or fingerprint scan, thereby signing digitally.

7.4 POST-COMPLETION MATTERS

After completion of the acquisition there are still a number of tasks to be undertaken by the solicitors for both the buyer and the seller.

7.4.1 Stamp duty and filing

On a share purchase of a company registered in England and Wales, the buyer's lawyers must ensure that the duly executed stock transfer forms are delivered to the HMRC Stamp Office within 30 days together with the requisite transfer duty. In practice this is usually undertaken immediately, as the buyer will want to be entered in the register of members as soon as possible and this can only be done after any stamp duty has been paid.

In addition, on a share purchase the buyer's lawyers may also need to file the following at the Companies Registry in relation to the target company and any of its subsidiaries:

(a)   forms notifying any change of registered office (CA 2006, s 87), changes of directors and secretary, and change of accounting reference period;

(b)   a copy of any special resolution of the company;

(c)   a print of any new articles of association of the company.

Where a company has issued shares as consideration, the buyer's lawyers may also need to file the following:

(a)   for a company incorporated under the CA 1985, a copy of any ordinary resolution triggering the directors' authority to allot shares pursuant to CA 2006, s 550, and a copy of any ordinary resolution necessary to remove the ceiling on issue of shares represented by the company's authorised share capital;

(b)   for a company other than a private company with only one class of shares in issue, a copy of an ordinary resolution authorising the directors to allot shares (CA 2006, s 551);

(c)   a copy of a special resolution suspending any applicable pre-emption rights;

(d)   a return of allotments (CA 2006, s 555) together with a statement of capital.

In addition, the buyer's lawyers should complete the statutory books of the target company, including the registers of members (after the stock transfer forms have been stamped), directors and secretary, and minutes.

Many European companies will not have internal company registers, and the buyer's lawyers will only have to file any changes to the management to the commercial register.

7.4.2 Matters outstanding on completion

There are often matters that may have been left outstanding on completion of a transaction. The parties may have agreed that part of the purchase price will be determined by accounts prepared after completion, or a particular release or transfer may have been left outstanding. The parties will have agreed timetables for dealing with these additional matters and will often have indemnities in place in relation to any costs that may be incurred. The buyer will also take practical steps after completion to implement any changes required to incorporate the target into its existing business, such as informing customers and suppliers of the acquisition.

7.4.2.1 'Bibles'

The parties' lawyers will often compile so-called 'bibles' after completion, containing copies of the complete set of documents used in the acquisition, which can be used as a source of reference should any problems crop up in the future (eg in relation to warranties).

VARIATIONS

CHAPTER 8

ASSET ACQUISITIONS

LEARNING OUTCOMES

After reading this chapter you will be able to:

- explain what is required to transfer the various types of asset on an asset sale
- describe the typical protections, by way of warranty and otherwise, that a buyer may require in respect of the assets to be acquired
- discuss how the TUPE Regulations protect the workforce on an asset sale
- explain the taxation implications of an asset sale for the buyer and seller.

8.1 AGREEING WHAT TO TRANSFER

The fundamental nature of an asset acquisition is that the buyer agrees to purchase a collection of assets, the make-up of that collection being dependent upon the negotiations between the buyer and seller, their respective commercial objectives and the applicable local laws governing the proposed acquisition. In this book, an asset acquisition is considered where the buyer's objective is to continue to run the target business after its acquisition, either as a stand-alone business or by incorporation of the acquired assets into the buyer's existing business operations. To achieve this objective, the buyer must ensure that it will acquire all the necessary assets, and that crucial trading arrangements will remain in place after completion of the purchase. The approach to achieving that objective may be very different depending on the underlying legal system governing the acquisition.

8.1.1 Approach under common law

In common law jurisdictions, the terms of the acquisition will be set out in the sale and purchase agreement, with further detail in the schedules to that agreement (see **4.4**) of the assets and liabilities (if any) that are to be included in the sale. Although ideally the parties should try to specify exactly which assets are to transfer, it is not always possible to identify every asset separately, so sometimes the buyer will seek to include more general provisions to encompass all assets used in the target business. It is therefore usual to include a definition of the 'business' of the target, together with provisions dealing with the transfer of goodwill (see **8.2.8**).

In addition to detailing the assets and liabilities included in the sale, the parties will often include a list of assets which are specifically excluded. For example, the seller may wish to retain certain assets for which it will continue to have use after completion, and some assets may simply be surplus to the buyer's requirements. Further, there is usually little point in including cash in hand or on deposit in the sale, since this would just involve the buyer paying an equivalent sum as part of the purchase price, and debtors and creditors are sometimes also left with the seller (see **8.2.7**).

In England and Wales, on an asset acquisition each of the assets and liabilities must be specifically identified and individually transferred in the manner required for the particular asset or liability, with the exception of certain obligations in relation to employees and environmental liabilities which transfer with the land. Although most common law jurisdictions recognise the concept of choice of assets, there are certain variations in common law jurisdictions. In Australia, for example, the liabilities for certain tax and utility charges attaching to the land (such as water rates, land taxes etc) will accrue with the land that is transferred in an asset acquisition.

A US asset acquisition requires compliance with applicable bulk sales statutes. The majority of US states have enacted bulk sales statues to protect the buyer in an asset acquisition. Though there are variations between the states, statutes detailing the legal requirements of a bulk sale (sometimes called a bulk transfer of assets) basically apply to the sale of all or most of the materials, supplies and inventory of a business other than in the ordinary course of the seller's business. In order to protect the buyer from claims made by the seller's creditors, the seller must usually complete a list (usually by way of affidavit) of existing creditors. The list is then registered with a government department, for example, a court office. Additionally, bulk sales statutes generally require that each of the creditors is given notice a certain period before the transfer of the business takes place. If the buyer does not complete the registration process for a bulk sale, creditors of the seller may obtain a declaration that the sale was invalid as against them, and the creditors may repossess their goods or obtain judgment for any proceeds the buyer receives from a subsequent sale of them. Moreover, pursuant to certain federal and state tax statutes, when the buyer acquires all or substantially all of the assets of a business it must assume the tax liabilities relating to the assets acquired.

8.1.2 Approach under civil law

Certain civil law jurisdictions do not recognise the concept of individual transfer of each of the specific assets (see **1.2.2.4**). A buyer of a business as a going concern can, in some civil law jurisdictions, also inherit business liabilities even if these are not specifically dealt with in the sale and purchase agreement.

Pursuant to French law, a business qualifies essentially as a going concern (*fonds de commerce*) when it includes goodwill (*clientèle*) which it owns. Assets in a French business may be sold separately. Nonetheless, if such assets include goodwill they qualify as a going concern and have to be subject to the statutory provisions. Certain assets such as goodwill, intangible assets, equipment and leasehold property are deemed to be part of a going concern. Other assets such as contracts, receivables and land, as well as liabilities, are not considered part of a going concern and their transfer must be explicitly stipulated in the required deed of sale.

The sale of a *fonds de commerce* is subject to detailed statutory provisions, including that the acquisition may only be realised by means of a specific deed (*acte de cession de fonds de commerce*) which is subject to publication and some other formalities. A French going concern cannot be validly transferred by any other means, for example by being part of a cross-border sale. The deed of sale of a *fonds de commerce* needs to include precise information as to the previous sale of that *fonds de commerce*, any registered liens and security interests, profit and losses as well as sales figures realised during the last three years of operation, and the terms and conditions of the lease. Omission of or inaccuracy in any of these compulsory issues may result in the buyer asking for a reduction of the purchase price or even a cancellation of the sale. The deed must be registered with the French tax authorities and has to be executed in the French language or, if in a foreign language, with a certified translation. The parties are bound to the agreement upon execution of the *acte de cession*. Following the execution, certain publications need to be made. These formalities are intended to protect the creditors of the business as, within a time frame of 10 days following publication, any creditor of the seller has the right to object to payment of the price. In practice, this means that, as long as the opposition period is running, the purchase price will be kept in escrow.

In Belgium, a similar procedure exists. The parties may decide to submit the transfer to a specific set of rules set out in the Belgium Company Code, provided that the assets can be typified as a branch of activity or universality of assets. Upon compliance with certain formalities as to the preparation of reports and notification or re-application by the buyer for permits and licences with the authorities, pursuant to the applicable Company Code provisions all operational activities, contracts, assets and liabilities relating to that part of the business are transferred automatically by operation of law without any additional requirements.

In certain civil law jurisdictions (such as Italy and Argentina), where part of the seller's business or one of the seller's businesses is transferred and it can be considered as 'the aggregate of assets and legal relationships organised for the operation of the business activity', this acquisition is considered as an acquisition of a going concern and will be regulated as such.

In Italy, when the acquisition involves at least two of the following elements: (i) assets, (ii) employees, (iii) contracts, (iv) know-how, (v) public licences and authorisations, (vi) a list of clients and suppliers, the transfer is considered as a going concern business transfer and the specific procedure pursuant to the Italian Civil Code applies. The Italian Civil Code requires that the transfer of a going concern is executed by a public deed or a private deed with legalised signatures. These transfer formalities may have a significant effect on the planning of a multi-jurisdictional acquisition as these types of acquisitions often involve simultaneous closing in various jurisdictions.

Pursuant to an Italian acquisition, the buyer and the seller are jointly and severally liable for debts incurred prior to the transfer if they are recorded in the accounting books and the creditors have not explicitly released the seller. This joint liability applies regardless of any express agreement reached by the parties. In addition, the buyer and seller are jointly and severally liable for taxes and sanctions originating from violation of tax laws in the two previous years and during the year the transfer of the going concern is executed. The seller is liable only for debts calculated until the date of transfer with, as a maximum amount, the value of the transferred business. The buyer may request the Italian tax authorities to certify the amount resulting from violation of tax law and the debts assessed to the seller.

8.1.3   The timing of the transfer

The sale and purchase agreement should also address the issue of the timing of the completion of an asset acquisition, and will usually specify that the transfer of all the required assets will take place simultaneously at completion. However, sometimes a formal transfer of an asset is not possible at completion, for example if consent to the transfer is required. In these circumstances, the sale and purchase agreement will usually provide that the seller will hold the asset on trust for the benefit of the buyer pending the formal transfer. The agreement will also provide that the buyer is able to use the asset for the purpose of running the business, thereby enabling the entire operation of the target business to transfer at a given moment in time. Many jurisdictions do not recognise the common law concept of a trust, so cross-border sale and purchase agreements will often resolve this issue by inserting a condition precedent clause into the agreement. In larger transactions, where it may be important to ascertain the exact moment that the business operation transfers from the seller to the buyer, the sale and purchase agreement will specify an 'effective time' (usually close of trade on the day of completion of the acquisition). In a multi-jurisdictional acquisition, the sale and purchase agreement will need to address the issue of varying 'close of business' times across the different countries and time zones involved. Any trade undertaken or costs incurred by the seller prior to the effective time will be allocated to the seller, and trade undertaken or costs incurred after this time will be apportioned to the buyer (see **8.2.7.4**).

8.2 TRANSFER OF ASSETS

In this section, consideration is given to the particular factors relevant on the transfer of each type of asset, including the nature of the warranties generally sought by the buyer (see **Chapter 5**).

8.2.1 Land and premises

8.2.1.1 General considerations under English law

Any freehold and leasehold premises which are to be transferred will normally be listed in a schedule to the sale and purchase agreement. The buyer will assume risk on the premises as from exchange of the agreement and should take out insurance from this date, or, in the case of leasehold property where the lease obliges the landlord to insure, have its interest noted on the landlord's policy. On completion of the acquisition, suitable transfer arrangements will be put in place for the formal transfer of the premises to the buyer.

8.2.1.2 Licence to assign

Requesting consent

Where the terms of a lease require the consent of the landlord to assignment, there is often considerable delay in obtaining a formal licence to assign. The seller should therefore request consent from the landlord as early as possible, in the hope that the licence will be available in good time for exchange of contracts. The buyer is also advised to give the seller details of referees so that these can be passed on to the landlord immediately (the provision and taking up of references is commonly a chief cause of delay).

The seller, as the existing tenant, does have some redress if the landlord acts unreasonably. Section 19 of the Landlord and Tenant Act 1927 provides that where the lease contains a covenant not to assign without the landlord's consent (such qualified covenants against assignment are standard in commercial leases), the landlord cannot unreasonably withhold its consent. The landlord is also under a duty to give its decision within a reasonable time and to give reasons for a refusal (Landlord and Tenant Act 1988, which entitles tenants to damages if the landlord unreasonably refuses or delays the granting of a licence to assign).

For leases granted on or after 1 January 1996, landlords are able to exercise greater control by stipulating in the lease any conditions which they will require the tenant to fulfil in order to assign the lease, or any circumstances in which a refusal of consent to assign will be deemed to be reasonable.

Guarantees

A landlord will often require that obligations under the lease are guaranteed by third party guarantors. The landlord will not normally be willing to grant a licence to assign and to release guarantors of the seller's obligations under the lease unless they are provided with equivalent guarantees of the buyer's obligations (eg from the directors of a corporate buyer). Indeed, the lease may stipulate that the landlord is not obliged to consent to the assignment unless this is done.

Conditional contract

If the licence to assign is not ready by the time the parties are in a position to sign the sale and purchase agreement, they may decide to make the agreement conditional on the consent of the landlord to the assignment and incorporate a right for the parties to rescind if this is not obtained within a specified time limit (see **7.1**).

Warranties

The buyer will seek to include warranties covering the state of the premises to be acquired and any relevant environmental matters.

8.2.1.3   Comparison with other jurisdictions

Some, but not all, civil law jurisdictions make the distinction between freehold and leasehold property. In the Netherlands, ownership can refer to freehold (*volle eigendom*) or to leasehold (*erfpacht*). Germany, on the other hand, does not make this distinction.

Many civil law jurisdictions require a notarial deed executed by a civil law notary in that jurisdiction to transfer the land or immovables. In the Netherlands, the buyer and seller can enter into a sale and purchase agreement relating to the property by a simple deed. However, according to Dutch law, it is mandatory to hire a civil law notary to perform the registration process of real property in the Netherlands. The civil law notary will conduct a title search at the land registry (*Kadaster*), verify the authority of the seller to dispose of the property, conduct research regarding the representation of the involved parties, prepare the deed of the transfer, provide for a transfer of the property free of mortgages and attachments, and carry out the final check for attachments before executing the deed.

In Germany, the notary will notarise the sale as well as the transfer agreement, which is a necessary requirement according to German statute.

A number of civil law jurisdictions (for example France and Luxembourg) make a distinction between general business leases, which are governed by the general provisions of the civil code, and business leases entered into for the purpose of business activities (such as retail and industry) (*baux commerciaux*) which are governed by derogatory provisions. These provisions generally relate to the length of the lease term, rent increases, tenants' rights to sell or sublease and transfer of the lease as a result of a change of control. Some countries require that leases with a duration of more than a certain length must be passed before a notary and registered with the authorities. The requirement for a document to be notarised can, in some jurisdictions, add a considerable amount of time to the acquisition timetable. Where an acquisition is likely to involve a notary, advice should be obtained early in the transaction as to the likely timescale for the notary's involvement.

8.2.2   Plant and machinery

8.2.2.1   General considerations

A schedule of the items of plant and machinery (including vehicles) which are part of the sale should be attached to the sale and purchase agreement. A buyer who wishes to purchase all of these assets of the business may seek to safeguard itself by providing that plant and machinery 'used in the business' are to be transferred, including those items listed in the schedule. Thus items omitted from the schedule by mistake (it may be difficult for the buyer to check the accuracy of the schedule) will, nevertheless, be included in the sale. No particular formalities are required for the transfer of plant and machinery which will pass on delivery at completion.

In the case of an international acquisition, the law of each relevant jurisdiction needs to be verified as to the appropriate formalities for transferring plant and machinery.

8.2.2.2   Warranties

The buyer will often seek to include the following warranties as to the state of the items of plant and machinery listed in the schedule:

(a)   they are in a proper state of repair and condition and in satisfactory working order;

(b)   they are not dangerous, obsolete or in need of replacement;

(c)   they have been properly and regularly maintained;

(d)   they are adequate for (and not surplus to) the needs of the business.

The seller should think twice before accepting these warranties and consider trying to restrict any liability to major defects. Also, in relation to (d), as it will have no control over how the buyer carries on the business after completion, it may wish to add the words 'as carried on by the seller prior to the agreement'.

8.2.3   Intellectual property

Ideally, all trademarks, service marks, registered designs, copyrights and patents which are to be included in the transfer should be listed in a schedule or an appendix to the sale and purchase agreement. Appropriate assignments of any licences and other intellectual property rights will be required to transfer title at completion.

The buyer may seek warranties in relation to the following matters:

(a)   that the seller is the beneficial owner or registered proprietor of the intellectual property rights (as defined in the interpretation clause);

(b)   that to the best of the seller's knowledge and belief those rights are valid and enforceable;

(c)   that the seller has not granted any person a right to do anything which would otherwise be an infringement of those rights;

(d)   that no licences for the use of intellectual property have been granted to the seller or are required to run the business;

(e)   that the operation of the business does not infringe the intellectual property rights of any other person.

The buyer may also insist on a warranty that the seller has not disclosed trade secrets, know-how or confidential information (eg customer price lists) except in the normal course of business.

Certain intellectual property rights, such as patents, trade marks and design rights, can be registered under the laws of many jurisdictions. On transfer of such a registered right, the relevant register will need to be notified, and the sale and purchase agreement should address this registration issue.

8.2.4   Leasing, hire-purchase and other finance contracts

Equipment employed by the seller in the business which is subject to hire-purchase, contract hire or leasing arrangements does not belong to the seller and cannot, therefore, be included in the transfer without the consent of the true owner. The owner may be prepared to consent to the assignment or novation of the agreement to the buyer, or may prefer to enter into a fresh agreement with it.

If these arrangements are not in place at completion the buyer may nonetheless be able to use the equipment from the completion date on the basis that it undertakes to discharge obligations under the contract (including payments due) on behalf of the seller until novation, or until a fresh agreement is entered into between the buyer and the third party .

8.2.5   Stock and work in progress

Stock will usually be defined as including raw materials, work in progress and finished goods. Since it is impossible to determine the level of completion stock in advance, it is unusual for the parties to agree a value for the stock prior to completion. They will often provide in the agreement for the stock to be valued at or shortly after completion, and for the price of the stock to be left outstanding until they have agreed the valuation.

Stock and work in progress will often be a significant element in the overall consideration for the target business, and the agreement should therefore specify who is to carry out the valuation, the basis on which the stock is to be valued, and the procedure to be followed if the parties dispute the valuation.

The parties may agree to carry out a joint stock-take, with the actual valuation to be prepared by the seller, or may provide for specified professional valuers to undertake the valuation.

The agreement may provide for the stock to be valued on the same basis as in the audited accounts (eg this will often be on the basis of the lower of cost or net realisable value); on some other general basis, such as market value; or in accordance with a detailed formula which, for example, takes account of slow-moving or obsolete stock.

Where the seller prepares the valuation, provision will usually be made for any dispute to be referred to an independent expert. The buyer may be obliged to pay a percentage of the valuation (eg 50%) immediately, with any balance payable within a specified time limit of its final determination – this should avoid the procedure being employed by the buyer simply as a method of delaying payment.

The buyer may wish to set a limit on the amount of stock it is obliged to purchase on completion and, in order to guard against the seller reducing stock to a level which will make it difficult for the buyer to meet orders, may also stipulate a minimum amount of stock. The buyer may also seek warranties that the stocks are of satisfactory quality and that none of the items is obsolete or unmarketable.

8.2.6   Contracts

8.2.6.1   Passing the benefit and burden – common law approach

The buyer should ensure that it receives the benefit of all contracts entered into between the seller and third parties which are important to enable the business to continue trading after completion of the acquisition, such as agency or distribution agreements, contracts with suppliers or customers, and licensing agreements. One way to achieve this under English law is to assign the benefit of the contract; if legal assignment is required, notice must be given to the other contracting party under s 136 of the Law of Property Act 1925. Such assignment is desirable since otherwise the third party can continue to make payments to the seller. The buyer should, however, check whether or not the terms of the contract prohibit assignment or require the consent of the other party. It is important to remember that this method will transfer only the benefit of the contract and that the seller will still be liable to the third party to fulfil any outstanding obligations. For example, in an exclusive distribution agreement, if the seller is the distributor, the benefit under the agreement is the receipt of goods for resale in a given territory; the burden is payment for the goods. Under English law, the right to receive the goods can be legally assigned by giving notice under s 136 of the Law of Property Act 1925 (unless the contract says consent is required), but the obligation to pay for the goods remains with the seller.

To get around this, the existing contract may be novated under English law. This involves the other party to the contract agreeing to release the seller from the contract, allowing the buyer to take over the benefit and burden of the contract. The parties to the novation agreement will be the buyer, the seller and the third party, the result being, effectively, a new contract between the buyer and the third party. Alternatively, the other contracting party may agree to enter into a fresh agreement with the buyer. This gives the buyer scope to negotiate new terms and conditions if the existing ones are commercially unacceptable in their present form.

As the co-operation of the other party to a contract is usually required, it is a time-consuming process to put all the necessary arrangements in place, and this may not coincide with the timetable the parties have agreed for the acquisition.

8.2.6.2   What if consents, etc are delayed?

Routine contracts

With some contracts (for example, minor or routine ones), a simple assignment of the benefit to the buyer will be required with, in many cases, no need for third party consent. Where third party consent is required, the parties may nonetheless be happy to proceed to completion on the basis of terms in the sale and purchase agreement to the effect that the buyer will take over the contracts at the completion date, and that both parties will use their reasonable endeavours to obtain the consents of third parties to the assignment of existing contracts. Since the seller will remain liable on existing contracts unless and until specifically released by the third parties, the buyer will usually undertake in the sale and purchase agreement to perform the contracts on the seller's behalf and to indemnify the seller against any liability which arises under them. It is unusual for the parties to take the trouble to novate or renegotiate minor or routine contracts if a straightforward assignment can be achieved.

Fundamental contracts

In relation to contracts which the buyer considers fundamental to the business, such as those with its main customers or suppliers, the buyer should ideally defer entering into the sale and purchase agreement until all necessary consents have been obtained. Novation may be more desirable in the case of fundamental contracts, and sometimes the buyer may even consider the negotiation of fresh agreements to be essential. As this is likely to be a time-consuming exercise, the parties may agree to the sale and purchase agreement being made conditional on the assignment, novation or conclusion of specified contracts. The buyer should, in these circumstances, seek an undertaking from the seller not to vary the terms of the original contracts during the period between exchange and completion without its consent.

8.2.6.3   Comparison with civil law jurisdictions

Common law principally favours the freedom of assignment, so assignment will generally be permitted unless it is expressly excluded in the contract.

In many civil law jurisdictions, the assignment of certain types of contracts may require precise formalities in order to be effective and enforceable against the other party. In many Continental European jurisdictions (the Netherlands, Denmark, German, Norway, Italy), a third party must give its consent before an assignment can take place. In this case, the assignor of a contract (ie the seller) is not released from its obligations until the third party has agreed to the release and has accepted that the assignee (ie the buyer) will assume the obligations under the contract. In France, generally, contracts can be assigned if they contain an assignment clause. In the absence of such clause, the prior authorisation of the other contracting party is necessary. This rule applies to the transfer of a going concern with some exceptions; contracts of employment, commercial leases and certain types of insurance policy are included in the transfer of a going concern and are automatically transferred to the buyer.

8.2.6.4   Warranties on contracts

In relation to the contracts which it is taking over, the buyer may require the following warranties:

(a)   that none of the contracts is of an unusual or onerous nature, or was entered into otherwise than in the ordinary course of business;

(c)   that the seller is not in breach of any of the terms of the contracts and has not waived any rights under the contracts;

(c)   that no event has occurred which entitles the other party to the contract to terminate or rescind the contract;

(d)   that the seller has not sold or manufactured products which, in any material respect, are defective or do not comply with warranties or representations made by the seller.

8.2.6.5 'No assignment' clauses

In some contracts, a clause may exist that restricts or prohibits assignment. The existence of such a clause is often driven by commercial reasons. For example, a manufacturer may have selected a specific supplier and it will not want that supplier to assign or subcontract the work to an unknown third party or another supplier. As a result, a clause may have been included limiting or prohibiting assignment.

Such arrangements may, however, be prohibited by the Business Contracts Terms (Assignment of Receivables) Regulations 2018 (SI 2018/1254), which came into force for contracts entered into on or after 31 December 2018. The Regulations invalidate restrictions on the assignment of 'receivables' in certain contracts for the supply of goods, services or intangible assets (a 'receivable' is the right to be paid under such a contract).

The Regulations, which apply only in England, Wales and Northern Ireland, are intended to facilitate access to finance by invalidating terms prohibiting the assignment of receivables. However, certain categories of contracts and certain types of companies are excluded from the application of the Regulations, most notably (in relation to acquisitions) (a) sale and purchase agreements for the sale of a business or for the sale of shares of a company, and (b) assignments by large enterprises. As such, while the Regulations require consideration during an acquisition, their impact may be limited.

8.2.7 Debtors and creditors

Sums owed to the seller by third parties (debtors) are an asset of the business; sums owed by the seller to third parties (creditors) are a liability of the business. Under English law, there are a number of ways in which trade debtors and creditors can be dealt with in the agreement.

8.2.7.1 Transfer to buyer

In many jurisdictions, including England and Wales, the debtors and creditors may be transferred to the buyer. In this case, full details should be included in a schedule or an appendix to the sale and purchase agreement. In order for the assignment of debts to be a legal assignment (as opposed to an equitable one) under English law, s 136 of the Law of Property Act 1925 requires, inter alia, written notice of the assignment to be given to each debtor. The seller will remain liable to its creditors after completion, however, unless they agree to release it. Accordingly, where the parties have agreed to transfer the creditors, the seller should seek an indemnity from the buyer against such liability.

In the case of a multi-jurisdictional acquisition, local counsel should be consulted as to the appropriate transfer formalities in respect of the debtors and creditors.

There are, however, several drawbacks to transferring debtors and creditors to the buyer. Apart from the complication of defining accurately the debts and liabilities involved, and of giving notice to all debtors, there is the difficulty of valuing the book debts. If these are transferred at their face value, the buyer will not only suffer a cash flow disadvantage but will also bear the risk of some of the debts proving irrecoverable. The amount of any discount on book value to reflect these uncertainties is likely to be the subject of much negotiation between the parties. Alternatively, the seller may be prepared to warrant that the debts are fully recoverable. The buyer should, however, be wary of any de minimis limit that applies to the warranties generally (see **6.2.1.2**).

8.2.7.2 Retention by seller

Under English law, it is possible for debtors and creditors to remain with the seller, although this can also give rise to a number of difficulties. The buyer will, for example, be keen to preserve the goodwill of the on-going business by maintaining good relations with suppliers and creditors of the business, and will, therefore, wish to ensure that the seller pays off its creditors promptly and is not too exuberant in chasing its debtors. The buyer may therefore insist on a retention from the purchase price which is to be released only once the creditors have been paid. It should also consider extracting an undertaking from the seller not to issue proceedings to recover debts for a specified period after completion, and to give the buyer the option to buy the debts from the seller at the end of this period (at least in relation to those debtors who continue to be customers of the business after the change in ownership).

A difficulty of this arrangement from the seller's point of view is that it may no longer have the means to collect the debts after completion, particularly where those employees responsible for debt collection have been transferred to the buyer. A solution to this problem, which often suits both parties, is for the buyer to agree to collect the debts as agent for the seller. The buyer will often be happy to assume this responsibility (usually on payment of a collection fee) as there will be less danger of the goodwill of the business being damaged if the process of collection of debts is undertaken by the buyer. The buyer will usually be required to use all reasonable endeavours to collect the debts but without being obliged to commence legal proceedings. As an incentive to the buyer, the collection fee may be based on a percentage of debts successfully recovered.

A complication which arises where debtors continue to deal with the business after its change in ownership is the application of sums received by the buyer after completion. For example, should such sums received reduce the debtor's original liability to the seller, or any liability of the debtor to the buyer incurred since completion? The sale and purchase agreement should specify the order in which the buyer should apply sums which it receives in these circumstances.

8.2.7.3   Who takes responsibility for on-going service and repair obligations?

Depending on the type of business, the seller may have entered into commitments to customers to provide an after-sales service in relation to products or services supplied prior to completion. It is in the interests of the buyer that these obligations are met in full, since a failure to do so may have a detrimental effect on goodwill and may reflect badly on the buyer. However, once it has disposed of the assets of the business, the seller is unlikely to be in a position to carry out repairs or provide an after-sales service. A solution to this problem is for the buyer to agree to perform the seller's obligations and to be reimbursed the cost of doing so by the seller (the buyer may also be able to negotiate a mark-up on the direct costs which it incurs).

8.2.7.4   Apportionment of outgoings and payments

The seller will have incurred various liabilities to, for example, utility companies for the use of gas, electricity, telephones, etc which have not been billed at the date of completion. Similarly, the seller may have made payments in advance which relate to periods after completion, for example rental payments or payments due under continuing contracts. Whichever method the parties choose to deal with the creditors and debtors, it will be necessary to apportion the outgoings and payments to the date of completion (or such other date agreed upon by the parties). The seller will usually be responsible for making the apportionments and providing full details with supporting documentation. As with the valuation of stock, the agreement may incorporate a system for resolving disputes between the parties. In any event, it is normally impractical for the apportionments to be made and agreed by completion, and consequently provision is usually made for the buyer to draw up a completion statement after completion and for adjustments to be made to the consideration when the parties have agreed the statement.

8.2.8 Goodwill, name and restrictions on the seller

8.2.8.1 Goodwill

Goodwill is an intangible asset of the business which is as difficult to define as it is to value. Where a business is sold as a going concern, a value is usually placed on the good name and reputation of the business and the likelihood that customers and suppliers will continue to deal with it in the future. In other words, the value of goodwill reflects the fact that the business is 'up and running', has traded successfully in the past and should continue to do so in the future.

A crude method of valuing goodwill is to apply a multiplier (usually between one and three) to the net profits of the business. In the case of a partnership, the net profit figure before any salaries or interest on capital payable to partners are deducted should be used for the calculation, as these items are merely allocations of the profit. However, the amount attributable to goodwill is extremely variable and, to a large extent, depends on the buyer's assessment of the potential of the business; the buyer may, for example, be prepared to pay a sum for the business which is well above its net asset value because it feels that it will fit in well with its existing businesses. Also, goodwill tends to be more of a factor in 'employee-orientated' businesses, ie those that rely on the flair and imagination of the employees, than in 'asset-orientated' businesses, such as property investment businesses, for example.

The buyer may try to negotiate the inclusion of a warranty that the seller is not aware of any matter arising since the date of the latest accounts which might adversely affect the trading prospects of the business and that the seller has not done anything (or omitted to do anything) which might adversely affect goodwill (see **8.2.8.3**).

The transfer of goodwill in some specific jurisdictions will be subject to regulatory provisions (see **8.1.2**).

8.2.8.2 Name

The goodwill to be acquired by the buyer will usually be defined to include the exclusive right of the buyer (or any assignee) to represent itself as carrying on the business in succession to the seller and to use the name of the business and all trade names associated with it. The seller will normally be required to undertake that it will not use the name, or any other name intended or likely to be confused with it, or hold itself out as being connected with the business, at any time after completion. The seller may even agree to covenant that it will endeavour to ensure that the buyer obtains full benefit of the goodwill and that customers, etc deal with the buyer instead of the seller.

On the acquisition from a company of its entire business, the agreement should provide that the seller changes its registered name to one that is acceptable to the buyer and does not suggest any connection with the business as transferred through the asset acquisition. As part of the completion arrangements, the buyer may require the seller to hand over the special resolution changing the name (and appropriate fee) and agree with the seller to file this at the Companies Registry or relevant register of the Chamber of Commerce or court of the jurisdiction involved.

Pursuant to German law, a buyer will be liable for the debts of the business if, after the transfer, the business is continued under the same or a similar name, unless the parties have expressly agreed otherwise in the sale and purchase agreement and a disclaimer has been published in the German commercial register.

8.2.8.3 Warranties on goodwill

A buyer acquiring the goodwill of the business has a legitimate interest in the way that the seller has conducted the business prior to completion. It will therefore require warranties from the seller that it has not conducted the business in any way that would damage its reputation or diminish the value of the goodwill (see **8.2.9.3**).

8.2.8.4 Restrictive covenants

The buyer will seek to protect the goodwill of the business by restricting the activities of the seller after completion, thereby preventing it from damaging goodwill. The seller will be prevented from competing with the business, soliciting customers, suppliers and employees of the business, and disclosing confidential information. The nature, extent and validity of such restrictions on the seller are dealt with in **5.10**.

8.2.9 General warranties

In addition to specific warranties about the assets to be acquired, in common law jurisdictions the buyer will also require some general warranties about the assets and, where the goodwill of the business is also being acquired, about the conduct of the business prior to completion.

8.2.9.1 Ownership of assets

The buyer will seek warranties that the seller owns the assets absolutely; that they are not subject to any charge, encumbrance, lien, option or retention of title provision; and that the seller has not agreed to dispose of them or grant security or any other encumbrance in respect of them.

8.2.9.2 Condition and adequacy

As mentioned above, whether the seller should give warranties as to the condition of, for example, fixed assets and stock, and as to the adequacy of the assets for the requirements of the business, will usually be a matter of much negotiation between the parties.

8.2.9.3 Trading and conduct of the business

The buyer will seek the following warranties:

(a)   that the business has been carried on in the ordinary course since the date of the last accounts, and that its turnover, financial or trading position has not deteriorated;

(b)   that the seller has obtained all licences and consents required to carry on the business properly and is not in breach of their terms;

(c)   that the seller is not aware of any suppliers or customers who will cease to deal with the business (or substantially alter their trading relationship with it) after completion;

(d)   that the seller has not been a party to any agreement, practice or arrangement relating to the business which contravenes, for example, the Competition Act 1998, the EA 2002 or the TFEU, or similar provisions in relevant jurisdictions;

(e)   that the seller is not a party to any litigation proceedings in relation to the business and no such proceedings are pending, threatened or, to the seller's knowledge, likely to arise.

8.2.9.4 Accounts

The buyer may have used the accounts as a basis for agreeing a valuation of the target business, in which case it will normally seek a warranty that the latest accounts (including, possibly, management accounts) give a true and fair view of the financial position of the business and are not affected by extraordinary or non-recurring items. The buyer will also wish to ensure that the financial books and records which the seller is obliged to deliver to the buyer on completion are complete and accurate in all material respects.

8.3 PROTECTION OF EMPLOYEES

The parties must consider the impact of an asset acquisition on the employees working in the target business. How does the transfer affect their contracts of employment? Can the buyer choose not to take on employees who are surplus to its requirements? What are the implications if the buyer wishes to integrate the terms and conditions of the target's employees with those of its existing workforce? What claims can employees bring against the seller or buyer if they are dismissed before or after the transfer? Can the employees object to working for the buyer? The buyer will often have a clear idea of which employees it wishes to retain and how it intends to integrate them with its current workforce. However, the employment consequences of the transfer do not always coincide with the expectations of the parties; this is an area which may impact significantly on the purchase price.

Under English law, an employer may be liable for contractual claims for wrongful dismissal as well as possible statutory claims relating to any employees' statutory protection with regard to unfair dismissal, redundancy or discrimination. In relation to an acquisition, the parties will generally seek the advice of employment law specialists. On a share acquisition, the buyer, in acquiring ownership of the target company, will indirectly acquire the target's liabilities to its employees, though the employer remains the same (ie the target company itself). On an asset acquisition involving employees working in a business situated in the UK, the parties must consider the impact of the Transfer of Undertakings (Protection of Employment) Regulations 2006 (SI 2006/246) (TUPE 2006).

8.3.1 Common law position

At common law the transfer of an undertaking from one employer to another automatically terminates the contracts of employment, which cannot be assigned as they are personal to the employer and employee. There is therefore a dismissal of the employees, and the seller of the undertaking may consequently be liable to the employees for contractual or statutory claims arising from that termination. In this situation, the reason for the dismissals would generally be redundancy (as the employer's requirement for employees to do work of a particular kind has ceased or diminished). However, the dismissed employees may also have claims under English law for wrongful dismissal (if the correct notice was not given) and unfair dismissal by reason of redundancy (if the employer acted unfairly). If the buyer of the undertaking requires the employees' services, it may offer new contracts of employment on its own terms.

In the US, the common law position applies to an asset acquisition involving employees. Generally, in the absence of a contractual agreement or collective bargaining agreement, most employees will be considered to be 'at will' employees. Broadly, this means that their employment may be ended with or without cause and they are not entitled to any compensation beyond payment for their last day of work.

In an asset acquisition, the status of a collective bargaining agreement will depend on whether the buyer is a 'successor', based upon the continuity of the business and the workforce or on the provisions of the seller's collective bargaining agreement. If the buyer is considered a successor, it must recognise and bargain with the union. Some US collective bargaining agreements or employment contracts may establish procedures as to the termination of the employment contracts involved. In certain US states, violation of these procedures may give rise to claims by the employees against the employer.

Canadian employment law is more protective of employees than is the case in the US. In certain jurisdictions (eg, the Province of Quebec), the buyer of a business is deemed to be a continuing employer and will therefore take over the employees under their current employment conditions, including compensation, seniority, holiday and other benefits. Unlike in the US, the employment contracts of an acquired business cannot in general be terminated at will, and substantial paid time in lieu of notice may be mandatory where contracts are to be brought to an end.

8.3.2   Application of TUPE 2006

The position in the UK is quite different, however, where there is a 'relevant transfer' under TUPE 2006 (see **8.3.4.1**). In that situation, the employees' contracts will automatically transfer with the undertaking and continue as if originally made between the employees and the buyer. The transfer does not terminate the employees' contracts of employment and does not, therefore, operate as a 'dismissal'. In fact, TUPE 2006 also provide protection for employees who are dismissed, whether actually or constructively, before or after the transfer, if those dismissals are by reason of the transfer (see **8.3.4.5**).

The 2006 Regulations came into force for transfers taking place on or after 6 April 2006, in order to comply with the EU Acquired Rights Directive 2001/23/EC. TUPE 2006 replaced the earlier Transfer of Undertakings (Protection of Employment) Regulations 1981 (SI 1981/1794) (TUPE 1981), which reflected the earlier EU Directive 1977/187/EC. The aim of the legislation is to protect the rights of employees where an undertaking is transferred from one employer to another. The 2006 legislation confirms and clarifies much of the old law, whilst also consolidating some of the existing case law in the area. Case law under the old Regulations is still relevant in many circumstances, as is the case law of the ECJ.

An update to TUPE 2006, implemented by the Collective Redundancies and Transfer of Undertakings (Protection of Employment) (Amendment) Regulations 2014 (SI 2014/16), came into force on 31 January 2014. The changes represent clarification of the existing Regulations, as well as a codification of recent case law and industry practice.

Unless otherwise specified, all discussion of the relevant regulations below relates to TUPE 2006 as amended.

8.3.3   Other European jurisdictions

The Acquired Rights Directive lays out mandatory provisions as minimum standards for the countries concerned. Each of the Member States of the EU and the European Economic Area (EEA) (EU countries plus Norway, Iceland and Liechtenstein) has a duty to implement the Directive's standards into its national legislation. Thus, although TUPE 2006 pertain only to the legal system in the UK, similar laws can be found in other Member States as well.

Member States are, however, allowed to promulgate legislation that is more favourable to employees in their jurisdiction. The Directive leaves room for flexibility in national law as to the definition of some of the concepts it uses, such as 'employee' and 'employment contract', and Member States are permitted to introduce or apply individual collective employment rules that are more favourable to the employee. Also, certain standards relating to the transfer of undertakings are optional and are therefore to be set out in the legislation of the Member States. One such standard concerns which obligations of the transferor will be maintained after the transfer, together with the transferee's rights to modify these obligations. So far, 14 Member States have made provision for the transferor to share liability with the transferee after the transfer, though this may, of course, be adjusted in the terms of a particular sale and purchase agreement.

As the laws of the EU and EEA countries vary by jurisdiction, expert and specific advice should be sought on the employment-related issues.

Other jurisdictions, such as Argentina, Chile and South Africa, have also implemented similar provisions.

8.3.4   TUPE 2006

8.3.4.1   A relevant transfer – reg 3

TUPE 2006 will apply only to a 'relevant transfer', which under reg 3(1) is a transfer of an undertaking, business or part of an undertaking or business situated immediately before the transfer in the United Kingdom to another person where there is a transfer of an economic entity which retains its identity.

An 'economic entity' is defined in reg 3(2) as 'an organised grouping of resources which has the objective of pursuing an economic activity, whether or not that activity is central or ancillary'. This provision effectively incorporates relevant case law on the definition of a transfer of an undertaking which developed since the implementation of TUPE 1981. The two key cases in the area are *Spijkers v Gebroeders Benedik Abattoir CV* [1986] ECR 1119 and *Dr Sophie Redmond Stichting v Bartol* [1992] IRLR 366.

In ascertaining whether there has been a relevant transfer, it is necessary to determine whether what has been transferred is an economic entity which is still in existence, and this will be apparent from the fact that its operation, with the same economic or similar activities, is being continued or has been taken over by the new employer. Clearly, a transaction involving the break-up of a business, with various assets sold to different buyers and no one buyer able to continue the business in its original form, will not constitute a relevant transfer for TUPE 2006 purposes.

As well as being the transfer of an 'economic entity', to come within the definition in reg 3(1) the transfer must be from one person to another. This can include a transfer between two companies in the same corporate group. Subsidiaries within a group of companies are all separate legal entities, so when employees are moved from one company to another within the same group, TUPE 2006 apply in so far as there is a transfer of an economic entity which retains its identity (per the ECJ in Case C-234/98 *Allen v Amalgamated Construction Co Ltd* [2000] IRLR 119). This means that TUPE 2006 also apply on any hive-down of assets to a subsidiary company in preparation for an onward share sale (see **1.4.2**) (although TUPE 2006 do not apply where a buyer acquires a majority shareholding in a company, since there is no change in the identity of the employer (see *Brookes v Borough Care Services and CLS Care Services Ltd* [1998] IRLR 636)).

In addition to the main description of a 'relevant transfer', reg 3(1)(b) contains a second definition which makes it clear that TUPE 2006 also apply to a 'service provision change', that is, where there is a change of service provider, eg in a situation where services, such as cleaning, catering or maintenance, are contracted out. The 2006 Regulations will apply to a service provision change if reg 3(3) applies, that is:

(a)   immediately before the service provision change:
   (i)   there is an organised grouping of employees situated in Great Britain which has as its principal purpose the carrying out of the activities concerned on behalf of the client;
   (ii)   the client intends that the activities will, following the service provision change, be carried out by the transferee other than in connection with a single specific event or task of short-term duration; and

(b)   the activities concerned do not consist wholly or mainly of the supply of goods for the client's use.

Therefore, TUPE 2006 will clearly apply to most situations involving the contracting out of services, save where the service is for a single event, is of short-term duration, or concerns the supply of goods. The recent reform of TUPE retains the service provision change test, but only in circumstances where activities carried out after the transfer are fundamentally the same as those carried out before the transfer.

The parties cannot agree to exclude the operation of TUPE 2006 (reg 18). Whether a transfer is a 'relevant transfer' is a question of fact. The court or tribunal will look behind the label which the parties put on the transfer and will instead examine the substance of the transaction.

If it is not a relevant transfer, any rights which the employees have (eg to claim wrongful dismissal, redundancy, or unfair dismissal) must be enforced against the seller. If the seller is insolvent, certain claims, such as redundancy and the basic award for unfair dismissal, will be met by the Secretary of State for Employment (ERA 1996, s 182). However, the employees will be unable to recover the compensatory award for unfair dismissal in these circumstances. It should be noted that TUPE 2006 include provisions governing the transfer by an insolvent transferor (regs 8 and 9) which are beyond the scope of this book.

8.3.4.2   Effect of a relevant transfer – reg 4

It is necessary to consider the effect of a relevant transfer on the employment relationship.

Automatic transfer of contractual rights and obligations

Regulation 4(1) protects the employees' employment in the event of a transfer, and reg 4(2) confirms that all the transferor's rights, powers and duties under the contracts of employment transfer to the transferee.

Regulation 4(1) provides that

> a relevant transfer shall not operate so as to terminate the contract of employment of any person employed by the transferor and assigned to the organised grouping of resources or employees that is subject to the relevant transfer, which would otherwise be terminated by the transfer, but any such contract shall have effect after the transfer as if originally made between the person so employed and the transferee.

In other words, an employee's contract of employment is not brought to an end by reason of the transfer but instead transfers from the old employer to the new. Employees do have the right, however, to object to the transfer of their contracts in this way (see **8.3.4.3**).

Regulation 4(2) states that, on the completion of a relevant transfer:

(a)   all the transferor's rights, powers, duties and liabilities under or in connection with any such contract shall be transferred by virtue of this regulation to the transferee; and

(b)   any act or omission before the transfer is completed, of or in relation to the transferor in respect of that contract or a person assigned to that organised grouping of resources or employees, shall be deemed to have been an act or omission of or in relation to the transferee.

Therefore, the employees have the same rights against the transferee as they had against the transferor, and their continuity of employment is not affected by the transfer.

8.3.4.3   Who is covered by reg 4(1)?

Regulation 4(3) states that any reference

> to a person employed by the transferor and assigned to the organised grouping of resources or employees that is subject to a relevant transfer, is a reference to a person so employed immediately before the transfer, or who would have been so employed if he had not been dismissed in the circumstances described in regulation 7(1), including, where the transfer is effected by a series of two or more transactions, a person so employed and assigned or who would have been so employed or assigned immediately before any of those transactions.

Regulation 4(3) clearly applies to all employees employed by the transferor immediately before the transfer. Where there is a gap between exchange of contracts and completion, it is the date of completion which is the date of transfer for the purposes of reg 4.

However, reg 4(3) also applies to employees who would have been so employed had they not been unfairly dismissed in the circumstances described in reg 7(1) (see **8.3.4.5**). Regulation 7(1) provides that the dismissal is automatically unfair where the dismissal was by reason of the transfer, unless the employer can show that the dismissal was for an economic, technical or organisational reason ('ETO reason') entailing a change in the workforce. This statutory provision encapsulates the House of Lords' judgment in *Litster v Forth Dry Dock and Engineering Co Ltd* [1989] IRLR 161, in which the employees were dismissed one hour before the transfer. The House of Lords made it clear that a transferee may still be liable for a pre-transfer dismissal, and reg 4(3) preserves this rule. This means that a transferee cannot circumvent TUPE 2006 by insisting that the transferor dismisses employees prior to completion.

Regulation 4 therefore applies to two groups of employees:

(a)   to those employees actually employed by the transferor at the time of the transfer. Their contracts of employment transfer to the transferee and they will work for the transferee under the terms of those contracts; and

(b)   to those employees who were dismissed by reason of the transfer where no ETO reason exists. Any rights they may have had with regard to unfair or wrongful dismissal, together with any claim for a redundancy payment, will transfer to the transferee.

Employees whose contracts would 'otherwise be terminated by the transfer'

Those employees whose contracts would not be terminated by the transfer do not come within reg 4. This may, for example, apply to an employee who is retained by the transferor and redeployed in some other part of its operation within the terms of the employee's contract or with the employee's consent. Such redeployment should take place before the transfer.

Where part of a business is transferred, employees will not be affected by reg 4 if they did not work in the part transferred. Even employees who perform duties in relation to the part transferred (eg administrative duties performed by a retained department) will not be covered unless they are assigned to the part transferred.

The question of whether an employee is assigned to the relevant part is a question of fact. Regard should be had to the test laid down in Case 186/83 *Botzen v Rotterdamsche Droogdok Maatschappij BV* [1986] 2 CMLR 50, ECJ. In summary, the test is whether there is a transfer of the part of the undertaking to which the employees 'were assigned and which formed the organisational framework within which their employment relationship took effect'.

Useful guidance on the *Botzen* test was given by the EAT in *Duncan Webb Offset (Maidstone) Ltd v Cooper* [1995] IRLR 633. In determining to which part of the employer's business the employee was assigned, a tribunal may consider matters such as:

(a)   the amount of time spent on one part of the business or the other;

(b)   the amount of value given to each part by the employee;

(c)   the terms of the contract of employment showing what the employee could be required to do; and

(d)   how the cost to the employer of the employee's services was allocated between different parts of the business.

In essence, then, the correct test is simply whether a person was assigned to an undertaking or a part. Note, however, that in *Carisway Cleaning Contracts Ltd v Richards* (EAT/629/97, 19 June 1998) the EAT held that an employer could not 'off-load' an unwanted employee by deliberately moving him to a part of the undertaking that the employer knew was about to be transferred. They held that such an act was fraudulent and, accordingly, void. The employee was not 'employed in the part of the undertaking' being transferred.

The employee's right of objection

The transfer of the contract of employment and rights, powers, duties and liabilities under and in connection with it will not occur if the employee informs the transferor or the transferee that the employee objects to becoming employed by the transferee (reg 4(7)). In that event, the transfer will terminate the employee's contract of employment with the transferor but the employee will not be treated for any purpose as having been dismissed by the transferor (reg 4(8)), that is, the employee will be regarded as having resigned.

The TUPE 2006 nevertheless include a provision in reg 4(9), whereby an employee whose contract of employment is or would have transferred under reg 4(1) may treat their contract as terminated and still be treated as having been dismissed by the employer, where the relevant transfer involves or would involve a substantial change in working conditions to the employee's material detriment. This preserves the common law right of an employee to resign and claim constructive dismissal for a fundamental breach of contract by the employer. However, the provisions of reg 4(9) provide two further advantages, in that there is no need to prove the dismissal and the wording appears to cover a wider set of circumstances than just the employer's repudiatory breach. This provision does not create any automatic unfair dismissal rights (see **8.3.4.5**) but simply provides that in certain circumstances an employee will have the right to object to becoming employed by the transferee and yet still retain the right to bring a normal unfair dismissal claim. To determine whether the dismissal was fair, the tribunal must still be satisfied that the employer acted fairly, and there is no presumption that it is unfair for the employer to make the proposed changes. Interestingly, the Court of Appeal has held that, as the effect of the objection was that the contract of employment did not transfer to the transferee, then neither did the liability for any claim arising from the constructive dismissal.

Neither the general application of the automatic transfer principle, nor the existence of the employee's right to object is subject to a precondition that employees have knowledge of the fact of a transfer and/or the identity of the transferee (*Secretary of State for Trade and Industry v Cook* [1997] ICR 288, EAT). In addition, if the identity of the transferee is not known to the employee, the employee can object after a transfer, provided the employee does so promptly (see *New ISG Ltd v Vernon* [2007] EWHC 2665 (Ch)).

Under the Acquired Rights Directive, Member States are allowed to provide for the legal consequences if an employee decides not to continue their employment with the transferee. The laws of some Member States (such as the UK and the Netherlands) state that, in this case, the employment contract will terminate as a matter of law from the date of the transfer; the laws of other Member States (Germany, for example) determine that such refusal means the continuation of the employment with the transferor.

8.3.4.4   What the transferee acquires

The transferee inherits those employees employed by the transferor immediately before the transfer on their existing terms and conditions, assuming that they do not object (reg 4(2)).

Changes to the employee's terms and conditions are possible only in limited circumstances (see **8.3.4.6** below), and the transferred employee has no right to insist that they be given the benefit of any superior terms enjoyed by the transferee's existing staff.

Rights transferring

The transferee inherits all accrued rights and liabilities connected with the contract of employment of the transferred employee, except for criminal liabilities and some benefits under an occupational pension scheme (see below). If, for example, the transferor was in arrears with wages at the time of the transfer, the employee can sue the transferee as if the original liability had been the transferee's. The transferor is relieved of its former obligations without any need for the employee's consent.

Equally, the transferee can sue an employee for a breach of contract committed against the transferor prior to transfer.

The transferee will also inherit all the statutory rights and liabilities which are connected with the individual contract of employment, for example to claims for unfair dismissal, redundancy and discrimination.

Regulations 11 and 12 contain provisions requiring the transferor to notify the transferee of 'Employee Liability Information' for employees who are the subject of the relevant transfer. The notification period is no less than 28 days before the transfer. If a transferor fails to give this information in whole or in part, the transferee can complain to the employment tribunal which can award compensation.

The transferred employee's period of continuous employment will date from the beginning of their period of employment with the transferor, and the statutory particulars of terms and conditions of employment, which every employer is obliged to issue, must take account of any continuity enjoyed by virtue of TUPE 2006.

Restrictive covenants

In the case of restrictive covenants, these will normally be expressed in terms of protecting customers of the transferor. In essence, following the transfer of an undertaking a restrictive covenant should be read as being enforceable by the transferee, but only in respect of customers of the transferor who fall within the protection. It may be necessary for the transferee to consider redrafting restrictive covenants, but this will be subject to the limits on the transferor's rights to make changes to terms of the employees' contracts (see **8.3.4.6**).

Collective agreements

Under TUPE 2006, any collective agreements made with a trade union by the transferor are deemed to have been made by the transferee (reg 5). Further, the transferee is deemed to recognise the trade union to the same extent as did the transferor (reg 6). In effect, the transferee steps into the shoes of the transferor. Neither TUPE 2006 nor the general law, however, prevent the employer from seeking to derecognise the union entirely, or from amending the basis of the recognition.

Individually, however, there may be 'hangovers' from previous union recognition. Of course, all terms of the individuals' contracts, including those pursuant to any collective agreements, will be deemed to have been made between the transferee and the employee. It follows that, notwithstanding withdrawal from collective bargaining by the transferee, the right to have pay determined by collective bargaining can persist.

This was considered in *Whent v T Cartledge Limited* [1997] IRLR 153, where not only the rate of pay and general terms which existed at the time of the transfer, but also the terms providing for the collective bargaining mechanism itself, transferred as a result of the transfer. The fact that the employer had derecognised the union was irrelevant. However, latterly, the Court of Appeal in *Parkwood Leisure Ltd v Alemo-Herron* [2010] EWCA Civ 24 has resolved this issue differently, overturning the decision in *Whent*. Rimer LJ followed the decision of the ECJ in *Werhof v Freeway Traffic Systems GmbH* [2006] IRLR 400, concluding that the benefit of an existing collective agreement does transfer but the transferee is only bound by it until such time as it lapses or is renegotiated. In the *Parkwood* case, the Supreme Court referred to the ECJ the question of how certain articles of the Acquired Rights Directive may be construed by national courts. The ECJ confirmed that the transferee should be fixed with the terms of a collective bargaining agreement only as they exist at the time of the transfer; it suggested that a more 'dynamic' approach, binding the transferee to future changes in the collective agreement, would undermine the fair balance between the interests of the transferee as employer and the interests of the employees. The ECJ said that the Acquired Rights Directive must be read subject to the Charter of Fundamental Rights of the European Union, and therefore some weight must be given to the transferee's 'freedom to conduct a business' under that Charter.

As part of the TUPE reform, the Government confirmed the 'static' approach reflected in the ECJ's decision in *Parkwood*. Regulation 4A provides that TUPE will not operate so as to transfer provisions of a collective agreement if the provision is agreed after the date of the transfer, and the transferee is not a participant in the collective bargaining for that provision.

Rights and liabilities which are not assigned under the Regulations

The Regulations do not have the effect of assigning:

(a)   criminal liabilities; or

(b)   rights and liabilities relating to provisions of occupational pension schemes which relate to benefits for old age, invalidity or survivors (although the Pensions Act 2004 does require a transferee to offer transferring employees who are members of the transferor's occupational pension scheme membership of another such scheme that meets requirements prescribed by regulations made under that Act).

8.3.4.5   Dismissal of an employee resulting from a relevant transfer – reg 7

Where an employee is dismissed (whether actually or constructively and whether before or after the transfer), if the sole or principal reason for the dismissal is the transfer and where that reason is not an ETO reason entailing a change in the workforce, the dismissal will automatically be unfair.

If the sole or principal reason for the dismissal is an ETO reason entailing changes to the workforce before or after the relevant transfer, there is no automatically unfair dismissal. The dismissal will be regarded as having been for redundancy where s 98(2)(c) of the ERA 1996 applies, or otherwise for some other substantial reason of a kind such as to justify the dismissal of an employee (reg 7(2) and (3)).

Regulation 7(4) states that reg 7 applies irrespective of whether the employee in question is 'assigned to the organised grouping of resources or employees that is or will be transferred'. This means that the protection of reg 7 on unfair dismissal is available to *all* employees. It is important, therefore, that transferees are aware that any remaining employees, as well as the transferring employees, are protected against TUPE-related dismissal. However, in order to bring a claim for unfair dismissal, an employee must have a minimum of one year's continuous employment if employment was started before 6 April 2012, and two years' continuous employment if employment was started on or after 6 April 2012.

When is a dismissal by reason of the transfer?

As emphasised by the ECJ in *P Bork International A/S v Foreningen af Arbejdsledere I Danmark* [1989] IRLR 41, it is a question of fact whether a transfer is the sole or principal reason for the dismissal. This approach was applied by the EAT in *Hare Wines Ltd v Kaur* (UKEAT/0131/17/JOJ). In this case, an employee was dismissed shortly before a transfer because of her difficult working relationship with a colleague. The EAT stated that as the employer had not taken action to resolve that relationship prior to the transfer, it was open to the tribunal to conclude that the reason for the dismissal was the transfer. It is therefore possible for a court to hold that the transfer is the 'sole or principal reason' for the dismissal if the employee is dismissed for a conduct or competency issue at the moment of, or shortly before, the transfer.

It less clear whether it is sufficient for the employee to show that the reason for their dismissal was transfers generally. In *Spaceright Europe Ltd v Baillavoine* [2011] EWCA Civ 1565, the Court of Appeal held that the employee may still have the benefit of protection where no specific transfer or transferee was identified at the time of the dismissal, but the reason for the employee's dismissal was transfers generally. However, the Court's analysis turned on the wording of the previous version of reg 7(1), which referred to dismissals 'connected with' the transfer. It is arguable that the result could be different under the current version of reg 7(1), which requires the transfer to be the 'sole or principal' reason for the dismissal.

Establishing an ETO reason

If the sole or principal reason for the dismissal is the transfer, and if this reason is not an ETO reason, the transferee (ie the buyer) will be liable for all claims by the dismissed employee (whether dismissed before or after the transfer – reg 4(3)). If the dismissal was for an ETO reason then liability for a pre-transfer dismissal will lie with the transferor (ie the seller).

If an ETO reason can be established, the dismissal will be deemed to be either for redundancy or for 'some other substantial reason' under s 98(1) of the ERA 1996 and s 135 of the ERA 1996. Even where the employer can show such a reason, the employment tribunal must still be satisfied that the employer has acted reasonably within s 98(4) of the ERA 1996.

The employer must show an ETO reason entailing a change in the workforce, otherwise the dismissal will be unfair.

There is no statutory definition of an ETO reason, but according to DBT guidance it is likely to include:

(a)   a reason relating to the profitability or market performance of the transferee's business (ie an economic reason);

(b)   a reason relating to the nature of the equipment or production process which the transferee operates (ie a technical reason); or

(c)   a reason relating to the management or organisational structure of the transferee's business (ie an organisational reason).

Although there is no statutory definition of the phrase 'entailing changes in the workforce', guidance issued by the DBT refers to previous interpretations of the phrase by the courts under TUPE 1981, which restricted it to changes in the numbers of employees employed or to changes in their functions. Regulation 4(5A) extends the meaning of this phrase to include 'a change to the place where employees are employed by the employer', so 'changes in the workforce' now specifically includes relocations.

To date, three cases, in particular, have provided authoritative guidance on what the ETO phrase means, as follows:

(a)   To be an ETO reason within reg 7, an 'economic' reason must relate to the conduct of the business as such, and does not include dismissing employees simply to obtain an enhanced price or to achieve an agreement for sale (*Wheeler v Patel* [1987] IRLR 211). An economic reason could, however, include an administrator dismissing employees of a business in order to keep that business afloat in the hope of a future sale, as decided in *Crystal Palace FC & Another v Kavanagh & Ors* [2013] EWCA Civ 1410. In *Hynd v Armstrong* [2007] IRLR 338, it was held that a transferor employer cannot rely on the transferee's reason in order to establish an 'economic, technical or organisational reason' so as to provide a potential defence under TUPE 2006. In this case a pre-transfer dismissal of a solicitor by the transferor because he was not required by the transferee was held to be automatically unfair. The Court of Session held that it is 'reasonably clear' that the Acquired Rights Directive would not 'permit dismissal in such circumstances'. A transferor can only rely on a reason of its own. In effect this means that where an employee is dismissed by the transferor prior to the transfer, the reason for the dismissal must relate to the transferor's future conduct of its business in order to be an ETO reason. That will never be the case where, as in *Hynd*, the transferor has no intention of continuing the business after the transfer. Although this was only a Court of Session case, and accordingly not binding on an EAT sitting in England, this approach has been followed by the EAT in practice.

(b)   The ETO reason must entail a 'change in the workforce'. For a change in the workforce there has to be a change in the composition of the workforce, or possibly a substantial change in job descriptions (*Berriman v Delabole Slate Ltd* [1985] IRLR 305, CA) or, subsequent to the TUPE reforms, a relocation of employees. Effectively, therefore, an ETO reason entailing a change in the workforce will usually involve a genuine redundancy situation. Although a real change in the functions of the workforce can satisfy the ETO requirement (*Green v Elan Care Ltd* [2002] All ER (D) 17), a mere change in the terms and conditions enjoyed by the workforce will not suffice. Consequently, a transferee who provokes an actual or a constructive dismissal by attempting to change the terms and conditions of the transferred employees to harmonise with those of the existing workforce, would be unable to rely on the defence.

Once an ETO reason has been established, the employer must still ensure that a dismissal for redundancy is fair within other legislative provisions, eg that the selection for redundancy is fair, and not based simply on the fact that the person is a transferred employee, and that the dismissal was handled fairly. In addition to any claim for unfair dismissal, dismissed employees may also be entitled to a redundancy payment if they have been employed for two years or more, and employers should ensure that any required periods of consultation with employees' representatives have been allowed (see **8.3.5**).

8.3.4.6   Changes to terms of employment

The 2006 Regulations provide that employees are entitled to retain the same terms and conditions post-transfer as they enjoyed pre-transfer, and that they are not penalised when they are transferred by being forced to accept inferior terms and conditions. This is achieved through two routes. First, TUPE 2006, reg 4(1) states that the contract of employment of any transferred employee 'shall have effect after the transfer as if originally made between the person so employed and the transferee', so effectively transferring the pre-existing terms and conditions (see **8.3.4.4**).

Secondly, by way of reinforcement, the Regulations also impose limitations on the ability of the transferee and employee to agree variations to those terms and conditions. In particular, reg 4(4) confirms that any alteration in the employees' terms of employment is void if the sole or principal reason for the variation is the transfer itself, unless one of the following applies:

(a)   the reason for the change is an ETO reason entailing changes in the workforce, provided that the employer and the employee agree the change;

(b)   the terms of the employment contract permit the employer to make such a change (for example there is a mobility clause); or

(c)   the term varied is one incorporated from a collective agreement, provided that the change takes effect more than one year after the transfer and that, following the change, the rights and obligations in the employee's contract, when considered together, are no less favourable to the employee than those which applied before the change.

The wording of reg 4(4) and reg 4(5) mirrors the wording of reg 7(1) and reg 7(2) (see **8.3.4.5**) and, accordingly, there will be an ETO reason only if there is a change in the numbers or functions of the workforce or a relocation of employees.

DBT guidance suggests that where an employer changes terms and conditions because of the transfer and there are no extenuating circumstances linked to the reason for that decision, such a change is prompted by reason of the transfer itself. Therefore any decision to 'harmonise terms and conditions' will be seen as arising from the transfer itself and so void unless the changes are shown to be for an ETO reason entailing changes in the workforce under reg 4(5), such as the need to relocate or to re-train staff.

In *Regent Security Services Ltd v Power* [2007] EWCA Civ 1188, the Court of Appeal held that this meant that the transferring employees could not be deprived of any rights that transferred with them but did not prevent the buyer being bound by favourable changes made to their terms of employment. This resulted in a change to the guidance given by the DBT on TUPE

2006, which now provides that the Regulations do not prevent changes to terms and conditions agreed by the parties which are entirely positive.

The restriction on the ability of employers to vary terms and conditions under TUPE 2006 has been evolving through case law in recent years, and there appears to be increasing scope for lawful variation of terms and conditions. In *Smith and Others v Trustees of Brooklands College* (UKEAT/0128/11), it was held that the correct test should not start with 'but for the transfer' but should start with 'what was the reason' for the variation. In that case it was held to be legitimate to make changes to the terms and conditions of employees in order to bring them in line with the industry standard. The same principle was followed in *Enterprise Managed Services Limited v Dance* (UKEAT/0200/11) where it was held that the test to be considered is 'What was the reason in the minds of the management invoking proposals to change terms and conditions'. The EAT concluded that change would be legitimate if it was aimed at improving performance and efficiency rather than 'harmonisation'. In *Tabberer v Mears* [2018] All ER (D) 180, the EAT held that contractual variation two years after the transfer to remove an outdated and unjustified payment was not because of the transfer. Based on this more recent case law, it would appear that there is scope for changes to terms and conditions on the basis that the reason for the change is not related to the transfer but is based on improving performance or complying with industry standards.

There is additional flexibility to agree changes in the employees' terms where a transferor is subject to relevant insolvency proceedings (basically, administration) at the time of the transfer. Regulation 9 allows the transferor, transferee or administrator to agree permitted variations to employment terms with collective representatives of the employees (ie variations cannot be agreed on an individual basis). A 'permitted variation' is one for which the principal reason is the transfer itself, and not an ETO reason, and one which is designed to safeguard employment opportunities by ensuring the survival of the transferred undertaking.

8.3.4.7 Summary of effect of TUPE 2006 on pre- and post-transfer dismissals

Pre-transfer dismissals

Reason for dismissal is not the transfer   Where the dismissal is not by reason of the transfer (eg for misconduct), the normal rules on employment claims apply. In this situation, reg 4(3) does not apply (because the dismissal is not within the circumstances described in reg 7(1)), and therefore liability remains with the transferor.

The transferee will be liable to the dismissed employee only if that employee was employed immediately before the transfer (ie at the moment of the transfer).

Reason is the transfer itself   The effect of reg 4(3) is that a pre-transfer dismissal, however long before the transfer, which is automatically unfair under reg 7, will result in liability passing to the transferee (but this does not alter the fact that the dismissal remains effective to terminate the contract). It is only where an ETO reason has been established that the transferee may escape liability, although this ETO reason must relate to the ongoing business as run by the transferor. Where the transferee does escape liability, liability will obviously fall on the transferor, who will have to make a redundancy payment if the employee has at least two years' continuous employment and, if the dismissal was not handled fairly, an unfair dismissal payment. Any wrongful dismissal claim would also be against the transferor.

So, in the context of a pre-transfer dismissal where the reason for dismissal is the transfer, the existence of an ETO reason for the transferor is essential to determine whether liability rests with the transferor or the transferee.

A genuine redundancy dismissal before the transfer should be for an ETO reason entailing a change in the workforce, provided it relates to the ongoing business of the transferor, and should not therefore involve the transferee in liability. However, where the transferee is identified and gets involved in the dismissal, the dismissal will be by reason of the transfer itself and the ETO reason will not be available, so liability will fall on the transferee.

Post-transfer dismissals

The liability for a post-transfer dismissal will obviously fall only on the transferee.

After the transfer, the transferee may wish to bring the contracts of the transferred employees into line with those of the existing workforce. An employer who expressly or constructively dismisses employees who refuse to accept new terms will encounter difficulty with reg 7. In addition, a purported variation of the terms and conditions enjoyed by the workforce will be void under reg 4(4) if the reason for the variation is the transfer itself unless the variation fits within one of the circumstances detailed in reg 4(5) (see **8.3.4.6**). If the agreed variation is an entirely positive change for the employees, though, TUPE 2006 will not prevent its taking effect.

Allocation of liability between transferor and transferee

Pursuant to regs 13 to 15, the transferor and transferee are jointly and severally liable in relation to any failure to comply with their duties to inform and consult employees under TUPE 2006 (see **8.3.5.1**). In other areas, joint liability is not possible: *Stirling District Council v Allan* [1995] IRLR 301. If the parties wish to allocate liability differently between themselves, they must do so by the inclusion of appropriate indemnities in the sale and purchase agreement. Where it may be unclear whether a claim should be made against the transferor or the transferee, an employee may bring a claim against both.

8.3.5   Consultation and allocation of risk

Regulations 11–16 of TUPE 2006 impose duties upon both the transferor and the transferee to provide information to each other, and to provide information to and consult with representatives of employees who may be affected by the transfer.

Following the Acquired Rights Directive, the seller and the buyer are required to provide certain items of information to the representatives of their respective employees. Member States may limit these obligations to undertakings or businesses which have more than a certain limited number of employees. In the UK, for example, micro-businesses (those with nine or fewer employees) are exempt from the requirement to elect and consult with employee representatives but can instead consult with the employees directly.

8.3.5.1   The duty to inform and consult trade unions

Regulation 13 of TUPE 2006 obliges both the transferor and the transferee to provide information to recognised trade unions or elected employee representatives in respect of any 'affected employee', ie any employee of the seller or buyer who may be affected by the transfer or measures taken in relation to it. The employer must supply specified information long enough before the transfer to enable consultation to take place. The information to be given includes the legal, social and economic implications for the employees, and the measures which the employer is proposing to take in relation to them (if there are no measures proposed, this should be stated). The seller must also inform the union or elected representative of any measures which it understands the buyer intends to take in relation to affected employees. 'Measures' in this context would appear to include proposed changes in the workforce or in their terms and conditions.

The employer is under an obligation to consult where it envisages taking measures in relation to the affected employees, with a view to reaching agreement on the measures to be taken. The employer must consider any representations made, respond to them and indicate the reasons for rejecting any of them.

Failure to comply with reg 13 may lead to the tribunal, on the application of the union or elected representative, awarding up to 13 weeks' pay in respect of each affected employee (reg 15). The employer has a defence if it can show that it was not reasonably practicable to perform the duties due to special circumstances, but that it took all such steps towards performance as were reasonably practicable in those circumstances.

Collective agreements and union recognition agreements will generally be transferred to the buyer (regs 5 and 6).

8.3.5.2   Obligation to provide information

Under reg 11, the transferor must provide the transferee with employee liability information about:

(a)   the identity and age of the employees who will transfer;

(b)   details contained in those employees' written statements of employment under s 1 of the ERA 1996;

(c)   any collective agreements affecting those employees which will continue to have effect after the transfer;

(d)   any disciplinary proceedings taken against, or grievance brought by, an employee in the preceding two years, to which a Code of Practice issued under the Trade Union and Labour Relations (Consolidation) Act 1992 applies;

(e)   any legal action brought by an employee against the transferor in the previous two years, and any such action that the transferor has reasonable grounds to believe may be brought against it.

The aim of this obligation is to help the transferee to prepare for the arrival of the transferred employees and to ensure that the transferee is fully aware of all its inherited obligations.

The information must be provided not less than 28 days before the transfer, or, if special circumstances mean this is not reasonably practicable, as soon as reasonably practicable (reg 11(6)). Once the information has been provided, the transferor is also obliged to notify the transferee in writing of any changes to it (reg 11(5)).

If the information is not provided, the transferee may bring a claim against the transferor in the tribunal (reg 12), and will receive compensation (subject to a minimum award of £500 per employee transferred) reflecting the losses sustained.

8.3.5.3   Allocation of risk

Although the parties cannot contract out of TUPE 2006, the buyer and seller will usually want to agree an allocation between themselves of liability for matters arising from the Regulations.

Due diligence

The parties will carry out the due diligence exercise in relation to the employees with the statutory obligations under reg 11 in mind. Since the buyer will inherit all liabilities in relation to the target's employees, arising under their contracts or otherwise, it is vital that full details of employment matters are obtained. The buyer must carefully examine the transferring employees' contractual terms in particular, as there will be little opportunity to vary those terms even with the employees' consent unless such variations are entirely positive.

The buyer will also want to ascertain which employees are working in or assigned to the undertaking being transferred. These employees will usually be specified in a schedule, although who is actually transferred is still a matter of fact for the EAT to determine.

The buyer will review this information to determine any likely costs it may incur in integrating these employees into its own business operations. This may involve the dismissal costs in relation to any surplus employees, or additional costs relating to more advantageous terms and conditions enjoyed by the transferring employees.

Warranties

The buyer should support the due diligence review with warranties in the sale and purchase agreement to the effect that:

(a)   the persons listed in the schedule of employees are the only employees working in or assigned to the undertaking being transferred and that all relevant terms and conditions of such persons have been disclosed to the buyer;

(b)   details of any collective agreements and whether there are any actual or threatened industrial disputes have been fully disclosed;

(c)   there are no outstanding or pending claims that have not been disclosed;

(d)   the seller has complied with its obligations to inform and consult with employee representatives and provided the required employee liability information; and

(e)   the information concerning the transferring employees provided in the disclosure letter is true and accurate.

In addition the buyer may also seek warranties relating to the operation of TUPE 2006. In particular, the buyer will seek a warranty that there have been no dismissals where the sole or principal reason for the dismissal is the transfer and there is no ETO reason, since liability in these circumstances will transfer to the buyer. For the same reason, the buyer will also require the seller to warrant that it has not made any changes to the transferring employees' terms of employment where the sole or principal reason for the changes is the transfer and there is no ETO reason. Subject to the exceptions in reg 4(5), such changes in terms would be void and the buyer bound by previous terms. Ideally the buyer will want both of these warranties to be supported by appropriate indemnities.

Indemnities

The buyer will usually also seek various indemnities from the seller, for example an indemnity against any costs or liabilities arising out of all outgoings in respect of the employees (eg salary, commissions, bonuses and holiday pay) up to the date of completion (an apportionment will be made to the date of completion). The buyer may also insist on an indemnity against any claims which are attributable to any breach by the seller of its employment obligations prior to completion (including claims arising on termination of any employee's employment) for which the buyer becomes liable through the operation of TUPE 2006.

Indemnities may also be appropriate in respect of any measures which may be taken in relation to the transferring employees both before and after the transfer date. For example, if redundancies are to take place before the transfer, the buyer may agree to indemnify the seller in respect of any claims arising out of such redundancies, although as discussed above it is more likely that liability will transfer to the buyer in any event through the operation of TUPE 2006. If employees are to be made redundant after the transfer, the parties may agree as part of the commercial transaction to provide a fund for redundancy costs rather than a straight adjustment of the price. This will usually be on the understanding that the dismissals will be for an ETO reason and that the buyer will act fairly in making the redundancies.

8.3.6   Pensions in the UK and EU

Where the transferring employees are members of a pension scheme, the parties will need to give careful thought to the pension aspects of the acquisition. This is a complex area, which often gives rise to more discussion and negotiation between the parties and their advisers than any other aspect of the transaction; this is understandable, since the value of the pension fund may even exceed the consideration for the acquisition itself. It may be necessary to have a specialist pensions lawyer as part of the legal team involved in an acquisition. It is not intended to deal with pension considerations in detail but merely to highlight a number of general points which may be relevant on an asset acquisition.

Pursuant to the Acquired Right Directive, unless member states provide an additional provision, the transfer does not apply to employees' rights to old age, disability or survivors' benefits under supplementary company or pension schemes outside the statutory social security schemes in member states. The transferor's obligations based on non-statutory schemes are not transferred. In some Member States, these rights are transferred just as any other right.

In certain Member States (such as France, Spain and Italy), pension contributions are largely made by compulsory contributions on behalf of employees to the national security system, which may also cover other social security benefits such as healthcare and/or welfare benefits. In addition to the mandatory contributions, the employee or employer may make voluntary contributions to supplementary pension schemes.

8.3.6.1   Money purchase or final salary scheme?

The buyer will require full details of any pension scheme benefiting the transferring employees; in particular, pre-contract enquiries will include requests for copies of the trust deed and rules under which the pension fund is administered, a list of the members of the scheme, and confirmation that the scheme is 'exempt approved', ie that it enjoys a privileged tax status. There are two main types of pension scheme: money purchase schemes and final salary schemes.

Money purchase

In a money purchase scheme, the employer and employee make fixed contributions into the fund which are invested and used to purchase benefits for the employee on their retirement. Employees are not guaranteed any particular level of benefit on retirement; the amount they receive will depend entirely on the return on the contributions made by them and by the employer on their behalf. This is the most common type of pension scheme.

Final salary

In a final salary scheme, the members are guaranteed a particular level of benefit on retirement; this will usually be on the basis of a fraction of their salary at the date of retirement for each year of completed service with the employer. Unlike money purchase schemes, there is no direct correlation between the contributions made to the fund (by employer and employee) and the benefits received by the employee. A final salary scheme may, consequently, be in surplus or deficit at the time of the acquisition; much will depend on the prevailing economic conditions which, of course, have an effect on investment performance. Whether the fund is in surplus or deficit and the amounts involved can be ascertained only by making a host of assumptions about future events. Such an exercise should be carried out by an actuary.

8.3.6.2   Is there a discrete pension scheme for the transferring employees or do they participate in a group scheme?

The pension implications of an asset acquisition are simplified if the transferring employees are members of a separate, self-contained pension scheme (a discrete scheme). However, it is often the case that they are members of a larger scheme involving other employees. For example, on an asset sale by a company, the selling company may be part of a group pension scheme.

8.3.6.3   Transferring the pension benefits

Discrete scheme

The assets in the pension fund do not form part of the assets of the business which are being acquired; the pension fund is a separate entity administered by the trustees. Where the transferring employees are members of a discrete pension scheme, they will remain in the scheme following the acquisition (usually, at least initially, even if the buyer has an existing scheme covering its own employees). If it is a final salary scheme, it is important for the parties to determine whether it is adequately funded or over-funded at the date of completion. The buyer will often commission an actuary to value the fund for this purpose.

If the scheme is revealed to be in surplus, the seller may seek an increase in the purchase price to reflect this. Although the buyer does not benefit directly from the surplus, it may enable a 'contributions holiday' to be taken, ie a period in which no contributions are made. If, on the other hand, there is a deficit, the buyer may seek a reduction in the price or require the seller to 'top up' the fund. If the actuarial valuation is not ready on completion, the agreement may provide for an adjustment of the price when it is to hand.

The sale and purchase agreement will usually contain a schedule setting out details of the scheme. Warranties relating to the scheme will include confirmation by the seller that all contributions have been paid to the date of completion and that there are no outstanding claims against the trustees.

Group scheme

Where the transferring employees are members of a group scheme, a transfer payment must be made from the group scheme to the buyer's scheme (whether an existing scheme or one established for the purpose). The amount of this payment is usually the subject of much argument and negotiation between the parties and their respective actuaries. The discussion often centres around who should have the benefit of any surplus in a final salary scheme. The different bases for calculating the transfer payment can produce vastly differing results. The calculation may, for example, be based on the benefits which the employees would receive on leaving employment, or on an apportionment of the fund between those leaving the scheme and those remaining (if the scheme is in surplus, the latter method will be more beneficial for the transferring employees).

The provisions relating to the transfer payment are normally contained in a pension schedule to the sale and purchase agreement. The parties' actuaries may not have agreed the amount of the payment by the date of completion, but the basis for calculating the payment is usually included in an 'actuary's letter' attached to the schedule.

It is important to appreciate that the trustees of the scheme will not be parties to the sale and purchase agreement, and can act only in accordance with the trust deed and rules. Since the seller cannot, therefore, force the trustees to make the transfer, the buyer is wise to insist on a guarantee by the seller to make up any shortfall if it is unable to procure the transfer of the full amount. Finally, if the buyer needs to establish a new scheme, the parties may agree that the target's employees should remain with the group scheme for a specified period after completion.

8.3.7   Flowcharts: unfair dismissal claims on transfer of an undertaking

8.3.7.1   Dismissals before the transfer

Is there a relevant transfer?

Reg 3(1)(a): business transfer: two limb test:
(a) Is there an economic entity? – question of fact;
(b) Has that entity transferred? – *Spijkers*

OR

Reg 3(1)(b) and reg 3(3) Service provision changes

NO → Usual employment rules apply

YES ↓

Effect of relevant transfer (reg 4) = Dismissal effective – liability **may** transfer (reg 4(3) and reg 7(1))

YES ↓

Check eligibility re UD – usual rules include **one year's continuous employment** (if employed before 6 April 2012) **or two years' continuous employment** (if employed on or after 6 April 2012) + **has there been a dismissal?**

NO → NO UD CLAIM

YES ↓

Was the transfer the sole or principal reason for the dismissal?

NO → Apply usual UD rules against **Transferor**

YES ↓

(Reg 7 provides that the dismissal = **AUTO UD** against the **Transferee** unless there is an ETO reason *entailing a change in the workforce)*

Was there an ETO reason entailing a change in the workforce?
- Must be reason of employer who dismisses employee and relate to ongoing conduct of **its** business (*Hynd*)
- Look for redundancy as the typical example – if established the dismissal will be deemed to be for redundancy/substantial reason [for purpose of ERA 1996, s 98]

NO → Dismissal is automatically **unfair** (**reg 7**) Claim against **Transferee** (**reg 4(3)**)

YES ↓

Claim against Transferor
Was dismissal handled fairly under s 98(4)?

NO → Dismissal unfair – claim against **Transferor**

YES ↓

Dismissal will be fair

NB – ALSO check for redundancy payment claims and/or WD claims. Claim will be against the same party as the claim for UD.

8.3.7.2   Dismissals on or after the transfer

NB – ALSO check for redundancy payment claims and/or WD claims. Claim will be against the Transferee.

8.4   TAXATION IN THE UK

8.4.1   Introduction

The sale and purchase agreement for an asset acquisition in the UK will usually provide for the total purchase price for all the assets. However, an asset acquisition is a series of separate disposals, and for tax purposes the amount of the consideration which is attributable to each separate asset must be specified in the agreement (the apportionment is often contained in a schedule). The parties have some flexibility in making this apportionment and are usually influenced heavily by taxation and stamp duty implications.

This section outlines the main tax consequences (including VAT and stamp duty) of an asset acquisition in the UK. It deals with the implications for a sole trader or partnership disposing of an unincorporated business, and for a company selling a continuing business. The tax position of the buyer is also considered.

It is not intended to explain in detail basic tax principles, such as the nature of the charges to income tax, CGT and corporation tax, and the main relieving provisions, but to deal with these in the context of an asset acquisition where the intention is to continue a business in succession to the seller.

8.4.2   Implications for the seller of an unincorporated business

It is assumed here that a sole trader or partnership is selling the whole of their or its business to an unconnected person at full market value; the buyer may be an individual, a partnership or a company. We are not concerned with the gift of a business or, indeed, with the incorporation of a business, ie where the proprietors sell their business to a company which they have formed or acquired specifically for this purpose.

8.4.2.1   Sales for cash

A sole trader or partnership disposing of the business in an arm's length deal must consider the income tax and CGT implications of the transaction.

Income tax

The closing year rules   The sale results in the discontinuance of the business carried on by the seller, so the seller will be assessed to income tax on the profits made from the end of the latest accounting period to be assessed until the date of the sale, less a deduction for overlap profit (ie any profit that has been charged to tax in two successive tax years).

Stock   The value at which trading stock is sold will affect the final profits of the business assessable to income tax. It will be seen at **8.4.4.5** that the parties have some flexibility in apportioning the global consideration for the business between individual assets. Clearly, the higher the value attributed to stock, the higher the final income tax assessment.

Balancing charges   The sale of the business may result in balancing charges arising in relation to assets on which capital allowances have been claimed (ie, items of plant and machinery). Most items of plant and machinery are 'pooled' together for the purpose of obtaining capital allowances, and it is only when the business is sold that HMRC calculates whether too much or too little income tax relief has been given on all the assets in the 'pool'. On the basis of the sale price attributable to those assets qualifying for capital allowances, HMRC will either make an income tax balancing allowance (where the pool is sold for less than its tax written-down value) or an income tax balancing charge (where the pool is sold for more than its tax written-down value).

In calculating such balancing allowances or charges, it should be noted that the capital allowances a business can claim are enhanced in the first year of ownership of any asset by virtue of the Annual Investment Allowance (AIA). The AIA can be applied against any asset in its first year of ownership, and is intended to act as an incentive for businesses to invest in their operations. While AIA rules, and their amount, have varied from year to year, from 1 January 2023 to 31 December 2024, businesses receive an AIA of £1 million, meaning that any expenditure up to £1 million incurred during this period on purchasing plant and machinery will be wholly deductible. Consequently, if an asset which benefited from the AIA is sold at a price exceeding its written-down value, it is likely to incur a balancing charge. In a recent budget announcement, the government has indicated that the AIA will remain at £1 million beyond 31 December 2024.

Apportionment of the global purchase price of the business between individual assets can thus have a significant effect on the tax position of the seller (and also the buyer, see **8.4.4.5**).

Relief for losses   The sale of the business will prevent any unrelieved losses from being carried forward under s 83 of the Income Tax Act 2007 (ITA 2007), since the provision only allows trading losses to be set against future profits of the trade. However, terminal loss relief under s 89 can be claimed if the taxpayer suffers a trading loss in the final 12 months in which they carry on the trade; unrelieved capital allowances in this period may be included for this purpose. The loss can be carried across against profits made in the final tax year and then carried back and deducted from profits of the same trade for the three years prior to the final tax year, taking the most recent years first. This may generate a repayment of tax.

The seller can also set a trading loss made in the year in which the sale takes place against any income or chargeable gains which they have in that year or the previous year under ss 64 to 71 of the ITA 2007. A loss relieved under ss 64 to 71 cannot form part of the terminal loss claim under s 89.

Capital gains tax

The seller will be liable to CGT at the following rates for the tax year 2023/24 on any gain that arises on the disposal of chargeable assets of the business, such as land, buildings and goodwill:

(a)   10% on any gains qualifying for business asset disposal relief (previously known as entrepreneurs' relief) (see below);

(b)   10% on any gains which fall within any unused portion of the seller's basic rate income tax band;

(c)   20% on any remaining gains which exceed the basic rate tax band.

Note that the basic rate tax band will be allocated first against taxable income, and then against any gains qualifying for business asset disposal relief, with any remainder being allocated against other capital gains.

On a sale of the business by a partnership, each partner is separately assessed to CGT and is treated as disposing of their fractional share of each chargeable asset (this is determined by the partner's capital profit sharing ratio).

The gain on the sale of a business may be considerable, particularly where the seller has built up the goodwill of the business. For a long-established business, rebasing to 31 March 1982 (ie substituting market value on this date for actual cost in calculating the gain) may reduce the gain significantly. However, it should be noted that for a business established since 31 March 1982, the goodwill will have no base cost, resulting in virtually the whole of its value becoming chargeable.

Business asset disposal relief (TCGA 1992, ss 169H–169S)   Business asset disposal relief was, until 6 April 2020, known as entrepreneurs' relief. The relief is designed to reduce the charge to CGT on gains realised on certain business disposals.

The relief will apply where there is a 'qualifying business disposal'. If the conditions for a qualifying business disposal are met, the amount of the capital gain chargeable to tax is reduced in two stages:

(1)   the gain arising from the qualifying business disposal is reduced by any losses made as part of the disposal; and

(2)   any net gain that remains after taking losses into account is charged to tax at only 10%. The relief is, however, subject to a maximum reduction of £1 million of qualifying net

gains realised after 11 March 2020. This represents a lifetime restriction so that only £1 million of net gains can qualify for the relief for each individual, whether those gains arise from a single disposal or several disposals spread over time. Until 11 March 2020, the lifetime restriction was £10 million.

Whether a 'qualifying business disposal' exists depends on whether the business interest being disposed involves (a) a sole trade or partnership interest, (b) company shares, or (c) an associated disposal, each of which has specific conditions that must be met for the relief to apply:

(a) Sole trade or partnership interests

(i)   The disposal of the whole or part of a business (whether by a sole trader or an individual partner) may qualify. This includes situations where:

    (a)   the business (or part of it) is disposed of as a going concern (not simply the disposal of individual asset(s) used in the business); or where

    (b)   assets are disposed of following cessation of the business (provided the assets were used in the business at the time of cessation).

(ii)   To be a qualifying disposal of part or the whole of a business, the interest in the business as a whole (as opposed to any one asset comprising it) must have been owned either:

    (a)   throughout the period of two years ending with the date of disposal; or

    (b)   throughout the period of two years ending with the cessation of the business (provided the disposal itself is within three years after that cessation).

(iii) Where there is a qualifying disposal of a sole trade or partnership interest, only assets used for the purposes of the business carried on by the individual or partnership are eligible for relief. Company shares and securities and any other assets held as investments are specifically excluded from this definition. Goodwill is also excluded from being a relevant business asset when the disposal is by an individual to a close company in which they or their associate(s) are participators.

(b) Company shares

(i)   A disposal of company shares (including securities) may qualify for relief if:

    (a)   the company is a trading company and is the selling shareholder's 'personal company' (so that they hold at least 5% of the ordinary share capital in the company and that holding gives at least 5% of the voting rights);

    and either or both of the following conditions are met:

        (i)   by virtue of that holding, the selling shareholder is beneficially entitled to at least 5% of the profits available for distribution to equity holders and, on a winding up, would be beneficially entitled to at least 5% of assets so available, or

        (ii)   in the event of a disposal of the whole of the ordinary share capital of the company, the selling shareholder would be beneficially entitled to at least 5% of the proceeds; and

    (b)   the selling shareholder is an employee or officer (such as a director) of the company.

(ii)   For a qualifying disposal, the requirements detailed in (i) above must have been satisfied either:

    (a)   throughout the period of two years ending with the date of disposal; or

    (b)   throughout the period of two years ending with the date the company ceased to be a trading company (provided that the disposal itself is within three years of that cessation).

(iii) To be a 'trading company', the company must not have activities that include 'to a substantial extent activities other than trading activities'. This will restrict the extent to which the company can hold cash reserves or investments whilst still meeting the definition.

(c) Associated disposals

(i)   Sometimes assets used by a business are not owned as part of the business but separately by an individual. Disposals of such assets owned by an individual outside of the business may qualify for relief if the asset was used for the purposes of the business run either by:

(a)   a partnership in which the individual was a partner; or

(b)   a company in which the individual's shares qualify under '(b) Company shares' above.

(ii)   Disposals of such assets qualify only if the disposal of them is associated with a qualifying disposal of the individual's interest in the partnership or company shares as the case may be, and if the disposal is part of the withdrawal of the individual from the business carried on by the partnership or company. (Withdrawal means reducing the partnership share by at least 5% of the partnership assets or reducing the shareholding by at least 5% of the share capital.)

(iii) To be a qualifying disposal, the asset in question must have been owned by the individual for at least three years and used throughout the period of two years ending with the earlier of:

(a)   the disposal of the interest or shares to which the disposal of the asset is associated; or

(b)   the cessation of the business of the partnership or company which used the asset.

(Note: further conditions apply if the shares being disposed of are in a company that is part of a group, or if the business or shares are owned as part of the assets of a trust).

Annual exemption   A sole trader, or in the case of a partnership each partner, will have the benefit of the CGT annual exemption (£6,000 for tax year 2023/24) if this has not otherwise been used up in the tax year.

Roll-over relief on replacement of business assets (TCGA 1992, ss 152–159A)   A sole trader or partner who reinvests the proceeds of sale of their business or partnership share in another business venture may be able to defer the charge to CGT if they fulfil the conditions for roll-over relief. The main features of the relief are set out below:

(a)   Where the business or partnership share comprises qualifying assets (or an interest in such assets), the sole trader or partner can elect to roll any gain on such assets into replacement qualifying assets acquired within one year before or three years after the sale of the business or partnership share (it is sufficient that an unconditional contract is entered into within these time limits). Capital gains tax is deferred until the replacement assets are disposed of (without themselves being replaced).

(b)   It is not necessary for the replacement asset to be of the same kind as the original asset. It is sufficient if both the 'old' and the 'new' assets come within the list of qualifying assets, which includes land or buildings occupied and used for the trade, goodwill, and fixed plant and machinery. Thus, an individual who sells one unincorporated business and then invests in another will be able to take advantage of this relief. However, shares are not qualifying assets for the purposes of this relief.

(c)   Relief is restricted if the old assets have not been used in the seller's trade (or trades which the seller carried on successively) throughout the seller's period of ownership, or if the whole of the proceeds of sale are not reinvested in new assets.

(d)   A partner who allows their firm to use the asset can claim relief on selling the asset if they reinvest in replacement assets.

(e)   Note that the seller cannot use their annual exemption to reduce the gain rolled over.

Deferral relief on reinvestment in EIS shares   An individual will be able to claim unlimited deferral of capital gains arising on the disposal, by sale or gift, of any asset when they invest the chargeable gain by subscribing for shares which qualify under the Enterprise Investment Scheme (EIS). This covers shares in qualifying unquoted companies which, if issued after 15 March 2018, satisfy the 'risk-to-capital' condition. This requirement was introduced by the Finance Act 2018 to ensure that relief is only available in relation to genuine investments where there is a real prospect of risk for the investor. It requires that, having regard to all the circumstances existing at the time of the issue of the shares, it would be reasonable to conclude:

(a) that the issuing company has objectives to grow and develop its trade in the long term; and

(b) that there is a significant risk that there will be a loss of capital of an amount greater than the net investment return.

The individual's chargeable gain on the disposal of the asset (up to the subscription cost) is deferred until they dispose of the shares. The relief is available where the EIS shares are acquired for cash within one year before or three years after the disposal. An individual may apply business asset disposal relief (above) before deferring any remaining gain by investing in EIS shares.

8.4.2.2   Sales in consideration for shares

On an arm's length sale of an unincorporated business (whether a sole trade or a partnership) to an existing company, the proprietors of the business may agree to take shares in the buyer company as consideration for the sale. Two special reliefs may be available to individual sellers in these circumstances.

Carry forward of unrelieved trading losses

Where a business is sold to a company wholly or mainly for shares, s 86 of the ITA 2007 allows the seller to carry forward any unrelieved trading losses and deduct them from income received from the company. The set off is available in any year in which the seller retains beneficial ownership of the shares. For the sale to be 'wholly or mainly' in return for shares, at least 80% of the consideration should be in shares.

CGT roll-over into shares

Section 162 of the TCGA 1992 enables the seller to roll any chargeable gains on the sale of the business into the shares issued by the company in consideration, thus reducing the CGT acquisition cost of the shares by the amount of the gain. The effect of the relief is to postpone the CGT until the former proprietor of the business disposes of their shares in the company.

For the relief to operate, all the assets of the business (although cash can be ignored for this purpose) must be transferred to the company; it is not necessary, however, to transfer all the liabilities. Since the nature of the relief is to roll the gain into shares, to the extent that the seller receives cash or debentures in part satisfaction of the purchase price, an immediate potential liability to CGT will arise. This may suit a seller if, for example, the seller has capital losses brought forward from previous years which the seller can use to offset the gain.

8.4.3   Implications on the sale of a business by a company

8.4.3.1   Corporation tax

A company is charged to corporation tax on both its income profits and its capital gains. Thus, on an asset sale by a company, the following will give rise to a corporation tax charge:

(a) capital gains (calculated in the same way as for CGT, save that companies are entitled to an indexation allowance to remove inflationary gains from the capital gains calculation) arising on chargeable assets of the business (profit on intangible fixed assets such as goodwill and intellectual property rights will generally be treated as income receipts in the hands of a corporate seller);

(b)   income profits on the sale of trading stock and intangible fixed assets (see above);

(c)   balancing charges. A company is entitled to capital allowances on plant and machinery in much the same way as an unincorporated business. The disposal of its business will entail an adjustment to the corporation tax relief given on those assets in the form of either a balancing allowance or a balancing charge. As for an unincorporated business, in computing any balancing allowance or charge, consideration should be given to Annual Investment Allowances, which a company will also benefit from. The AIA will operate in the same manner, and at the same allowance limits, as described in **8.4.2.1**.

For the tax year 2023/24, the rate of corporation tax for companies is determined by the level of their taxable profits in the accounting year:

- companies with taxable profits of up to £50,000 are subject to the standard small profits rate of 19%;

- companies with taxable profits of more than £250,000 are subject to the main rate of 25% (on the taxable profits in their entirety);

- companies with taxable profits above £50,000 but not exceeding £250,000 are subject to the marginal rate. The complexity of the formula used to arrive at the marginal rate is beyond the scope of this book.

The company does not have the benefit of an annual exemption to reduce its capital profits. However, if the selling company reinvests the proceeds of the asset sale in a new business, roll-over relief from corporation tax on replacement of business assets is available in much the same way as already described in relation to CGT.

If a company sells its business, it will lose the right to carry forward trading losses which arose in accounting periods beginning before 1 April 2017, since such losses may only be set against subsequent profits of the same trade. In contrast, and subject to the limitations discussed in **9.3.3.1**, trading losses arising in accounting periods beginning on or after 1 April 2017 may be carried forward against any profits made by the company in subsequent years, even if such profits do not relate to the same trade.

Where a company ceases to trade, any trading losses sustained in its final 12 months may be carried back for up to three years against previous profits of the same trade.

To the extent that losses have been carried forward into the company's final 12 months but not set against profits, the company may carry those unrelieved losses back and set them against profits of the preceding three years. However, no such deduction may be made for any accounting period beginning before 1 April 2017.

The reliefs discussed in **8.4.2.1**, business asset disposal relief and deferral relief on reinvestment in EIS shares, are not available to a corporate seller.

8.4.3.2   Extracting the cash from the company

One of the attractions of selling a company by way of share transfer is that the sale price is received directly by the owners of the company, whether they are individual or corporate shareholders. Where, on the other hand, the assets of the company are sold, it is the company itself, rather than the owners of the company, which receives the price. Consider, for example, a company (A Ltd) with a single business which has two individual shareholders (Bob and Charlie). D Ltd, which is aware that Bob and Charlie wish to sell A Ltd, agrees to buy its business as a going concern. On completion of the sale of its business to D Ltd, A Ltd will be a mere 'cash shell' in which the net proceeds of sale (ie after deduction of corporation tax) are deposited (see **Figure 8.1** below). Further steps involving an additional tax charge must be taken for this money to end up in the hands of Bob and Charlie (see below). If, instead, D Ltd acquired A Ltd's shares, Bob and Charlie would receive the consideration direct, subject only to paying CGT (see **Figure 8.2** below and **9.4**).

Figure 8.1   Asset sale

leads to:

Figure 8.2   Share sale

leads to:

Liquidating the company

The shareholders may extract the proceeds of sale of the assets of the business by putting the company into voluntary liquidation. On a winding up, however, the shareholders are treated as disposing of their shares, and individual shareholders will be liable to CGT on any resultant gain. A corporate shareholder will be liable to corporation tax on any such gain if the disposal is not exempt from tax as a disposal of a substantial shareholding (ie broadly 10% or more of the ordinary share capital – see **9.4.2.4**). There is, accordingly, a potential double charge to tax where an asset sale is followed by the liquidation of the company: a corporation tax charge on the company on the sale of the assets of the business, and a CGT (or corporation tax) charge on the shareholder on the winding up.

Distribution by dividend

The shareholders may find it more tax efficient for the company to declare a dividend before it is put into liquidation. However, for individual shareholders, this will, once again, involve a second charge to tax (ie in addition to the corporation tax payable by the company on the sale of the assets of the business). It is also worth bearing in mind that a pre-liquidation dividend may be less attractive to individuals, as their available reliefs (eg business asset disposal relief) in respect of chargeable capital gains may be more advantageous.

If a pre-liquidation dividend is paid, individual shareholders are liable to income tax on the gross dividend (being the net dividend plus the tax credit), after application of the dividend allowance.

Corporate shareholders will not pay corporation tax on the receipt of a dividend from a subsidiary. Where a shareholding will not qualify on disposal for exemption from tax as a substantial shareholding, a pre-liquidation dividend will be the most tax-efficient method of distributing the proceeds of sale, provided there are genuine distributable profits (see **9.4**).

Where the shareholders have extracted cash from the company in the form of a pre-liquidation dividend, the ensuing liquidation is less likely to give rise to a charge to CGT (or corporation tax) since the distribution by the company will have reduced the value of the shares.

8.4.4   Implications for the buyer of a business

The great advantage to the buyer of acquiring the business of a company rather than its shares under English law is that it does not assume responsibility for all the hidden liabilities of the company. It can therefore save the cost and time involved in carrying out an in-depth investigation into the tax affairs of the company, and in negotiating extensive warranties and indemnities.

The tax consequences of acquiring the assets of a business are similar whether the buyer is an individual or a company.

8.4.4.1   Capital allowances

Capital allowances, as well as the Annual Investment Allowance described in **8.4.2.1** above, are not restricted to the purchase of brand new assets. The allowances also apply to 'second-hand' purchases as they are available for any assets that are newly introduced into a business, irrespective of whether the asset was bought from another party (such as a seller) that previously owned the assets.

Consequently, the buyer will be able to claim capital allowances on, for example, plant and machinery which it acquires from the seller. The allowances are calculated on the price the buyer pays for them and not their tax written-down value in the seller's hands. Assume, for example, that the seller originally acquired an item of plant and machinery for £8,000 and has received writing-down allowances totalling £6,000 up to the date of the sale. On an asset sale of the business, £4,000 is attributed to this item (ignore the effect of pooling for this purpose). As the seller has sold the asset for more than its tax written-down value (ie £2,000), a balancing charge will be levied on it. In the year of the sale, the buyer will receive an allowance based on the purchase price of £4,000.

8.4.4.2 Trading stock

The amount which the buyer pays for stock or work in progress will be a deductible expense in working out income profits liable to income tax or corporation tax as appropriate.

8.4.4.3 Base cost for capital tax

The price paid by the buyer for chargeable assets of the business will form its base cost for CGT or corporation tax purposes. This contrasts with a share acquisition, where the base cost of the chargeable assets of the target company for capital gains purposes will be their original cost to the target. This may be relevant if the buyer is proposing to dispose of certain unwanted assets soon after the acquisition.

8.4.4.4 Roll-over relief from CGT (or corporation tax) on replacement of qualifying assets

If the buyer has disposed of qualifying assets in the previous three years, or is intending to do so in the next 12 months, it will be able to roll any chargeable gain arising on such a disposal into those assets of the acquired business which are themselves qualifying assets.

8.4.4.5 Apportioning the purchase price

The parties will usually agree initially upon a global consideration for the assets of the business. For tax and stamp duty purposes, however, they will need to negotiate the apportionment of this overall figure between the various assets transferred. Although s 52(4) of the TCGA 1992 requires that any method adopted for this apportionment must be 'just and reasonable', in practice the parties have some flexibility as to the figures upon which they settle.

It will be clear from what has been said above that the seller and buyer may be pulling in different directions on this issue. For example, the buyer may prefer the consideration to be balanced in favour of goodwill, which will not attract stamp duty, and also stock, which will form a deduction from its income profits, and plant and machinery, on which capital allowances and the Annual Investment Allowance will be available. By contrast, the seller may prefer the apportionment to be weighted more in favour of qualifying assets for roll-over relief if it is proposing to reinvest the sale proceeds. Much will depend, of course, on the individual circumstances of the parties. If, for example, the seller has unrelieved trading losses which it would not otherwise be able to use, it may be happy for a relatively high value to be attributed to stock and plant and machinery. The carried forward losses would then be available to absorb some or all of the resulting trading profit.

8.4.4.6 Value added tax

A taxable person must charge VAT on taxable supplies of goods and services made in the UK in the course or furtherance of a business carried on by them (Value Added Tax Act 1994 (VATA 1994), s 4(1)). Prima facie, therefore, on the sale of a business, VAT is chargeable on the stock and capital assets (including goodwill) of the business.

There is, however, a special exemption contained in Art 5 of the Value Added Tax (Special Provisions) Order 1995 (SI 1995/1268). This treats the transfer of the whole or part of a business as a going concern as being outside the scope of VAT. See further below.

Transfer as a going concern

For the Art 5 exemption to apply, the following two important conditions must be satisfied:

(a)   the assets must be used by the buyer in the same kind of business as that carried on by the seller with no significant break; and

(b)   the buyer must be a taxable person, or become a taxable person as a result of the transfer.

In determining whether the sale is of a business as a going concern or merely assets in the business, regard must be had to all the circumstances, including, for example, the following:

(a)   the wording of the sale and purchase agreement (however, the label which the parties put on the transaction is not conclusive);

(b)   whether goodwill (and the right to use the business name), contracts and customer lists are transferred;

(c)   whether the workforce is transferred;

(d)   whether the buyer can carry on the same type of activities without interruption;

(e)   where part of a business is transferred, whether it is a severable unit, capable of standing on its own.

It is very important to distinguish between the sale of a business as a going concern and a mere transfer of assets for VAT purposes (see **1.2.3.3**). It used to be common practice where there was any doubt (and particularly in the case of a sale of part of a business) for the parties to a transaction to seek a ruling from HMRC as to whether the proposed sale would come within Art 5. Now, however, HMRC will not consider routine clearance applications and will only give an opinion when the transaction has unusual features, to which attention should be drawn in the application. This strict approach requires lawyers to take great care in applying Art 5 in order to determine the nature of the transaction for VAT purposes.

Provision in the sale and purchase agreement

The seller's lawyers should ensure that in the sale and purchase agreement the consideration is stated to be exclusive of VAT. Otherwise, if HMRC argues successfully that VAT is chargeable because the Art 5 conditions have not been satisfied, the purchase price will be deemed to be inclusive of VAT (VATA 1994, s 19(2)). The unfortunate result will be that the seller must account for the VAT to HMRC but is unable to recover this from the buyer. In the absence of advance clearance from HMRC, even if the seller believes that the sale comes within Art 5, the seller should seek an indemnity from the buyer against any VAT charge arising from the sale (plus any penalty or interest payable).

If the seller wrongly charges VAT on a sale in respect of which Art 5 applies, the buyer may be unable to recover the tax from HMRC by claiming an offset against input tax (although the buyer should have a right of recovery from the seller).

8.4.4.7   Stamp duty land tax

Stamp duty land tax (SDLT) is a tax that is payable by the buyer on transactions involving the transfer of land.

Rate of duty

SDLT is payable by the buyer on commercial property on a sliding scale at the following rates:

(a)   nil where the consideration does not exceed £150,000;

(b)   2% on consideration that exceeds £150,000 but does not exceed £250,000;

(c)   5% on consideration that exceeds £250,000.

On the acquisition of a business, the relevant consideration for SDLT is the aggregate consideration for all of the properties transferred. The Finance Act 2003 provides that where partnership property includes land, there will be no SDLT charged on the transfer of an interest in that partnership where the partnership's main activity is the carrying on of a profession or a trade (other than a trade of dealing in or developing land).

8.4.4.8 Financing the acquisition by borrowing: is tax relief available?

Individual buyer

If an individual borrows money to purchase a share in a partnership, they can obtain relief for interest payments they make under the loan by treating the interest payments as an income tax deduction. This enables the interest payments to be set off against the total income of the individual. Alternatively, the interest payments can be treated as a deductible expense in arriving at the profits of the partnership (Income Tax Act 2007 (ITA 2007), s 383).

Corporate buyer

Tax relief on interest payable by a company on a loan to acquire a business will normally be available as a deductible expense under the loan relationship legislation contained in the Corporation Tax Act 2009 (CTA 2009), subject to certain restrictions introduced in 2017 (which are complex and outside the scope of this book).

8.4.5 Warranties

Since the buyer does not 'inherit' any of the tax liabilities of the seller of the business (whether the seller is an individual or a company), it does not need the protection of extensive warranties and indemnities in the sale and purchase agreement.

Any warranties that are included are likely to be aimed at eliciting disclosures from the seller, particularly with regard to any concessions or dispensations agreed between the seller and HMRC (eg in relation to benefits provided to employees). The buyer will usually also seek assurances that PAYE, National Insurance and VAT records are complete and up to date.

SHARE ACQUISITIONS

LEARNING OUTCOMES

After reading this chapter you will be able to:

- discuss the nature of a share sale
- describe the typical protections, by way of warranty and otherwise, that a buyer may require in relation to its acquisition of the target company
- explain the application of the FSMA 2000 to a share sale transaction
- understand the compliance aspects of the CA 2006 in the context of a share acquisition
- explain the taxation implications of a share sale for the buyer and seller.

9.1 THE TRANSFER OF SHARES

In a share acquisition the only asset being transferred is the shares of the target company, the effect of the transfer being to transfer ownership of the company. The buyer usually seeks to acquire the entire issued share capital of the target company, thus making it the sole owner of the company, though the buyer can acquire effective control by acquiring a majority holding of the target's shares.

In a share sale and purchase agreement the buyer will seek reassurances both about the actual shares being transferred and about the company over which it will acquire ownership.

9.1.1 Shares

The share sale and purchase agreement will provide for the sale and purchase of the shares within its operative terms (see **4.3.3**). The shares to be acquired will be specified, and if there are a number of sellers, details of their relative shareholdings will normally be contained in a schedule.

In some European and Latin American countries, such as Brazil, ownership of a private limited company is held through 'quotas'. The capital of the company is divided into quotas of either equal or unequal par value. These quotas may be assigned to another party, thereby transferring ownership in the company to the buyer in a similar manner to the transfer of shares. In international acquisitions, the transfer of such quotas is usually referred to as a transfer of shares.

The shares will be expressed as being transferred free from all charges, encumbrances, liens, etc. If the shares of the target are owned by a holding company, it is likely that they will be subject to a charge, and accordingly arrangements should be put in place to ensure their release from the charge prior to the sale.

Shares in a private company registered in England and Wales are likely to be subject to restrictions on transfer contained in the company's articles. It is common for the articles of a private company to oblige a member proposing to transfer its shares to offer them pro rata to the existing members. Although the articles invariably allow for the pre-emption provisions to be overridden by special resolution, it is usually easier for the sellers to waive their rights. The sale and purchase agreement will often contain a clause whereby the sellers agree to waive any pre-emption rights they may have, whether conferred by the articles or otherwise (the rights may be incorporated in a shareholders' agreement rather than in the articles).

In the US, it is more common for share transfer restrictions to be embodied in a shareholders' agreement executed by shareholders holding a majority of the shares of the target company, rather than in its articles.

9.1.2   The company

In taking ownership of the target company, the buyer will indirectly be acquiring all the assets and liabilities in that company. As considered in **Chapter 5**, the buyer will want to seek reassurances about the target company through the provision of warranty statements. Although many of the warranties considered in the context of an asset acquisition will be equally appropriate on a share acquisition, the list of warranties in a share sale and purchase agreement is likely to be longer due to the greater degree of risk which the buyer of shares assumes. Set out below are some of the areas where the buyer will wish to have warranty cover, together with, in each case, the typical warranties sought in the UK.

9.1.2.1   Constitution of the company

The buyer will seek to include the following warranties in relation to the constitution of the company:

(a)   that the statutory books of the company have been properly kept and are accurate and up to date;

(b)   that the memorandum and articles (in the disclosure letter schedule) are true and complete;

(c)   that all documents and returns required to be filed with the Registrar of Companies or the jurisdictional equivalent have been duly filed and were correct;

(d)   that the directors listed in the agreement (usually in a schedule) are the only directors of the company.

9.1.2.2   Accounts

The buyer may seek to include the following warranties in relation to the most recent set of audited accounts:

(a)   that they have been prepared using the same bases and policies of accounting as were used in preparing the accounts for the previous three accounting periods;

(b)   that they comply with the CA 2006 and with all relevant standards set by the accountancy profession and contained in Financial Reporting Standards and Statements of Standard Accounting Practice or the jurisdictional equivalent, and are not affected by any exceptional or non-recurring item;

(c)   that they give a true and fair view of the assets and liabilities (including contingent, unquantified or disputed liabilities) of the company at the date of the balance sheet and of its profits for the relevant accounting period.

The seller is advised to be wary of the scope of warranties relating to the accounts. For example, the seller will often resist the inclusion of a warranty that management accounts are accurate or give a true and fair view. It is arguable that the buyer is not justified in placing much reliance on management accounts, which will have been drawn up for a specific management purpose and will not have been audited.

9.1.2.3 Financial matters

The buyer may seek assurances from the seller that the company has not done any of the following, for example, since the last accounts date:

(a)   incurred any liabilities except in the ordinary course of business;

(b)   incurred or agreed to incur any capital expenditure or disposed of any capital assets;

(c)   paid or declared any dividend or made any other distribution.

The buyer may also seek warranties in relation to the debtors and creditors revealed in the accounts, for example, that the company has paid its creditors in accordance with their credit terms and that the debtors have paid their debts in full. It may also ask for assurances that any amounts owing to the company on completion will be fully recoverable in the ordinary course of business (possibly with a long-stop date of, say, three months) and that no amounts owing by the company on completion have been due for more than a specified period (eg two months).

9.1.2.4 Trading

The buyer may seek warranties in relation to the trading position of the company, for example:

(a)   that the business of the company has been carried on in the ordinary course and that its turnover, financial position or trading position has not deteriorated since the date of the last accounts (the seller should resist the extension of this warranty to include 'trading prospects');

(b)   that the company is not engaged in any litigation or arbitration proceedings as claimant or defendant, and that no such proceedings are pending, threatened or, to the seller's knowledge, likely to arise;

(c)   that the sellers have no knowledge, information or belief that any supplier will cease to supply the company (or substantially reduce supplies) after completion;

(d)   that the sellers have no knowledge, information or belief that any customer will cease to deal with the company (or substantially reduce the level of business) after completion;

(e)   that compliance with the terms of the agreement will not result in a breach of any agreement to which the company is a party, relieve any person from any obligation to the company, or enable any person to determine any right or benefit enjoyed by the company or to exercise any right;

(f)   that the company has obtained all licences and consents required to carry on its business properly and is not in breach of their terms;

(g)   that the company is not a party to any contract or arrangement of an unusual or loss-making nature or which it cannot terminate on 60 days' notice or less;

(h)   that the company has not supplied or manufactured products which, in any material respect, are defective or do not comply with any warranties or representations made by it (whether express or implied);

(i)   that the company has conducted its business in accordance with all applicable laws and regulations.

9.1.2.5 Assets other than land

The buyer may seek warranties in relation to the underlying assets of the company other than land, for example:

(a)   that the company still owns and has good title to all the assets included in the latest audited accounts (except for current assets subsequently sold in the ordinary course of business) and has good title to all assets which it has since acquired;

(b)   that plant, machinery, vehicles, etc are in a good state of repair, and have been properly and regularly maintained;

(c)   that the stock-in-trade of the company is in good condition and capable of being sold in the ordinary course of business by the company at prices contained in its current price list;

(d)   that the stock of raw materials and finished goods held by the company is adequate (and not excessive) in relation to the trading requirements of the business on completion.

The particular warranties that are sought will take into account the nature of the target business and any specific concerns of the buyer.

9.1.2.6   Insurance

The buyer will usually require warranties that full particulars of the company's insurances are included in the disclosure letter, that they are in full force and effect, and that they contain adequate cover against such risks as prudent companies carrying on the same type of business would normally cover by insurance. The buyer will also seek a warranty that no insurance claims are outstanding or pending, and that the seller is not aware of any circumstances likely to give rise to a claim.

9.1.2.7   Intellectual property

Details of patents, trademarks, service marks, design rights and copyrights owned or used by the company will often be contained in the disclosure letter (with copies of agreements relating to these intellectual property rights attached). Warranties will be included that there are no outstanding claims against the company for breach of the intellectual property rights of any other person and that, to the seller's knowledge, the company is not in breach of any such rights in operating the business. The buyer may also require the seller to warrant that it is not aware of any infringement of the intellectual property rights of the company by any third party.

9.1.2.8   Land

The scope of the warranties in relation to land will depend on the extent of the buyer's property investigation and on whether the seller's solicitor is prepared to give certificates of title (see **3.5.6**). The following are some examples of the warranties that may be sought by a buyer in this area:

(a)   the company has good title to each of the properties and has possession or control of all deeds and documents necessary to prove title;

(b)   each property is free from any mortgage, charge, lien or other encumbrance;

(c)   the current use of each property complies with town and country planning legislation, and all necessary planning and building regulation consents have been obtained;

(d)   all obligations, restrictions, conditions and covenants affecting any of the properties (leasehold or freehold) have been observed and performed, and no notice of breach has been received;

(e)   the company has vacant possession of each of the properties;

(f)   there are no outstanding disputes affecting any of the properties and no outstanding orders, notices or demands have been made by local or other authorities;

(g)   each of the properties is in good and substantial repair and fit for the purposes for which it is presently used;

(h)   each of the properties is free from any notice, inhibition, caution, land charge, or local land charge not of general application to the area.

9.1.2.9   Employees

When control of a company is acquired by share transfer, this has no direct effect on the employees of the target company. There is no change of employer in these circumstances and the employees retain exactly the same rights against their employer company, even though ownership of its shares has changed hands. In the UK, the fact of the share acquisition will not of itself give rise to any employment claims as there is no dismissal either at common law or within the statutory definition. All the contractual rights of the employees are therefore preserved, TUPE 2006 do not apply and, unlike on an asset acquisition, there is no obligation for either the buyer or the seller to inform and consult with trade unions.

As the buyer will indirectly assume liability for the target's workforce, it will require confirmation of the particulars of all directors and employees, including dates of commencement of employment and remuneration (including bonuses, etc). The buyer will normally insist on a warranty that the particulars provided by the seller (either in a schedule to the agreement or in the disclosure letter) are true and complete.

The buyer may also seek warranties as to the following:

(a)   that all subsisting contracts of service can be determined at any time by the company on three months' notice or less (this warranty should prompt disclosures of any fixed-term or 'evergreen' contracts, or contracts with a substantial notice requirement);

(b)   that the company has not given notice terminating the employment of any employee;

(c)   that no employee of the company is entitled to give notice terminating their employment as a result of the agreement (this warranty should 'flush out' any 'golden parachute' clauses);

(d)   that there are no outstanding claims against the company by any current or former employee;

(e)   that no changes have been made to the terms and conditions of employment of any employee over a specified period (eg within three or six months of completion).

Lastly, the sale and purchase agreement may provide for new directors to be appointed, or for existing directors to enter into fresh service contracts on completion (the terms will usually be agreed prior to completion and annexed to the contract).

In other jurisdictions, the appropriate warranties to be sought will depend on the relevant employment regulations. For example, in Germany, any termination of employment must comply with the Termination Protection Act, which provides that the termination must be 'socially justified' based on the person, their conduct or compelling business requirements. In addition, works councils have to be informed of the proposed termination before it occurs, and failure to do so will make the termination invalid.

9.1.2.10   Pensions

Many of the pension considerations discussed in **Chapter 8** in the context of an asset acquisition are equally applicable to a share acquisition. The buyer of shares will similarly seek reassurances about the pension arrangements for the employees of the target company, the precise warranties sought being dependent upon how the company has organised its pension provision.

In most jurisdictions, the pension fund is a separate entity from the target company, and is administered by trustees who are obliged to act in accordance with a trust deed or jurisdictional equivalent. The trustees will not be parties to the sale and purchase agreement, so suitable arrangements must be made to notify them of the change in ownership of the company. The buyer will acquire the target company with its inherent obligations in relation to payments into its pension scheme. Therefore, the buyer will seek appropriate reassurances about the current state of the pension scheme, including, for example (if the scheme is a final salary scheme), whether there is a deficit or a surplus in the fund. If there is a significant deficit, the buyer may ask the seller to make a payment into the fund, or, alternatively, seek to reduce the purchase price of the target. Where the scheme is in surplus, on the other hand, the seller may seek an increase in the purchase price to reflect this.

If the target company does not have its own discrete pension scheme but is a member of a group scheme (see **8.3.6.2**), the sale and purchase agreement must also provide for the transfer of the target company employees' pension entitlement. The parties must agree a basis for making a transfer payment from the group scheme to the buyer's scheme. The buyer should insist on a guarantee from the seller to make up any shortfall if the seller cannot procure that the trustees transfer the agreed amount.

Details of a discrete pension scheme or provisions relating to a transfer payment out of a group scheme are normally included in schedules to the sale and purchase agreement.

9.1.2.11 Taxation

Most tax matters will be dealt with separately, either in a deed of tax indemnity or by means of tax covenants. Whichever method is employed, the seller will often be obliged to compensate the buyer for any breaches on an indemnity basis (see **9.3**).

Where, however, the buyer is keen to elicit disclosures from the seller, it will include some tax warranties; problems may then be revealed which it is able to use as a lever to renegotiate the purchase price (or which may even prompt it to withdraw from the acquisition). In particular, the buyer will want confirmation that the company is not in dispute with HMRC in the UK, or the jurisdictional equivalent elsewhere, and has complied with obligations, inter alia, to file returns, make payments and operate the PAYE system in the UK, or complied with equivalent obligations in other jurisdictions. The buyer may also require a warranty that the latest accounts make full provision or reserve for all taxation which could be assessed on the company in respect of the period covered by the accounts.

9.1.2.12 Information disclosed

Two controversial warranties that a buyer may seek relate to information disclosed by the seller to the buyer. First, the buyer may include in the initial draft of the agreement a warranty that all information about the target company provided to the buyer or its advisers prior to the parties entering into the contract is true and accurate in all material respects. This is clearly a wide-ranging warranty which would involve the difficulty of identifying the information which the seller and its advisers have passed to the buyer. A compromise might be for the warranty to be restricted to information contained in the disclosure letter.

Secondly, the buyer may seek to impose a warranty that the seller has disclosed everything which might materially affect the value of the shares, or which might influence a buyer in deciding whether to proceed with the acquisition. This 'catch-all' warranty should be resisted by the seller on the basis that it would cover matters which the buyer can be expected to find out for itself (eg information in the public domain) and information which the seller may not realise is significant.

Such a warranty obligation would be unusual in a civil code jurisdiction. Under the duty of good faith, each party to the transaction is under an obligation to inform the other party of any material information that it could not obtain itself. An obligation relating to information which it could find out itself, or where the materiality of such information could not be known to the seller, would be perceived as unfair and, as such, void.

9.1.3 Directors and senior managers

Directors of the target company who are also employees, and senior managers, are subject to the same employment obligations as all other employees; however, their important position in the company requires that the buyer gives them careful consideration. The strengths and weaknesses of the management team should be analysed, and the buyer should identify those managers and directors it considers important to the future success of the company and those whom it does not wish to retain. Where the buyer is a company, part of its strategy for improving the performance of the company may be to introduce some of its own managers or managers from other parts of the group. Similarly, individual buyers may insist on becoming directors on completion. As early as possible in negotiating the acquisition deal, the buyer should consider how the key managers will be retained and what will be the costs and consequences of dispensing with others.

9.1.3.1 Removing 'surplus' directors and managers

The buyer should check whether the articles of the target company give weighted voting rights to directors on any resolution to remove them as directors or to change the article conferring those rights. Under English law, such provisions may have the effect of entrenching the directors by preventing their removal by ordinary resolution under s 168 of the CA 2006.

The buyer will often be concerned about the cost to the target company (and, therefore, indirectly, to itself) of removing directors and managers, and the possibility that those dismissed may damage the company by their activities after leaving.

Cost to the target company

The target company may face substantial claims for wrongful dismissal from directors or managers who are removed prior to the end of a fixed term or without proper notice. The cost of removing a director who is, for example, in the early stages of a five-year fixed-term contract which entitles them to a lucrative package of salary and benefits, may be prohibitive. Similarly, it may prove expensive to remove a director or manager who has a so-called 'evergreen' or 'rolling' contract. This is a contract for a fixed term which, on each anniversary of the commencement date, is automatically renewed for a further fixed term; automatic renewal will be avoided only if the employer gives notice before the anniversary of the commencement date that the contract will determine at the end of the current period.

Under English law, for directors who have been granted (before 1 October 2007) service contracts for over five years, or (from 1 October 2007) service contracts for over two years, the buyer should check that the term was authorised by ordinary resolution of the members in accordance with either s 319 of the CA 1985, in the case of the pre-October 2007 contracts, or s 188 of the CA 2006, in the case of those contracts entered into on or after 1 October 2007. In the absence of such approval, the contract can be terminated by the company at any time on reasonable notice.

In the UK, payments to directors in lieu of notice or payments of damages to directors may be treated as earnings and subject to income tax. In reaching any settlement in relation to a director, the likely tax treatment should be considered and any amount 'grossed up' to the extent appropriate to take account of this liability. On the other hand, in determining damages or an agreed settlement amount, significant reduction may be made to take account of accelerated receipt and the duty on the employee to mitigate their loss by seeking suitable alternative employment.

Restrictive covenants

The buyer should check whether the service contracts of the directors and managers of the target contain effective restraints on their activities after termination of their contracts. Typical clauses include covenants by the employee not to work in a competing business and not to solicit or entice away customers of the target company. The employee may also be prohibited from using or disclosing confidential information about the business of the target. In the absence of express terms, few post-termination restraints are implied into an employment contract (there is an implied term, however, that the employee will not reveal highly confidential information).

In the UK, restraints of this nature are valid and enforceable at common law only if they protect a legitimate trade interest of the employer (eg they protect the goodwill of the business), are not against the public interest and are reasonable between the parties, as was recently confirmed in *Tillman v Egon Zehnder* [2019] UKSC 32. A non-competition covenant, for example, is likely to be considered void as being in restraint of trade unless its scope is limited in terms of duration and the geographical area which it covers. Similarly, a non-solicitation clause should be limited to customers who have recently dealt with the target (eg within the previous 12 months). It is now well established that clauses preventing the disclosure of information after termination can be effective only in relation to highly confidential information or trade secrets (*Faccenda Chicken Ltd v Fowler* [1986] IRLR 69, CA).

If any of the directors who are leaving are also selling shares in the target, the buyer should ensure that they agree to restrictive covenants in the sale and purchase agreement (see **5.10**). The courts will more readily uphold restraints which have been freely negotiated between parties to an acquisition than those included in employment contracts.

Even if restrictive covenants are prima facie valid, they will not survive a repudiatory breach of contract by the employer. This is on the basis that, by committing such a breach, the employer is indicating that it no longer considers itself to be bound by the contract and cannot, therefore, hold the other party to obligations contained within it. There is a danger here for buyers proposing that the target dismisses some of the management team; if dismissals are carried out in breach of contract, this may discharge the former employees from compliance with restrictive covenants (*General Billposting Co Ltd v Atkinson* [1909] AC 118, HL). Even if the covenant purports to enable the employer to enforce the covenant whatever the reason for the termination of the contract, this will not be effective (*Briggs v Oates* [1991] 1 All ER 411). Some directors' service contracts, however, permit the company to pay them salary in lieu of notice. Since, in this event, the company is not in breach of contract in terminating the contract without notice, it should be able to rely on post-termination covenants.

9.1.3.2   Retaining directors and managers

The buyer should consult with those directors and managers whom it is keen to retain as early as possible in the negotiations for the acquisition of the target company (subject to considerations of confidentiality). It may be able to negotiate a term in the sale and purchase agreement that certain key personnel enter into new service contracts on completion. If a director or manager chooses to leave, however, the rights of the parties will, inter alia, depend on the terms of any existing contract.

'Golden parachute' clauses

A director's service contract may include a so-called 'golden parachute' clause, entitling the director to treat themselves as dismissed without notice on a change of control of their employer company and to receive a specified payment from the company in this event.

A disadvantage for the director of receiving a contractual payment is that it is taxable in full as income. The first £30,000 of a claim for damages for breach of contract or a settlement of such a claim would, in contrast, be tax free within s 403 of the Income Tax (Earnings and Pensions) Act 2003.

'Garden leave' clauses

A 'garden leave' clause is intended to enable the employer to hold an employee to their contract if, for example, the employee attempts to resign in breach of contract. Although the employer must continue to pay the employee for the notice period, the employer will not usually intend to provide the employee with work. The advantage to the employer is that the employee is unable to work for anyone else during the notice period and must comply with all obligations of confidentiality, etc which apply during the contract, which can be more extensive than those imposed after termination of the contract. However, the enforceability of clauses of this nature is still open to question, particularly where the employer refuses to provide work for the employee.

9.2 REGULATORY PROVISIONS IN THE UK

On a share acquisition in the UK, consideration has to be given to relevant provisions of the Financial Services and Markets Act 2000 (FSMA 2000) and the Companies Act 2006 (CA 2006).

9.2.1 Compliance with the Financial Services and Markets Act 2000

Financial services regulation in the UK has undergone a major overhaul in recent years. The regime set out in FSMA 2000 was updated by the Financial Services Act 2012, which created three new regulatory bodies and abolished the previous regulator, the FSA.

The Financial Policy Committee (FPC) sits within the Bank of England (BoE) and considers macro-prudential issues, that is, affecting economic and financial stability. The Prudential Regulation Authority (PRA) is a subsidiary of the BoE, and it is responsible for the micro-prudential regulation of the investment and financial services sector, including banks, building societies, insurers and certain investment firms (including certain private equity funds – see **10.1**). The Financial Conduct Authority (FCA) is responsible for the conduct of business regulation of all firms (including those also regulated by the PRA) and is responsible for market regulation. It is also responsible for the prudential regulation of firms not regulated by the PRA.

In addition to creating new regulatory bodies, the legislation gives additional powers to the new bodies, including enabling the FCA to block the imminent launch of financial products, to require firms to withdraw or amend misleading financial promotions, and to publish details of enforcement proceedings.

9.2.1.1 Financial promotions and unsolicited calls

The proposal to acquire the shares of a private company may arise in a number of ways: the seller may, for example, have a particular buyer in contemplation, or the initial approach may come from the buyer. It may be, however, that the seller is searching for potential buyers for the company and wishes to bring the possibility of a sale to their attention. In these circumstances, the seller and its advisers must be careful not to contravene the provisions of the FSMA 2000 relating to financial promotions and unsolicited calls.

The basic restriction

Section 21 of the FSMA 2000 makes it a criminal offence for any person other than an authorised person to 'communicate an invitation or inducement to engage in investment activity' unless its contents have been approved by an authorised person. Any investment agreement entered into as a result of the breach is rendered unenforceable (although the court has discretion to permit enforcement in certain circumstances).

What sort of activities are covered by the restriction?

The restriction would seem to include approaches by a seller to potential buyers in the hope of inducing them to enter into negotiations for the acquisition of shares in the target company. The consequences of breach are serious, so the seller should seek the approval of an authorised person if there is any possibility of the section applying. An example of an authorised person used in these circumstances would be a merchant banker.

It should be noted that the Financial Services and Markets Act 2023 introduces additional regulations governing when and how an authorised person may approve financial promotions for unauthorised persons. The additional regulations are intended to ensure that approval for financial promotions is provided only after extensive enquiries have been made by an authorised person.

Where there is a sale of a body corporate, an exemption from the restrictions on financial promotions is provided by Art 62 of the FSMA 2000 (Financial Promotion) Order 2005 (SI 2005/1529). The conditions under which this exemption applies are the same as those mentioned at **9.2.1.2** below in relation to the exclusion from regulated activities under Art 70 of the FSMA 2000 (Regulated Activities) Order 2001 (SI 2001/544).

9.2.1.2 Regulated activities

If a firm finds that it is involving itself in 'regulated activities', it must obtain authorisation, direct from the Financial Conduct Authority, for each specific type of activity with which it is involved.

'Regulated activities' are activities involving defined financial matters as a stand-alone service. Although advising on and arranging a share purchase would constitute 'regulated activities' as defined by s 22 of the FSMA 2000, there are a number of helpful exclusions under the FSMA 2000 (Regulated Activities) Order 2001. The most significant exclusion in the acquisitions context is provided by Art 70. This excludes from regulation activities carried on in connection with the sale of a body corporate if that sale will result in the buyer owning 50% or more of the company's voting shares, or if the transaction is designed to enable the buyer to obtain day-to-day control of the company's affairs. Most company acquisitions will clearly fall within the parameters of this exclusion.

9.2.1.3 Comparison with the United States

In the US, there are no equivalent provisions covering communications relating to investment activity. These concerns are primarily addressed in the US securities laws, which prohibit the public offer or sale of securities unless such offer or sale is registered with the Securities and Exchange Commission or falls within one of many exemptions. Federal and state laws also regulate activities with respect to certain products, such as insurance and investment property, and activities, such as brokerage services.

9.2.2 Compliance with the Companies Act 2006

9.2.2.1 The financial assistance rules

Under s 151 of the Companies Act 1985, all companies registered in England and Wales were prohibited from giving financial assistance for the purchase of their own shares. The rules were complex in their application and extended to financial assistance given before, at the same time as, and after the acquisition. The application of these financial assistance rules meant that arrangements such as the target company's assets being offered as security for loans to buy shares in the target, or parts of the purchase price being left outstanding at completion, could have serious consequences, including rendering the agreement for the purchase of shares void. As such provisions are often an integral part of a private company acquisition, a special relaxation procedure (known as 'the whitewash procedure') was available to authorise financial assistance for the acquisition of shares in the context of a private company. The prohibition on private companies giving financial assistance for the purchase of their shares, and the associated whitewash procedure, were abolished by Ch 2 of Pt 18 of the CA 2006.

However, the prohibition on giving financial assistance is retained for public companies under s 678 of the CA 2006, and s 679(1) restates the previous prohibition on the provision of financial assistance by a public company subsidiary for the purpose of an acquisition of shares in its private holding company. The exceptions from the prohibition are set out in s 678(2) (the principal purpose exceptions), s 681 (unconditional exceptions) and s 682 (conditional exceptions) of the CA 2006.

In accordance with EC directives, all EU Member States restrict the ability of a target company or its subsidiaries to give financial assistance in connection with the acquisition of the target's shares, at least where the company is a public-type company, such as an NV in the Netherlands and an AG in Germany. In a few jurisdictions, such as France, the restrictions apply to all companies, private and public, though some jurisdictions, such as Germany, provide that a company with limited liability (GmbH) can give such assistance but usually only from retained earnings.

There is no concept of financial assistance under the various corporate laws in the US, although disclosure requirements may arise where such assistance is given.

9.2.2.2 Directors' interests

A director of a company registered in England and Wales who is directly or indirectly interested in a contract or proposed contract with the company should declare their interest to the board in accordance with s 177 of the CA 2006 and comply with any relevant provisions of the company's articles (eg restricting the director from voting or counting in the quorum of a board meeting discussing the contract).

On completion of a share acquisition, the target company must hold a board meeting in order effectively to transfer control of the newly-acquired company (see **7.3.3.2**). If a director has any interest in the proposed acquisition, this may give rise to a requirement to declare their interest (unless a general notice has already been given or the directors ought to have already have been aware of the interest – CA 2006, s 177). This may arise where a director of the target company (or of its holding company) is also a party to the sale and purchase agreement or connected with such a party.

Where a director is a party to any share or asset acquisition, consideration should also be given to the wider considerations of directors' duties.

If a director, or a person 'connected' with a director (this includes families and companies with which the director is associated), is buying a substantial non-cash asset from or selling such an asset to the company, the approval of the members by ordinary resolution is required (CA 2006, s 190) (see **7.3.3.3**). The requirement for authorisation under s 190 of the CA 2006 applies to both asset and share acquisitions but is often hard to identify on a share acquisition. Consider, for example, the following transactions:

EXAMPLE 1

A Ltd is acquiring the entire share capital of Target Ltd. B is a shareholder in Target Limited and a director of A Ltd.

A Ltd is acquiring a non-cash asset (the shares) from one of its directors. If B's shares in Target Ltd are 'substantial', an ordinary resolution of the shareholders of A Ltd is required to authorise the transaction.

EXAMPLE 2

A Ltd is acquiring the entire share capital of Target Limited. B is a director of A Ltd. C, who is B's son, is a shareholder in Target Limited.

Consent of the shareholders of A Ltd may again be required because A Ltd is acquiring a non-cash asset from a person 'connected' with one of its directors (the definition of 'connected persons' for this purpose is contained in s 252(2)(a) and s 253(2)(c) of the CA 2006).

EXAMPLE 3

D Ltd sells shares in Target Limited to E Ltd. F is a director of D Ltd and is also a 30% shareholder in E Ltd.

D Ltd is disposing of a non-cash asset (the shares) to a person 'connected' with one of its directors. The definition of 'connected persons' for this purpose is contained in s 252(2)(b) and s 254(2)(a) of the CA 2006. E Ltd is a company 'connected' with the director by virtue of F's 30% shareholding. If D Ltd's shares in Target Limited are 'substantial', consent of the shareholders of D Ltd is required by s 190.

In other jurisdictions, directors are under similar obligations. Directors of US companies owe a duty of care and loyalty to the company. Under these duties, a director must act in an informed and deliberate manner and refrain from taking actions that are adverse to the company and its shareholders. This would include any action taken purely for the directors' own benefit.

9.2.2.3 Payments to directors in connection with the transfer of shares by way of compensation for loss of office

Payments made to a director of a company registered in England and Wales in connection with a transfer of the company's shares by way of compensation for loss of office may be governed by s 219 of the CA 2006. Any proposed payment for loss of office in connection with a transfer of shares in the company (or its subsidiary) which results from an acquisition must first be approved by an ordinary resolution of the holders of the shares to which the purchase relates.

A director who receives a sum in breach of these requirements holds it on trust for the shareholders who have sold their shares as a result of the offer. Section 219 does not apply to bona fide payments by way of damages for breach of contract.

It is also provided (s 216(2)) that if the price which is offered to the director for their shares is in excess of the price obtainable by other holders of like shares, the excess is deemed to be a payment for loss of office. This provision is designed to prevent compensation to a director being 'dressed up' as part of the purchase price of their shares.

9.2.2.4 Service contracts for directors

After a target company has been acquired, or as part of the completion arrangements, new directors may be appointed and granted service contracts, or existing directors may be awarded fresh contracts. Under English law, if these contracts are to last for more than two years, consent of the members by ordinary resolution is required under s 188 of the CA 2006.

9.2.2.5 Interests of employees

Section 172 of the CA 2006 obliges directors to have regard to the interests of, amongst other stakeholders, the company's employees in general. The directors of a target company should therefore try to strike a balance between the interests of the members and those of the employees when taking decisions relating to the share acquisition (eg at the completion board meeting). The directors owe this duty to the company and not to the employees, who are unable, therefore, to take any direct action to enforce it.

9.3   ACQUIRING TAX LIABILITIES

On a share acquisition, the buyer is acquiring an entity with a tax history and with all its tax liabilities intact. This obliges the buyer to carry out a more detailed investigation into the tax affairs of the target than on an asset acquisition (when tax liabilities remain with the seller) and to seek protection in the sale and purchase agreement by negotiating numerous warranties and indemnities. In some cases, the buyer may be attracted to a particular company because of its tax status; the target company may, for example, have unrelieved trading losses which the buyer intends to use to shelter future profits. In these circumstances, the buyer would wish to ensure that nothing has happened in the past which would mean that anticipated reliefs are prejudiced by the change in control of the company.

9.3.1 Warranties

Warranties are appropriate to deal with compliance requirements of the target, such as the proper submission of returns and the correct implementation of the PAYE system or its jurisdictional equivalent.

Tax warranties will also be used to obtain as much information as possible about the tax history of the company. This tax history may be relevant to potential future liabilities of the target. For example, the buyer will want to know the base cost of chargeable assets owned by the target, particularly if it is intended that the target will sell assets after completion.

9.3.2 Indemnities

The buyer will be keen to ensure that the target company has accounted for all outstanding taxes and has no hidden tax liabilities. Appropriate indemnities will be included in the sale and purchase agreement to cover specific tax charges which may arise over and above those provided for in the accounts and which are referable to the seller's period of ownership. Tax indemnities may be incorporated in a separate deed (often referred to as the 'Tax Deed' or 'Tax Covenant'), or embodied in a schedule to the sale and purchase agreement. It is helpful if the tax warranties are in a separate part of the sale and purchase agreement as a different (longer) limitation period will apply for claims brought by the buyer under these warranties.

In the UK, tax indemnities, whether in the body of the agreement or in a separate deed, should be expressed to be in favour of the buyer and not the target company. This avoids the target being assessed to tax on an indemnity payment (see *Procter (Inspector of Taxes) v Zim Properties Ltd* [1985] STC 90); instead, the price of the target will be adjusted for capital tax purposes if the liability crystallises (see **5.7.2**).

9.3.3 Redress for loss of reliefs

The buyer may also negotiate an indemnity provision to enable it to obtain redress from the seller if expected reliefs, such as the target's ability to carry forward unrelieved losses, are forfeited on the change in ownership of the target as a result of events prior to completion.

9.3.3.1 Carry forward of trading losses

The target company may have unused trading losses which the buyer intends to offset against future profits of the company. Section 45 of the CTA 2010 normally allows trading losses of a company to be set against future profits. For accounting periods beginning on or after 1 April 2017, this permits deduction of up to a maximum of £5 million initially, in the form of a deduction allowance, plus a further deduction of 50% of any remaining profits in excess of the £5 million deduction allowance. Losses may be set against future profits of the same trade in respect of losses arising prior to 1 April 2017 and, in most cases, against total profits in respect of losses arising after 1 April 2017. Sections 673 and 674 of the CTA 2010 restrict this right if there is a major change in the nature or conduct of the target company's trade within a five-year period which includes a change of ownership.

For accounting periods ending on or after 1 April 2020, amendments to Part 7ZA of the Corporation Tax Act 2010 mean that the £5 million deduction allowance can also be set against chargeable gains. Furthermore, from 1 April 2020, companies making chargeable gains will only be able to offset up to 50% of those gains using carried forward capital losses.

The buyer should seek assurances from the seller that there has been no such major change in the nature and conduct of the trade before the acquisition, and must keep an eye on the position after the acquisition. What, then, amounts to a 'major change in the nature and conduct of the trade'? Section 673(4) states that it would include a major change in the type of property dealt in, or services or facilities provided, in the trade, or a major change in customers, outlets or markets of the trade.

9.4 TAXATION ON A SHARE ACQUISITION IN THE UK

In the UK, the tax position on a share acquisition is relatively straightforward as the transaction involves the sale and purchase of only one type of asset – the shares.

The shares will be a 'chargeable asset', and the seller will be liable to tax (either CGT for an individual or corporation tax for a company) when the seller disposes of a chargeable asset (ie the shares) at a price higher than its value when the seller acquired it.

9.4.1 Liability of the seller on the sale of shares

9.4.1.1 Individuals

Subject to available reliefs and exemptions, an individual shareholder pays CGT on the gain arising from the disposal of their shares at the rate of either 10% (on gains falling within their available basic rate tax band) or 20% (on gains in excess of the basic rate tax band) for the tax year 2023/24. The date of the disposal for CGT purposes is the date on which the parties enter into the acquisition agreement (or, if the agreement is conditional, the time when the condition is fulfilled) and not, if later, the date of completion.

9.4.1.2 Companies

A company which sells a shareholding, the disposal of which does not qualify for exemption from tax as a disposal of a substantial shareholding, pays corporation tax on any chargeable gain which arises on the disposal of the shares at the rate of 19%, 25% or its marginal rate of tax (as explained at **8.4.3.1**). The company pays the tax nine months after the end of the accounting period, unless it is a large company.

For large companies (those with taxable profit of at least £1,500,000), corporation tax will be paid in instalments, calculated according to the anticipated final tax bill for the accounting period. The first instalment is payable six months and 13 days into the accounting period. There are provisions for HMRC to repay tax to a company that believes it has over-estimated the instalments that become due. Interest will be payable on late paid instalments and HMRC will pay interest on overpaid tax.

9.4.2 Reducing the charge

There are a number of provisions in the TCGA 1992 enabling shareholders selling shares to exempt either the whole or part of the gain, or at least to postpone the occasion of the charge. There may also be scope for corporate sellers to take steps prior to entering into the contract which have the effect of reducing liability on the disposal.

9.4.2.1 Business asset disposal relief

Business asset disposal relief (previously known as entrepreneurs' relief) may be available where the share sale represents a 'qualifying business disposal' for an *individual* seller.

If the conditions for the relief are met (see **8.4.2.1**), the seller's gains on the sale of the target's shares are reduced by any losses made as part of the disposal, and any net gain is charged to tax at 10%. The relief is subject to a lifetime restriction, however, of £1 million of qualifying net gains realised after 11 March 2020.

Deferral relief on reinvestment in EIS shares

This relief will avail an *individual* who, for example, disposes of shares of any kind and reinvests the chargeable gain by subscribing for shares which qualify under the EIS. The individual's chargeable gain on the disposal of the original shares (up to the subscription cost) is deferred until they dispose of the EIS-qualifying shares. The EIS shares must be acquired within one year before or three years after the original disposal. The seller can apply any available business asset disposal relief before deferring any remaining gain by investing in the EIS shares.

The relief will not avail a corporate shareholder.

9.4.2.2   Emigration

An *individual* seller who sells shares whilst neither resident nor ordinarily resident in the UK can avoid a charge to CGT. The requirements for an individual to establish that they are neither resident nor ordinarily resident are set out in s 10A of the TCGA 1992 (as inserted by the Finance Act 1998 and amended by the Finance Act 2013) and are stringent. The rules are outside the scope of this book.

9.4.2.3   Share for share exchanges (TCGA 1992, s 135)

Section 135 of the TCGA 1992 provides another form of roll-over type relief where the seller of shares (*individual or corporate*) receives shares issued by an acquiring company as consideration for the sale.

Nature of the relief

The effect of the relief is to roll any gain on the target company's shares into the shares in the acquiring company which are issued in consideration. The seller pays no capital tax on the sale of the target company's shares as it is treated as not making a disposal at this stage; it is deemed, however, to have acquired the consideration shares at the same time and for the same price as the original shares. The effect is to postpone any CGT or, in the case of a corporate seller, corporation tax until the disposal of the new shares.

This relief cannot be used in conjunction with the annual exemption.

Conditions for the relief

The buyer must hold a minimum stake in the target   For the relief to operate, the buyer must hold over 25% of the ordinary shares of the target company, either before or in consequence of the share exchange. Alternatively, the exchange must result from a general offer made to the shareholders of the target conditional on the buyer obtaining control of the target.

The exchange must be effected for bona fide commercial reasons   Section 137 of the TCGA 1992 provides that, for s 135 relief to be available, the exchange must be effected for 'bona fide commercial reasons' and must not form part of a scheme or arrangement of which the main purpose, or one of the main purposes, is to avoid CGT or corporation tax. This provision does not, however, affect the availability of the relief to a shareholder who holds 5% or less of the shares or debentures (or any class of shares or debentures) in the target company (s 137(2)).

A clearance procedure is contained in s 138, under which HMRC can be asked to confirm that it is satisfied that the exchange is effected for bona fide commercial reasons and not for a tax avoidance motive. It must notify its decision within 30 days of the application for clearance, unless it requires further information. Although it is clearly in the seller's interest to obtain a clearance, the section provides that the application for clearance must be made either by the target company or by the acquiring company. Another curious feature of the procedure is that clearance from HMRC does not guarantee that relief will be granted; it confirms that s 137 will not prevent the relief, but not that the conditions for the relief are met.

Other paper-for-paper exchanges

Relief is generally available in the same way if the shares in the target company are exchanged for debentures or loan notes issued by the acquiring company. There are two caveats, however: first, special rules apply to certain debentures which come within the definition of 'qualifying corporate bonds' (these rules, which are contained in s 116 of the TCGA 1992, are outside the scope of this book); secondly, HMRC is unlikely to give advance clearance where loan notes issued in exchange can be redeemed by the holder within six months of issue. Subject to this, it may suit a seller to receive staggered payments (loan notes will often be redeemable at six-monthly intervals), thereby effectively enabling it to pay the CGT or corporation tax in instalments.

9.4.2.4 Exemption for company gains on substantial shareholdings

The Finance Act 2002 introduced legislation to facilitate corporate restructuring. The effect of the legislation was to exempt from tax capital gains arising on the disposal by corporate shareholders of substantial shareholdings in trading companies. From April 2017, the exemption has been reformed by, amongst other things, removing the original 'trading company' condition, so allowing a wider use of the exemption within groups of companies and by institutional investors. Since the reforms, the main conditions attached to the provisions are as follows:

(a)   The selling company must have held at least 10% of the ordinary share capital of the company being disposed of for at least 12 consecutive months in the six years prior to the sale.

(b)   The company whose shares are being disposed of must be a trading company or qualifying holding company throughout the shareholding period and, if the disposal is to a connected person, immediately after the disposal. (The provision extends to cover gains only (ie losses are not allowable) on shares in a company which is not a qualifying trading or holding company immediately after the disposal by reason only of it ceasing to trade/being put into liquidation at the date of disposal, and, where the disposal is to an unconnected person, there is no requirement that the company sold meet the trading condition immediately after the disposal.)

   A qualifying holding company is a company the activities of which, together with those of its 51% subsidiaries, do not to any substantial extent include non-trading activities.

(c)   The extension of the exemption is broader in the case of companies owned by qualifying institutional investors, where there is no requirement that the company sold be a trading company or qualifying holding company. Gains/losses are fully exempt where the target is owned as to 80% by qualifying institutional investors, and there is proportional relief for ownership between 25% and 80%.

It should be noted that although the test for 'substantial shareholding' is measured by reference to ordinary shares only, if the test is satisfied, relief will be available in relation to disposals of any class of, or interest in, shares.

9.4.3 How is the seller taxed when the consideration is deferred?

It is common for some part of the purchase price to be left outstanding on completion. The seller may have agreed to receive payment by instalments, or to the buyer retaining a specified amount as security for breaches of warranty. The price may even be determinable by reference to future profits (an 'earn out', see **4.3.4.2**). What, then, are the tax implications of such arrangements?

9.4.3.1 The general rule

The general rule, stated in s 48 of the TCGA 1992, is that even if some part of the consideration is deferred, CGT (or corporation tax) is payable on the total consideration by reference to the date of the sale. This applies even if the seller has only a contingent right to receive part of the price (although, if the amount is uncertain, special rules apply, see **9.4.3.3**). The section does provide, however, that if the seller does not in fact receive the full amount of the deferred consideration, an appropriate adjustment will be made to the tax payable, thus entitling the seller to a tax refund.

The contingent liability which the seller has to the buyer in respect of warranties and indemnities will not affect the calculation of the gain. However, any payment which the seller makes to the buyer after completion under a warranty or indemnity will have the effect of reducing the proceeds of sale and, consequently, the gain for capital tax purposes (see **5.7**).

9.4.3.2 Payment of the consideration by instalments

Where the consideration is payable in instalments over a period exceeding 18 months, the tax may be paid by instalments at the option of the taxpayer, who must agree the instalment schedule with HMRC.

9.4.3.3 Where the amount of deferred consideration is uncertain

The tax position is complicated if the amount of the deferred consideration cannot be determined on completion; the most obvious example is on an 'earn out', where the total amount payable by the buyer depends on the profits earned by the target company in the two or three years following completion.

Following the English case of *Marren (Inspector of Taxes) v Ingles* [1980] 3 All ER 95, HMRC charges tax on the basis of the consideration actually received at the time of the disposal plus a current valuation by HMRC of the right to receive the future consideration. It regards this contingent right to future consideration as a future right to something which may be recovered (*chose in action*) which is itself a chargeable asset. Thus, when the seller receives the deferred consideration, it is treated as disposing of the chose in action and may face a further charge to CGT (or corporation tax).

Although no HMRC guidance has yet been published on the point, it is thought that the disposal of the chose in action will not constitute a qualifying business disposal for the purposes of business asset disposal relief, so an individual seller will only be able to claim this relief, if available, to reduce the charge to CGT on the gain made as at the date of completion of the acquisition.

Consider, for example, an individual seller who disposes of their shares this year and who has agreed to receive £250,000 on completion plus 20% of profits (as defined) of the target for the next two years; the base cost of the seller's shares is £30,000.

In calculating the capital gain on the disposal of shares, HMRC will deduct the base cost of the shares (£30,000) from the consideration received on completion (£250,000) plus its valuation of the seller's right to the deferred consideration.

The 20% of profits of the target for the next two years is treated as the seller's right to the deferred consideration. HMRC will estimate the value of this right as, say, £200,000. In this example, this would produce a gain of £420,000, which may be subject to applicable reliefs, such as business asset disposal relief.

When the individual seller receives the deferred consideration (at the end of the two-year period), they are treated as making a chargeable disposal of a chose in action (ie their right to receive that deferred consideration). A further gain may arise, resulting in a subsequent CGT payment being made.

Let us assume that the consideration received at the end of the two-year period is, in fact, £350,000. The individual seller's gain is arrived at by deducting from this figure the base cost of the chose in action (ie £200,000) to produce a gain of £150,000. Again, this gain may be reduced by available reliefs, though as mentioned above this will not be a qualifying business disposal for business asset disposal relief.

If the amount of deferred consideration received by the seller is less than the value placed on it by HMRC, a loss will accrue to the seller on the disposal of the chose in action. A capital loss can, of course, be relieved if the seller makes gains in the future against which the loss can be set. In addition, a recent measure allows an individual seller to elect for a loss arising in these circumstances to be treated for CGT purposes as though it arose in an earlier year (in practice, the seller will generally elect for the loss to be treated as having arisen in the year of the original disposal of shares).

The rule in *Marren (Inspector of Taxes) v Ingles* applies where the consideration is unascertainable at the time of completion. It would not apply if, for example, some part of the consideration is left outstanding pending the drawing up of completion accounts. In this case, although the consideration is not known on completion, the information is available for it to be ascertained.

9.4.3.4   Deferred consideration satisfied in shares

Where the deferred consideration is to be satisfied by the acquiring company issuing shares to the seller, the seller can elect to treat the chose in action as a security for capital tax purposes, with the result that it should not be charged to tax in respect of the deferred consideration until disposal of the shares issued in satisfaction of this deferred element. Instead, roll-over relief on a share for share exchange is available, provided the seller does not have the option to take cash instead.

9.4.4   Tax implications for the buyer

9.4.4.1   Stamp duty

In the UK, the buyer pays stamp duty on the price paid for the shares, which also forms their base cost for CGT (or, in the case of a company, corporation tax) purposes.

If the price paid for the shares is over £1,000, the buyer pays stamp duty at the rate of 0.5% of the consideration, rounded up to the nearest £5. The buyer should present the stock transfer forms for stamping within 30 days of completion. Where completion accounts are to be drawn up, the buyer should present the stock transfer forms to the Stamp Office within 30 days but undertake to pay the duty when the price has been determined. Stamp duty reserve tax (SDRT) is chargeable (at the rate of 0.5% of the consideration) on an agreement to sell shares. The tax is payable on the seventh day of the month following that in which the agreement was made or became unconditional. Any SDRT charge will, however, be cancelled (and any SDRT paid refunded) if the transfer is executed and stamped within six years of the agreement.

9.4.4.2   Financing the acquisition by borrowing: is tax relief available?

Close companies

An individual who takes out a loan to buy ordinary shares in a close trading company will obtain tax relief on the interest as a charge on income if they either control more than 5% of the ordinary share capital (shares acquired as a result of the borrowing are included), or work for the greater part of their time in the management of the company (ITA 2007, s 383).

Enterprise Investment Scheme (ITA 2007, Part 5, as amended)

The Enterprise Investment Scheme was introduced to encourage individuals to invest in shares issued by a qualifying unquoted trading company. In respect of shares issued on or after 15 March 2018, there must be a real risk to the capital being invested (see **8.4.2.1**). If certain conditions are fulfilled (eg the shares must be held for three years), income tax relief (at 30% for shares issued after 6 April 2011) is available on up to £1 million worth of investment for shares issued on or after 6 April 2012.

In addition, any gains on disposal of the shares are exempt from CGT and relief is given for any losses. Shares traded on the Alternative Investment Market are treated as 'unquoted' for this and other tax purposes.

Corporate buyer

A company will generally receive tax relief as a debit under the loan relationship rules contained in the Corporation Tax Act 2009 on the interest which it pays on a loan to acquire shares. Consequently, funding an acquisition with debt financing tends to be cost effective. However, in 2017, in the UK, new corporate interest restriction rules were introduced to restrict the amount of interest that could be deducted and benefit from tax relief, particularly if the interest exceeds £2 million. The rules are complicated and outside the scope of this book but, very broadly, limit tax relief. A buyer may therefore need to factor into its financial assessment the extent of borrowing it uses to acquire a target, given that not all interest may be deductible.

PRIVATE EQUITY ACQUISITIONS

> **LEARNING OUTCOMES**
>
> After reading this chapter you will be able to:
>
> - understand the structure of a private equity transaction
> - explain the issues raised by a management buy-out and by a leveraged buy-out
> - appreciate the nature of the documents that may be required for an acquisition funded by private equity.

10.1 PRIVATE EQUITY OVERVIEW

Private equity transactions are full of terminology such as 'sweet equity' and 'subordination'; it is easy to become bewildered as you try to learn the language of the private equity world. However, the basic premise of private equity is actually very straightforward. It is simply an investment in the share capital of a private company.

By acquiring shares and thereby ownership rights in a company, an investor hopes to receive income from the profits generated by that company (often through dividends) and to make a capital gain from the onward sale of those shares.

Making an investment in a private company is an inherently risky venture, but one where the potentially high risks may be matched with potentially high returns. Shares in a private company cannot readily be sold if the venture does not prove to be successful, so an investment of this nature should be based on expert advice and the use of appropriate strategies to try to minimise the possible risks. Over recent years expertise has developed in this type of investment and, as a result, many investors have seen great success.

The development of private equity began with the provision of finance to new developing businesses, and in particular with business managers seeking to finance the purchase (or 'buyout') of the business in which they worked (**10.2**). The provision of such finance was often referred to as 'venture capital' and usually involved the investor taking a minority stake in the developing company. This type of financing is still made available by private equity investors in the form of start-up or developmental funds and traditional management buyouts.

However, as the private equity market has developed, some private equity providers have become interested in seeking wider investment opportunities by acquiring a majority stake in an underperforming company, in the hope that the investor's involvement will turn the company's fortunes around and it can then be sold on for a profit. In these circumstances, the private equity provider is actively seeking a company whose performance it believes can be improved either through the introduction of new management, or through the use of the existing management in a restructured company. Once the company has returned to optimum performance, the investor can realise its investment at a profit. This has proved to be a very successful strategy, with private equity providers seeking out bigger and better investments. The expansion of the private equity market has even led to 'public to private transactions', where private equity providers consider underperforming listed companies as potential acquisition targets. Whilst historically the private equity industry has been lightly regulated, increasing concerns in recent years about the development of the private equity markets in the UK have led to the introduction of some regulations to address possible conflicts of interest, as well as the extent to which acquisitions by private equity providers have been funded by excessive borrowing (or, in private equity terminology, 'overleveraged').

As the result of a number of commissioned reports on the issues arising from large-scale transactions by investment funds, such as private equity funds, the EU has passed the Alternative Investment Fund Managers Directive (2011/61/EU), which was implemented in the UK by the Alternative Investment Fund Managers Regulations 2013 (SI 2013/1773) (AIFMR 2013) which came into force on 22 July 2013, the required date for implementation.

The Directive implements a harmonised regulatory framework across the EU for EU-established managers of alternative investment funds (AIFMs); this includes any legal or natural person whose regular business is to manage one or more alternative investment fund, which includes a range of investments including private equity funds. The Directive imposes a number of requirements including that AIFMs are authorised, adhere to strict capital requirements and have systems to manage risk, liquidity and conflicts of interest. Significantly, it also imposes new obligations in respect of disclosure about the investments the fund has made. The AIFMR 2013 include a number of amendments to the FSMA 2000 (Regulated Activities) Order 2001, including the addition of the new regulated activity of managing an alternative investment fund

10.1.1 The private equity provider

So what are a private equity fund and a private equity provider? The private equity fund is the pool of money that is to be invested. The money may come from a variety of sources, such as particular individuals or companies, or from institutional investors like pension funds, banks and insurance companies, as well as sovereign wealth funds. Specialist private equity funds are created whereby these investors agree, usually (primarily for tax reasons) in the UK through the form of a limited partnership, to provide funds to be invested in particular types of private companies. In 2017, the Legislative Reform (Private Fund Limited Partnerships) Order 2017 created a new class of limited partnerships – private fund limited partnerships – which are subject to a simplified regulatory regime, making them the most suitable vehicle for the majority of modern transactions.

The private equity fund will usually have a statement as to the type of investments it can (and cannot) make. The allocation (ie the investment) of the money within the fund will be a decision that is effectively made by a private equity provider (sometimes referred to as the private equity house or private equity fund manager). Typically, the private equity fund will delegate its investment management duties to the private equity fund manager, thereby benefitting from the expertise of the private equity investment professionals which the private equity fund manager has. The private equity fund delegates its duties in such a manner because, as a mere investment vehicle, it lacks the investment professionals with the necessary expertise required to manage the fund.

The private equity provider makes its profit by identifying opportunities for investing, by making investments into such opportunities and then managing them on an ongoing basis and, finally, by divesting (or exiting from) investments already made, all of which are services it provides to the private equity fund, in return for which the private equity provider/fund manager receives fees. The fees typically comprise an annual management fee (based on the total value of the fund being managed) and a performance fee (calculated by reference to the growth in net asset value of the fund over the course of a year).

Whereas it is fees that generate profit for the private equity provider/fund manager, the investors in the private equity fund make their profit primarily in the form of capital growth of the fund, which is achieved by the fund investing in suitably lucrative opportunities – and which it can only do provided the advice and decisions of the private equity provider/fund manager lead to successful investments being made. Consequently, it is vital for the private equity provider to identify and undertake successful investments since, if the funds it invests do not generate acceptable returns, the investors are unlikely to put money into funds run by that provider again.

10.1.2   The decision to invest

Before undertaking an investment, the private equity provider will usually follow an agreed internal procedure for the approval of the investment. As an acquisitions lawyer working on a private equity transaction, it is important to appreciate any requirements there may be for such internal approvals before funds are placed, as this can have a significant impact on the timetable of a proposed acquisition. The internal procedure will usually involve the production of an investment paper which will then be presented to an investment committee of the private equity provider. This paper will set out the proposed structure for the transaction and the anticipated rate of return on the investment. Where the funds to be provided are for a buyout (**10.1.3**), an offer for the acquisition will be made on the basis of this initial approval, and final approval of the investment committee may also be required when the detail of the proposed acquisition has been agreed. The investment of the funds will often be provided through particular corporate investment structures. If the transaction is large this may involve the use of a number of corporate entities in order to layer the input of the required finances (a method known as 'structural subordination') and may also involve the use of overseas holding companies (for tax and investment planning purposes).

10.1.3   Types of investments

Private equity investments broadly fall into three categories: start-up capital (providing financing at the outset of a business); development capital (providing finance for expansion); and buyouts (where finance is provided for the acquisition of a business). For both start-up capital and development capital, the investment will usually take the form of a subscription for shares in the existing company. Where funds are to be provided for a buyout, the investment may take a variety of forms depending of the nature of the buyout that is proposed. This chapter covers two different types of buyout that are common in practice: a traditional management buyout, and an institutional leveraged buyout.

On a buyout, the method by which the investment is made will vary depending on both the type and size of the buyout. For a small management buyout, a direct subscription for shares may be made in the company undertaking the target business. In the case of a large management buyout, it is likely that there will be a substantial amount of debt finance as well, so a corporate structure may be created in order to undertake the acquisition; and on large institutional leveraged buyouts it is likely that a fairly complex corporate structure will be used to cope with the numerous layers of investment and debt finance.

10.2   MANAGEMENT BUYOUT

A management buyout ('MBO') is a transaction by which the target is acquired by some or all of its management, usually through the vehicle of a new company established for this purpose ('Newco'). Management buyouts may proceed as share or asset acquisitions. The prospective management team is unlikely to be able to generate sufficient capital itself to finance the acquisition and will therefore usually seek funding elsewhere. The management team draws up a business plan designed to attract investment by a private equity provider. Often, several private equity providers will be invited to bid for the opportunity to be involved in the deal.

The financing for the acquisition will comprise a combination of equity finance provided by the management team and the private equity provider, and debt finance to be secured on the assets of the target company. In a management buyout that has been instigated by the existing management team, the private equity provider will expect the management team to provide a substantial investment, primarily to ensure that the team is heavily committed financially as well as commercially to the success of the venture. The private equity provider will usually prefer to take a majority shareholding in the venture, but may be prepared to accept a minority shareholding on certain MBOs provided it can also negotiate measures to allow it more control if it becomes concerned that the venture is failing.

10.2.1   The investment

As indicated above, the investment by the private equity provider will often be made through a new corporate vehicle established for the purpose ('Newco'). Both the private equity provider and the management team will subscribe for ordinary shares in Newco, although each party will have carefully negotiated the rights attaching to those shares. The private equity provider will also make a large proportion of its investment in return for redeemable preference shares that carry preferential rights to receive income by way of dividends and to the return of capital on a winding up of Newco (to try to minimise its exposure should the venture prove to be unsuccessful).

In addition to requiring particular class rights in relation to the issued shares, the parties to the venture will expect to enter into an 'investment agreement' (see **10.4.1** below). This agreement will set out the basis on which the investment has been made, any required restrictions on the running of the acquired company and relevant provisions governing the realisation of the investment through an onward sale or listing. On a traditional MBO the investment agreement will also include extensive warranties given by the management team about the target business and also the business plan drawn up by the team to attract the investment. Where a company is being sold to its own management, the seller will often be able to resist giving extensive warranties (see **10.2.3**). However, the private equity provider will not be satisfied with the seller's limited warranties and will require the management team itself to provide comfort by warranting all key information about the target business.

10.2.2   Conflict of interest

When a management team is contemplating a buyout, it must take great care to ensure that its actions do not breach any obligations of good faith or confidentiality owed to the target company. The management team, in negotiations for the purchase of the target, will inevitably try to achieve the best price possible, and this may place them in a position of conflict with their duties to the company, its shareholders and employees. If a management team member is also a director, consideration should be given to their statutory duties. As soon as a director has decided to initiate a MBO, an approach should be made to the board to declare the director's interest and to seek consent to proceed. Even where the management team member is not a director, an approach to the board is still advisable as the MBO process is otherwise likely to involve breaches in the terms of the employment contract, in particular any terms as to confidentiality.

Under English law, management buyouts may also give rise to consideration of s 190 of the CA 2006 and the need for shareholders' approval where a company buys an asset from or sells an asset to a director (see **9.2.2.2**). If the director will hold shares in the corporate vehicle created for the purpose of the buyout (Newco) then this could fall within the classification of a company 'connected' with the director under s 254 of the CA 2006. Although a single director is unlikely to hold the relevant 20% holding required for Newco to be a company connected with the director under s 254(2), the legislation refers to a 20% holding by a director and/or the director's connected persons. Consideration should always be given as to whether any of the other shareholders of Newco are 'connected' with the director resulting in a holding of

20% or more of Newco's shares. Where the management team will have a shareholding of 20% or more in Newco, a detailed review should be undertaken to ascertain whether or not shareholders' approval under s 190 of the CA 2006 will be required for the sale.

10.2.3 Warranties

As indicated above, another feature of MBO transactions is the issue of warranty provision, which may involve more negotiation than on a traditional asset or share sale. The seller is likely to resist extensive warranties being included in the sale and purchase agreement on the basis that the managers who are buying the target are likely to have more knowledge about the business than the seller. On the other hand, warranties are designed to allocate risk between the seller and the buyer, as well as to elicit information about the business. The seller will, of course, be receiving full consideration whether or not the buyers are part of the management team, and should arguably, therefore, be prepared to give full warranties.

10.3 INSTITUTIONAL LEVERAGED BUYOUT

On an institutional leveraged buyout, the private equity provider will hope to acquire a majority shareholding in a private company (or even an underperforming public company that could be converted into a private company) that has the potential to generate substantial profits. The private equity provider will be managing funds created by institutional investors such as pension funds, banks and insurance companies. These institutional investors in the private equity fund will be seeking to achieve good returns whilst trying to minimise potential risks. Having identified a possible target company as the proposed investment opportunity, the private equity provider will follow its internal procedures for approval of the proposed investment. In recent years many companies have been sold through the auction process (**2.4.2**), and on some such transactions there may be a number of private equity providers who are bidding for the right to acquire the company.

10.3.1 Debt/equity ratio

In arranging the structure of a leveraged buyout, consideration will be given to the overall arrangement for financing the acquisition. The private equity provider will try to achieve the optimal blend of debt and equity in order to maximise its profit. As part of its investment decision, it will consider its internal rate of return (how much gain will be achieved on the sale based on projections for the increase in value of the target company). This will be dependent on how much equity needs to be provided: the lower the amount of equity, the greater the gains per share.

A feature of such private equity-led acquisitions has been a very high level of borrowing, given the plentiful supply of cheap debt funding in recent years. One advantage of private company investments is that they are not subject to prohibitions on the provision of financial assistance (see **9.2.2.1**). Consequently, any borrowing for the acquisition of the target company's shares can be secured on the assets of the target company. Provision of security in this way is not possible on the acquisition of a public company, so where a public company is to be acquired through a private equity-led investment, the public target will immediately be converted into a private company.

10.3.2 The management team

On a leveraged buyout, the management team will not be the driving force behind the acquisition but will still be instrumental in that it will usually have the expertise necessary to maximise the investment potential of the target company. The management team selected may be the existing managers, external managers brought in by the private equity provider or a combination of the two. The managers will usually be provided with some form of financial incentive in order to achieve a successful exit from the target company. This will usually be in the form of a class of equity shares (often called 'sweet equity') that the management team will be able to sell when the target company is sold. As with a traditional MBO, the management team will be expected to give warranties in relation to its business plan and information provided by it about the target. The provision of warranties in this case, though, is usually driven more by a concern to establish the management team's full commitment to the process rather than as a risk allocation exercise. Unlike on a traditional MBO, the seller will usually provide full warranties, and any claims will be made by the buyer under those warranties rather than by pursuing the management team.

10.3.3   Common structures on leveraged buyout

In order to accommodate the varying interests of the parties involved in a leveraged buyout and to maximise the security and tax planning opportunities, the private equity provider will not invest directly into the company to be acquired. Instead, a corporate structure will be put together to receive the investment initially, the complexity of which will vary according to the particular circumstances of the transaction.

At its most straightforward the structure will consist of a holding or 'top' company which will act as the investment vehicle for all the equity funds (ie those provided by the private equity provider and any provided by the management team). This top company will usually then have a wholly-owned subsidiary that will undertake the bank borrowing needed to provide the balance of the acquisition cost. The actual purchase of the target company may be made by this wholly-owned subsidiary, or by the subsidiary of that wholly-owned company if that suits the tax and other circumstances of the transaction.

The layering of the corporate structure used for the acquisition relates primarily to considerations of tax and structural subordination which are outside the scope of this book. The companies undertaking the debt finance and the purchase of the target company will be wholly-owned subsidiaries of the top company. The equity investment is placed in the top company, which will be responsible for overseeing the operation of the investment, as governed by the terms of the investment agreement and by appropriate provisions in its articles.

10.4   KEY DOCUMENTATION

On any buyout there will essentially be three key parties: the private equity provider; the debt financiers (there may be several); and the management team. Each of these parties will have its own aims and objectives in the transaction, though they will all seek to manage the risks that they agree to take on as part of the buyout arrangement. This will be achieved in part by the corporate buyout structures discussed above, but also by the terms of the documentation governing the investment (the investment agreement) and the rights attaching to the equity shares that are acquired.

10.4.1   The investment agreement

The investment agreement is a contractual document that will set out the agreed terms of the proposed investment, the ongoing management of the target company and the terms of any proposed realisation of the investment. The agreement will usually expressly state that its terms take precedence over any other documentation that may be required to govern individual relationships between the various parties to the transaction, such as loan agreements, constitutional documents or service contracts.

Although the investment agreement is intended primarily to cover the terms of the equity investment (it is sometimes referred to as the subscription and shareholders' agreement), the providers of the debt finance will often also be a party to it. On a straightforward management buy-out, the providers of the debt finance will simply enter into facility agreements setting out the terms on which they are prepared to lend the required funds and the terms of any charges or other security that will be taken over the assets of the target company. In this case, there is no real need for the debt financiers to be party to the investment agreement, though they will want to ensure that any relevant provisions in it are not inconsistent with the agreed security provisions. On the other hand, on larger leveraged buy-outs, in addition to simple loans the debt providers may also provide debt with an option to convert into equity, or even a level of debt which is unsecured. In these circumstances it is appropriate for the debt financiers to be party to the investment agreement.

The terms of the investment agreement will cover three key areas, as set out below.

10.4.1.1   The terms of the investment

The investment agreement will specify how the money required for the proposed purchase will be raised. This will include how much money is being invested by the private equity provider and the management team, as well as the proportion of funds to be raised by borrowing. The investment by the private equity investor will often take the form of different classes of shares. A relatively small proportion of the funds will be invested in ordinary shares, with the remainder invested in shares carrying particular rights in terms of dividend payments and the return of capital. The private equity provider may also provide some of its investment in return for debt securities.

The agreement will also provide details of the proposed acquisition. The acquisition will proceed only if all elements of the proposed investment proceed. The terms of each separate investment will usually be described as 'conditions precedent' to the transaction. This means that the various parties will all sign the investment agreement but each party will become committed to making its investment and proceeding with the acquisition only once all the other parties have also made their respective investments. On a traditional MBO, the management will also be required to give the specified management warranties (**10.2.1**). Management warranties will also be expected on an institutional leveraged buyout if the existing management team are being given the opportunity to take an equity stake in the venture.

10.4.1.2   Governance of the investment

The investment agreement will set out the agreed structures for the ongoing management of the target business. This structure will vary depending on whether the private equity provider has taken a minority or a majority stake in the venture. If the private equity provider has taken a minority stake, directly into the target company itself or a corporate vehicle created for the purpose of the acquisition in a traditional MBO (see **10.2**), then that provider will want very strict restrictions on the activities of the target company in order to protect its investment. If the provider has a majority stake it is likely to be more relaxed about restrictions, as it should be able to take over effective control of the company if necessary. On an institutional leveraged buyout the provider will usually require a majority stake, but will still require provisions to be put in place to monitor the investment and enable it to step into place if it needs to take control of the top company or any of its subsidiaries as a matter of urgency.

The particular type of restrictions imposed will vary with each transaction. However, the agreement will usually provide for the right to appoint board members, the right to dismiss all board members (this will be a point of negotiation on a traditional MBO), the right to obtain information and the right to veto certain decisions. The restrictions provided for in the investment agreement will be reflected in the articles of the top company (or the target company on a direct investment) and will usually be expressed as rights attaching to the particular class of shares issued as part of the investment.

10.4.1.3   Realisation of the investment

The investment agreement will usually include provisions relating to the intended realisation of the investment. The private equity investor will want to realise its investment within a specified period of time, usually about five years. There are a number of ways in which the investment may be realised. A listing is usually the most desirable outcome for the private equity provider and the documentation will often provide for the conversion of particular classes of shares, such as preference shares, into ordinary shares, prior to those shares being admitted onto a public market such as the London Stock Exchange. If a listing is not possible the private equity provider will seek to realise the investment through a trade sale, or even a sale to another private equity provider. With these forms of sale the buyer will usually expect the seller to provide warranties about the company being sold. However, a private equity provider will not be prepared to give such warranties, as the money it realises from the investment must be returned to the private equity funds and cannot be subject to a possible later charge. In the investment agreement, therefore, the private equity provider will include a statement as to the intended length of its investment and that it will not be prepared to give any warranties on any subsequent sale.

The investment agreement will usually include agreed forms of the constitution of the company in which the investment is to take place. In particular, these constitutional documents will include extensive provisions governing the transfer rights of the different classes of shares. The constitution will usually prohibit the transfer of any shares taken by the management team, but will also provide for the mandatory sale of those shares if a director leaves whether through dismissal, retirement or death. The price paid for the shares in those circumstances will usually depend on whether the manager is considered a good or a bad leaver, usually roughly correlating to whether they left under amicable circumstances or were dismissed for poor performance or behaviour. On a traditional MBO these provisions will be heavily negotiated, as a considerable amount of money may depend on whether the manager is classified as a good or a bad leaver.

The agreed constitution of the target will usually also include provisions relating to the permitted transfer of shares, known as 'drag along' and 'tag along' provisions. A drag along provision will usually be imposed on any minority management shareholders. When the private equity provider is seeking to realise its investment through the onward sale of the company, it will want to ensure that it can force the minority shareholders to sell their shares at the same time. Drag along provisions in the constitution mean that the company can act as agent for the minority shareholders by automatically offering their shares to a buyer who has made an offer for a majority shareholding in the company. However, the minority shareholder will also usually require a reciprocal arrangement whereby it is able to 'tag along' or join in any sale of shares where an offer has been made to the private equity provider.

10.4.2   Associated documentation

In addition to the investment agreement, the parties to a private equity-led acquisition will enter into a number of associated documents covering their individual relationships. This documentation will cover the three different aspects of the transaction: the investment; the debt finance; and the acquisition.

10.4.2.1   The investment

The parties to the transaction must agree the terms of the constitution of the top company. This constitution will usually be agreed between the parties and attached to the investment agreement. The constitution will set out the agreed class rights of each type of share that is to be issued, including rights to income and return on capital, and any rights relating to the governance of the company. The constitution will also include any agreed restrictions on the transfer of shares and provisions regarding mandatory sales where a manager is dismissed or an offer to purchase the shares is received.

If the private equity provider is also providing funds using debt securities (such as loan notes, for example), the form of these must also be agreed.

The managers will usually be employees of the top company, and the terms of their service contracts must be negotiated. These contracts will usually include detailed provisions governing confidentiality and restrictive covenants.

10.4.2.2   The debt finance

The bank may be a party to the investment agreement on an institutional buyout if it is subscribing for debt securities that can be converted into equity securities, but there will also be separate banking documentation to govern the provision of the pure debt finance. This documentation will usually include a bank facility agreement specifying the amount of money being lent, which usually covers both the balance of the purchase price for the acquisition and the provision of working capital for the new venture. The bank will also require a package of documentation detailing the security it will have over the assets of the target business. If there are a number of providers of debt finance, there will also be an inter-creditor agreement setting out an agreed order of priority between the debt financiers for the different security taken over the target company's assets.

10.4.2.3   The acquisition

The acquisition process will be exactly the same as on a trade acquisition; it is simply that the focus of the buyer on a private equity acquisition will be firmly on the investment potential of the target rather than on trade implications.

The scope of the due diligence exercise will be determined by, amongst other things, the nature of the private equity transaction (venture capital, growth capital or buy-out) and whether the investor will acquire a minority or majority shareholding. Many private equity deals progress by way of structured auction where the seller controls the process and provides summaries of the due diligence information. Buyer-led due diligence may also give rise to particular issues, notably on warranty provision, if the management team comprises existing managers (**10.2.2**). It is increasingly common for investors to take out warranty and indemnity insurance to cover an element of the risk inherent in private equity transactions.

Following the due diligence review, the buyer and seller will enter into a sale and purchase agreement in the usual way, together with any associated documentation that may be required, such as the disclosure letter, tax covenant, pension transfer provisions, etc.

GROUP REORGANISATIONS

LEARNING OUTCOMES

After reading this chapter you will be able to:

- understand the nature of groups of companies and how they may arise
- appreciate how some of the main regulatory provisions apply in a group context
- understand the potential company law issues that may arise on an intra-group transfer of assets
- understand the main tax implications of intra-group transfers.

11.1 INTRODUCTION TO GROUP COMPANIES

Groups of companies involving a parent (or holding) company, one or more subsidiaries and, sometimes, sub-subsidiaries, are popular structures for the carrying on of business enterprises both in the UK and abroad. It is not only well-known public companies listed on The Stock Exchange which avail themselves of this structure, groups are also common among smaller concerns and private companies.

The attraction of operating through a group of companies rather than divisions of a single company has much to do with the fact that each company within the group is a separate legal entity with limited liability. The parent company, for example, is not liable for the debts of its subsidiaries unless it has agreed to assume responsibility for them or there are other special circumstances (see **11.1.3**).

The group structure enables risky businesses or activities to be packaged into separate subsidiaries so that their failure will not impact too heavily on the remainder of the group. The valuable, asset-rich parts of the enterprise can be isolated from more speculative and uncertain ventures.

A group arrangement will often prove less cumbersome than having all activities under the umbrella of one company. It may be convenient for separate businesses or parts of a business to be run as identifiable units with their own management teams. Another factor is that a group structure provides greater flexibility where acquisitions and disposals are contemplated, since it is usually easier to transfer a subsidiary than part of the business of a company.

11.1.1 How do groups come about?

A group can come into existence in a number of ways.

11.1.1.1   Enterprise formed as a group

The promoters of a business venture may decide from the start to incorporate a parent company and several subsidiaries (which may be wholly owned by the parent) to carry on different aspects of the enterprise.

11.1.1.2   Splitting up a large concern

A company may decide to transfer certain sectors of its business (eg manufacturing, retail, distribution, etc) to subsidiaries specifically formed for this purpose. Similarly, where a number of different businesses are being run under the umbrella of a single company, these may be separated out and hived down to subsidiaries (**1.4**).

11.1.1.3   Mergers and acquisitions

Where a company acquires control of another company by share acquisition, the relationship of parent and subsidiary is created between the acquiring company and the target company; if the entire issued share capital of the target changes hands, it becomes a wholly-owned subsidiary of the acquiring company. Where the target company itself has subsidiaries, the acquisition brings into existence a group with three levels (and so on). The buyer will often be content to maintain this structure rather than incur costs in transferring the businesses out of the subsidiaries. A group which expands in this way by making acquisitions rather than by achieving 'organic' growth of its core business may end up with an array of diverse activities under its wing (such a group is known as a conglomerate group).

11.1.2   Company law status of groups

Company law makes very little specific provision for groups of companies. Each company within the group is treated as a separate entity with its own assets and liabilities. Generally, a company (even the parent company of a wholly-owned subsidiary) does not have any additional liabilities or obligations imposed on it, or benefits granted to it, through being a member of a group. Some provisions of the CA 2006 do, however, make specific reference to groups.

11.1.2.1   Extension of restrictions to group companies

Membership of holding company prohibited

Section 136 of the CA 2006 prohibits a subsidiary or its nominee from being a member of its holding company and renders any transfer or issue of the holding company's shares to a subsidiary or its nominee void, except where the subsidiary is acting as a trustee or as an authorised dealer in securities.

Substantial property transactions involving directors

Section 190 of the CA 2006 requires the passing of an ordinary resolution of the members of a company where a director of the company or its holding company acquires an asset from the company or disposes of an asset to the company which is 'substantial' (see **9.2.2.2**). If the director is a director of its holding company, an ordinary resolution of the holding company is also necessary to approve the transaction. No approval is required under s 190, however, by any company which is a wholly-owned subsidiary (s 190(4)(b)).

Loans to directors

Under s 197 of the CA 2006, shareholder approval is required for a company to make loans to its directors; and similarly, if a loan is to be made to a director of the company's holding company, the approval of the members of the holding company must also be sought.

11.1.2.2   Definition of group

Section 1159 of the CA 2006 defines the terms 'holding company' and 'subsidiary' used in the provisions outlined above. A company is a 'subsidiary' of another company, its 'holding company', if that other company:

(a)   holds a majority of the voting rights in it; or

(b)   is a member of it and has the right to appoint or remove a majority of its board of directors; or

(c)   is a member of it and controls alone, pursuant to an agreement with other members, a majority of the voting rights in it,

or if it is a subsidiary of a company that is itself a subsidiary of that other company.

In determining the voting rights for this definition, indirect holdings are taken into account, so this may include voting rights held through other subsidiaries, certain nominees and trustees.

11.1.3   Group indebtedness

One of the consequences of treating each member of the group as a completely separate entity is that a parent company is not liable for the debts of an insolvent subsidiary; the parent may even take priority to other creditors if, for example, it has loaned money to the subsidiary and taken security over its assets. Intra-group loans are common within groups of companies, as are group banking arrangements. In the event that a company is sold out of the group, steps must be taken to settle any intra-group debts and release the company to be sold from any forms of security that have been given in relation to the group finances.

11.1.3.1   Guarantees

Often, when a subsidiary company is entering into an agreement, a creditor may seek some form of guarantee or security from the parent company or other company in the group which has a stronger financial standing. This may extend to a guarantee of provisions in a sale and purchase agreement. For example, if part of the purchase price is to be left outstanding at completion, the seller may want to make the buyer's parent company a party to the agreement in order to guarantee the payment (**4.3.5.2**).

11.1.4   Group accounts

One area where the CA 2006 does impose additional obligations on group companies is in the preparation of accounts.

11.1.4.1   Definition for accounting purposes (CA 2006, s 1162)

A slightly different definition of a group is used for accounting purposes from that used for other purposes. Broadly, the differences are as follows:

(a)   the terms 'parent undertaking' and 'subsidiary undertakings' are employed. The definition of 'undertaking' includes companies, partnerships and unincorporated associations;

(b)   a parent/subsidiary relationship arises in a similar way to a holding company/subsidiary relationship as described at **11.1.2.2** above. In addition, a company will be a parent undertaking for accounting purposes if:

(i)   it has the right to exercise a dominant influence over the 'subsidiary undertaking', or

(ii)   it is managed on a unified basis with the 'subsidiary undertaking'.

11.1.4.2   Obligation to prepare accounts

A parent company constituted in England and Wales is obliged to prepare consolidated annual accounts for the group, ie a profit and loss account and balance sheet incorporating the results, assets and liabilities of the parent and all the subsidiary undertakings in the group; this is in addition to preparing its own annual accounts. Group accounts must be approved by the directors of the parent company and audited by its auditors; they must be laid before the members of the parent company and filed with the Registrar of Companies (at the same time as the parent company's own accounts). The purpose of these provisions is to enable the members of the parent company to obtain an overall impression of the prosperity (or otherwise) and prospects of the group as a whole.

There is no obligation to produce group accounts where the group comes within the definition of a 'small' group. Also, an intermediate parent company which is itself included in consolidated accounts does not generally have to produce group accounts; it must, however, file a copy of these consolidated accounts with the Registrar of Companies together with its own accounts.

Lastly, certain information must be included in notes to the accounts. For example, parent companies must list their subsidiary undertakings and give details of their shareholdings, whilst subsidiaries are obliged to reveal the name of their ultimate parent company.

11.1.5   Taxation

Although each company in a group is a separate legal entity, the group is treated as a single entity for certain tax purposes. This has the advantage of avoiding a plethora of tax charges on intra-group transactions and enables the group as a whole to take greater advantage of reliefs (**11.4**). Indeed, if each member of the group were treated as independent for tax purposes, the group structure, which has proved so popular commercially, would compare very unfavourably with the divisional structure. Inevitably, the legislation is complex and the companies within a 'group' must meet the specific definitions in the tax legislation.

11.1.5.1   VAT group registration

Tax legislation recognises that group companies will supply goods and services to each other, or even on behalf of each other. Two or more companies which are UK resident can apply to HMRC for a group VAT registration if, inter alia, one controls each of the others (VATA 1994, s 43). Broadly, control is defined as holding a majority of the voting rights or controlling the composition of the board of directors.

Group registration is in the name of a 'representative member'. Any supply made by a group member to a person outside the group is deemed made by the representative member. Equally, any supply made to a group member by a person outside the group is deemed made to the representative member. This does not mean that other group members escape liability; all members of the group registration are jointly and severally liable for VAT due from the representative member.

The other main consequence of registration is that supplies between members of a group registration are disregarded for VAT purposes.

Once a group registration is in place, other companies may be included, or existing companies may be excluded from the group on application to HMRC. This will be a relevant factor if a subsidiary which is a member of a group registration is transferred outside the group. The buyer of a subsidiary should always check its VAT status and seek warranties that VAT has been properly accounted for (whether or not the subsidiary is part of a group registration).

In the Finance Act 1996, HMRC was given wide discretionary powers to counter avoidance schemes. These include, for example, the power to direct that supplies between group companies are to be subject to VAT.

11.2   OVERVIEW OF GROUP REORGANISATIONS

Group reorganisation is a generic term that can be used to describe anything from the transfer of a couple of assets to a complete restructuring of an entire group of companies. On an initial consideration it may be thought that if a transfer is between companies under common ownership there is no need for a formal acquisition process. However, each company is a separate legal entity and should enter into an agreement for the transfer of assets only after due consideration. Any such transfer should be properly documented and any tax considerations carefully examined. Although there may be no need for lengthy negotiations on the allocation of risk in the transaction, other concerns may need to be addressed. This is the case particularly if the intra-group transfer of assets is to be followed by a sale to an external third party. The third party buyer should investigate the terms of the intra-group transfer in its due diligence investigations in case there are any latent tax liabilities or breaches of company law provisions.

11.2.1   Why companies transfer assets intra-group

Many businesses develop through a series of acquisitions or internal expansion and so are not necessarily well-organised, self-contained units. Within a group, assets may be used by a number of different group companies and a variety of services may be provided across the group. This situation may not be regularised until a restructuring of the group becomes necessary, whether to improve efficiency, to prepare a group company or division for sale to an external third party, or to accommodate a new acquisition.

11.2.1.1   Transfers before a sale to third party

A transfer of assets between group companies may be required if a prospective buyer has identified that a particular asset or service that it requires is actually held by another company within the group.

A transfer may also be required in order to create a packaged unit for sale to an external third party. For example, the buyer may want to acquire a division but the parties prefer the transaction to proceed as a share acquisition. The seller may undertake a hive-down (**1.4.2**) by which it transfers the assets of the division into a newly-created subsidiary, the shares of which are then sold on to the buyer. Alternatively, it may undertake a hive-up (**1.4.3**).

11.2.2   Documenting the transfer

As with a sale to an external third party, an intra-group transfer should be properly documented with details of the assets being transferred. This is relatively straightforward where the transfer is of a shareholding in a subsidiary from one group company to another. However, contracts held by that subsidiary company should still be checked to confirm that they will not be affected by clauses that may enable termination in the event of a change of control of the company (although such clauses usually exclude transfers within the same group of companies). Where the transfer is of other assets, the details of those assets should be specified in the contract and the appropriate individual transfers undertaken. This may involve obtaining consents from third parties as in an asset acquisition with a third party (see **8.2**).

11.3   REGULATORY ISSUES ON INTRA-GROUP TRANSFERS IN THE UK

On transfers between group companies in the UK, consideration has to be given to the potential company law issues that may arise on the transfer. Although these are unlikely to be of practical significance whilst the companies involved are under the same ownership, these issues will be the subject of careful scrutiny in the event that any company is subsequently sold out of the group or becomes subject to insolvency proceedings.

11.3.1   Directors' duties

11.3.1.1   Duty owed to own company

The board of directors of every company involved in an intra-group transfer should give formal approval for the transfer in the same manner as required for an acquisition with a third party. The directors of each company owe a duty to their own company, so the intra-group transfer should be such as the directors consider 'would be most likely to promote the success of the relevant company for the benefit of its members as a whole' (CA 2006, s 172). Each company must be treated as a separate legal entity, and the directors of a particular company are not entitled to sacrifice the interests of that company for the interests of other members of the group (*Charterbridge Corporation v Lloyds Bank Limited* [1970] Ch 62).

As with any other acquisition, the directors must ensure that in approving the transfer they are complying with their statutory duties and that consideration of the interests of the company is recorded in the minutes. However, even if the transfer does give rise to a potential breach of duty, if it is in the interests of other companies within the group, the breach may be ratified by the shareholders (*Rolled Steel Products (Holdings) Ltd v British Steel Corporation* [1986] Ch 246), provided that the transaction is lawful (**11.3.2**), within the objects of the company and that the company is solvent at the time of the transfer (**11.3.1.2**).

11.3.1.2   Transfer at book value

Intra-group transfers have traditionally been undertaken on the basis of the value of the assets as specified in the company's accounts ('book value'). This avoids the need for any separate valuation to ascertain the actual value; however, it does mean that the company may well transfer the assets at less than their market value.

A transfer at book value is potentially a breach of duty and the directors should, for their own protection, seek confirmation from the holding company that the reorganisation is in the best interests of the group. The holding company's assent to the transaction, as the sole shareholder, will protect the directors against a potential claim for breach of duty, including a transfer at an undervalue. However, it should be noted that shareholder assent or ratification will not be effective if the company is insolvent at the time of the breach, because in these circumstances the duty to the company would also extend to the creditors (*West Mercia Safetywear Ltd v Dodds* [1988] BCLC 250). There may also be specific problems with transfers at an undervalue under insolvency law and therefore, if there are any concerns about the solvency of the transferring company, the assets should either be transferred at market value or evidence of the solvency of the transferring company should be obtained.

11.3.2   Distributions in kind

An intra-group transfer at an undervalue can also give rise to company law issues as a distribution in kind (that is, a dividend that is paid in assets other than cash). A transfer of an asset at an undervalue from a subsidiary to its holding company will be treated as a distribution in kind, as will a transfer between two subsidiaries that have the same holding company.

For this deemed distribution in kind to be lawful, it must be made in accordance with the statutory provisions governing distributions, ie there must be sufficient distributable profits available for the distribution to be made. A distribution will usually be declared by the company, but a deemed distribution in kind can be ratified by the shareholders, thereby rendering the distribution lawful. However, if the amount of the distribution exceeds distributable profits then the amount of the excess will be regarded as an unlawful reduction of the transferor's capital and this will not be capable of ratification (*Aveling Barford v Perion Ltd* [1989] BCLC 626).

In order to determine whether a distribution in kind can lawfully be made, the amount of that distribution has to be established.

How the amount of the distribution in kind is determined will depend on the distributable profits of the transferring company. Section 845 of the CA 2006 provides that the amount of the distribution is calculated by reference to the book value of the asset. The amount of the distribution will be zero if the asset was transferred at book value, or, if transferred for less than book value, the distribution will be of the amount by which the book value exceeds the consideration actually received for the asset. However, this section applies only if the transferring company has distributable profits at the time the asset is transferred and could lawfully make a distribution of the amount calculated under the provisions of the section.

If the company had no, or insufficient, distributable profit available, the distribution will be unlawful and the amount of the unlawful distribution will be the full difference between the market value of the asset and the consideration actually received by the company (s 846). This is significant, because any member of the company who knows or has reasonable grounds for believing that the distribution is unlawful is liable to repay the distribution (s 847(2)(a)). Where both companies had common directors (as is often the case with group companies) the requisite awareness might be implied. Such a request for payment would not usually arise between group companies, but if one of the companies is sold out of the group, there is a risk that the new shareholders will make a request for repayment.

11.4   TAX IMPLICATIONS OF INTRA-GROUP TRANSFERS IN THE UK

A transfer of assets between group companies is subject to the same general taxation principle as a sale to an external third party. A transfer of assets is taxed according to the nature of the asset transferred. For example, a transfer of shares in a subsidiary company will be the transfer of a capital asset and the transfer of a division may involve the transfer of a number of different types of assets, each taxed according to the nature of that asset, such as land (capital), intellectual property rights (intangible) and stock (income). However, as highlighted earlier, a group of companies may be treated as a single entity and such transfers may be treated as 'tax neutral' if they are within a particular tax group. Unfortunately there is no single universal definition of a 'group' for tax purposes. Whether the relationship between the transferring companies is sufficient for them to obtain, or indeed be subject to, group provisions will vary depending on the tax legislation in question. However, in determining these relationships, a common system of classification of subsidiaries is employed within tax legislation.

11.4.1   Classification of subsidiaries for tax groups

Groups are defined for tax purposes by reference to the percentage of ordinary share capital which companies hold in their subsidiaries. Subsidiaries are described, inter alia, as '51% subsidiaries', '75% subsidiaries' and '90% subsidiaries' (CTA 2010, ss 1154–1157). For a company to have a 51% subsidiary, it must own, directly or indirectly, over 50% of the ordinary share capital of the company; for a 75% subsidiary, the holding must be not less than 75%; and for a 90% subsidiary not less than 90%. Clearly, a 75% subsidiary also qualifies as a 51% subsidiary. Certain 'economic ownership tests' must also be satisfied (see **11.4.1.4**).

11.4.1.1   'Ordinary share capital'

The definition of ordinary share capital is wide; it includes all the issued share capital of a company (whatever it is called), other than capital the holders of which have a right to a dividend at a fixed rate but no other right to share in the profits of the company (s 1119). Thus, shares with no voting rights or carrying no rights to a dividend may still be classed as ordinary shares for this purpose.

11.4.1.2   Owned 'directly or indirectly'

Ownership may be direct or indirect. Indirect ownership means ownership through another company. Consider the examples below (which assume that the relevant 'economic ownership tests', as discussed at **11.4.1.4**, are satisfied).

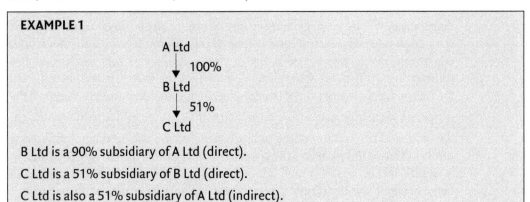

EXAMPLE 1

A Ltd
↓ 100%
B Ltd
↓ 51%
C Ltd

B Ltd is a 90% subsidiary of A Ltd (direct).

C Ltd is a 51% subsidiary of B Ltd (direct).

C Ltd is also a 51% subsidiary of A Ltd (indirect).

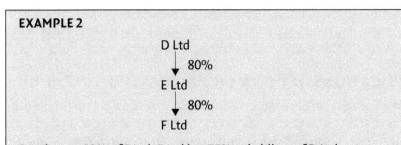

EXAMPLE 2

D Ltd
↓ 80%
E Ltd
↓ 80%
F Ltd

D Ltd owns 80% of E Ltd. E Ltd is a 75% subsidiary of D Ltd.

E Ltd owns 80% of F Ltd. F Ltd is a 75% subsidiary of E Ltd.

D Ltd owns 80% × 80 = 64% of F Ltd. F Ltd is a 51% subsidiary of D Ltd (but not a 75% subsidiary).

EXAMPLE 3

A Ltd owns 70% of B Ltd. B Ltd is a 51% subsidiary of A Ltd.

B Ltd owns 60% of C Ltd. C Ltd is a 51% subsidiary of B Ltd.

A Ltd owns 20% (directly) and 70% × 60 = 42% (indirectly) of C Ltd. C Ltd is a 51% subsidiary of A Ltd.

11.4.1.3   Beneficial ownership

The company must be the beneficial owner of the appropriate percentage of the share capital in the other company. A company which enters into an unconditional contract (or a conditional contract if the condition can be waived by the buyer) for the sale of the entire share capital of a subsidiary ceases to have beneficial ownership of the shares. It is important, therefore, that any intra-group transactions take place before this happens.

11.4.1.4   'Economic ownership tests'

In order to prevent the creation of artificial groups, 'economic ownership tests' must also be satisfied for a company to come within the definition of a 75% or 90% subsidiary (CTA 2010,

Pt 5, Ch 5). In addition to owning beneficially the required percentage of the ordinary shares of the subsidiary, the parent company must fulfil the following two requirements:

(a) be beneficially entitled to not less than 75% (or, in the case of a 90% subsidiary, not less than 90%) of the profits available for distribution to equity holders of the subsidiary; and

(b) be beneficially entitled to not less than 75% (or, in the case of a 90% subsidiary, not less than 90%) of any assets of the subsidiary available for distribution to its equity holders on a winding up.

Beneficial entitlement to profits and assets may arise directly or through intervening companies. Special rules for determining this entitlement are contained in ss 165 and 166 of the CTA 2010.

11.4.2 Transfer of income assets

The transfer of a division is likely to involve the transfer of income assets such as stock or work in progress. In a group reorganisation such assets will often be transferred at cost and so would not give rise to a taxable profit. However, it should be noted that for certain large corporations the transfer of goods will be deemed to have been at market value regardless of the actual price paid if the parties are deemed connected under Part 4 of the Taxation (International and Other Provisions) Act 2010, the details of which are outside the scope of this book. In the event that an income profit has been made, there is scope to offset this profit against any trading losses that may have been made in another company.

11.4.2.1 Group relief (CTA 2010, s 131)

Group relief enables a company (the surrendering company) which has incurred a trading loss in an accounting period, or which has charges on income or loan relationship debits, such as interest payments, to surrender these to another member of the group (the claimant company). This enables the claimant company to set the loss or charges on income or debits against its own taxable profits (ie income profits and chargeable gains), thus reducing its liability to corporation tax. The claimant company must first deduct its own charges on income and any current or brought forward losses. Historically, the surrendering company could surrender only trading losses, etc of its current accounting period. The claimant company could set them against profits of the corresponding accounting period and could not carry them forward or back. However, in relation to accounting periods beginning on or after 1 April 2017, the Finance (No 2) Act 2017 now allows losses carried forward to subsequent accounting periods to be surrendered to other group companies. There are special rules which regulate the amount of losses which can be surrendered and claimed by companies with different accounting periods.

The whole of the trading loss, etc does not need to be surrendered and partial surrenders may be made to different members of the group. If the claimant company pays the surrendering company for the use of the trading losses, etc, the payment itself does not affect the tax position of either company, provided it does not exceed the amount of losses surrendered (CTA 2010, s 183).

11.4.2.2 Applicable groups

Two companies are members of a group for the purposes of this relief if one is a 75% subsidiary of the other, or if both are 75% subsidiaries of a third (CTA 2010, s 152). Generally, for the relief to apply, the surrendering and claimant companies should both be 'UK related' (CTA 2010, s 134) (though since April 2006, companies may, in certain circumstances, claim relief for losses incurred by subsidiaries resident in the European Economic Area – see *Marks & Spencer plc v Halsey (Inspector of Taxes)* [2007] EWCA Civ 117 and CTA 2010, s 136). Consider Example 4 below.

EXAMPLE 4

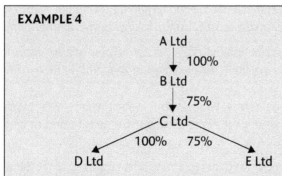

D Ltd is a 90% subsidiary of C Ltd and a 75% subsidiary of both B Ltd and A Ltd. A Ltd, B Ltd, C Ltd and D Ltd are members of a 75% group.

E Ltd does not form part of such a group since A Ltd and B Ltd own only 75% × 75 = 56.25% of E Ltd.

E Ltd is a 75% subsidiary of C Ltd. C Ltd, D Ltd and E Ltd form a 75% group.

11.4.2.3   Example of group relief

EXAMPLE 5

A Ltd owns 100% of B Ltd. Both companies have the same accounting reference date of 30 September. In the accounting period ending 30 September 2019, B Ltd makes a trading loss of £50,000 (and no chargeable gains), whereas A Ltd makes total profits of £150,000.

B Ltd can carry the loss back against any profits of the preceding year, thus entitling B Ltd to reclaim tax (CTA 2010, ss 35–44). Carry forward relief against trading profits is also available to B Ltd to reduce future corporation tax assessments (s 45). B Ltd may, however, choose to surrender all or part of the trading loss to A Ltd. If the whole of the loss is surrendered, A Ltd's profits liable to corporation tax for the year ended 30 September are reduced to £100,000.

11.4.2.4   Companies joining or leaving the group

As an anti-avoidance measure, s 154 of CTA 2010 is designed to prevent the artificial manipulation of group relief by the forming of groups on a temporary basis in order to obtain relief. In other words, a company with a loss arising, or due to arise, cannot join an unconnected group, surrender its losses and then depart from the group afterwards.

A company will not be regarded as a member of the group if 'arrangements' are in existence for the transfer of that company to another group: relief is not available during any period when such arrangements are in force (*Shepherd (Inspector of Taxes) v Law Land plc* [1990] STC 795).

In the context of an acquisition, therefore, losses will generally be available for surrender between other members of the group only if they arose *before* 'arrangements' are in place for the sale of the target.

So, when do 'arrangements' come into existence for this purpose? It is clear that there does not have to be a binding contract for the acquisition of the shares; the signing of heads of agreement may, for example, be sufficient to prevent group relief. Although there is no statutory definition of 'arrangements', HMRC provides some guidance in a Statement of Practice (SP 3/93). The main points arising from the Statement are as follows:

(a)   arrangements will not normally come into existence in the case of a straightforward sale of a company before the date of the acceptance (subject to contract or on a similar conditional basis) of the offer;

(b)   where a disposal of shares requires approval of shareholders, no arrangement will come into existence until that approval has been given or the directors are aware that it will be given;

(c)   'arrangements' might exist if there is an 'understanding between the parties in the character of an option' for a potential buyer to acquire shares.

When a company joins or leaves the group, CTA 2010, ss 138–141 provide for the group relief to be apportioned.

11.4.3   Transfer of capital assets

11.4.3.1   Tax neutral

If capital assets are transferred within a defined group then the transfer will be deemed as tax neutral (TCGA 1992, s 171). Such a disposal is treated as being for such a consideration (whatever the actual consideration passing) as not to give rise to either a capital gain or a loss. (In other words, the consideration is treated as being equal to the original acquisition cost of the asset.) However, if that asset is transferred out of that defined group, or the company that received that asset leaves the defined group within six years of receiving that asset, then a tax charge will arise.

11.4.3.2   Definition of 'group'

The definition of a group for the purposes of the provisions on the transfer of capital assets is contained in s 170 of the TCGA 1992. The following rules apply:

(a)   a company (the 'principal company') forms a group with all its 75% subsidiaries;

(b)   the group also includes any 75% subsidiaries of those subsidiaries (and so on) if they are 'effective 51% subsidiaries' of the principal company;

(c)   for a subsidiary to be an 'effective 51% subsidiary', the principal company must be beneficially entitled to more than 50% of any profits available for distribution to equity holders of the subsidiary and more than 50% of any assets available for distribution to equity holders on a winding up;

(d)   a company which is a 75% subsidiary of another company cannot itself be a principal company unless it is prevented from being part of a group because it fails the 'effective 51% subsidiary' test.

All companies must be UK tax resident. See Example 6 below.

EXAMPLE 6

A Ltd (Principal company)

↓ 75%

B Ltd

↓ 75%

C Ltd

↓ 75%

D Ltd

A Ltd, B Ltd and C Ltd form a group (C Ltd is a 75% × 75% = 56.25% subsidiary of A Ltd).

D Ltd is not part of the group as it is not a 51% subsidiary of A Ltd (A Ltd indirectly owns 75% × 75% × 75% = 42.18% of the shares in D Ltd).

As D Ltd cannot be part of the group it can be a principal company of its own group. Thus if D Ltd has a 75% subsidiary, E Ltd, D Ltd and E Ltd form a group.

Note that B Ltd and C Ltd cannot be principals of their own groups because they are 75% subsidiaries of other companies and do not fail the 51% subsidiary test.

11.4.3.3   Degrouping charge on company leaving the group

A potential corporation tax charge on the postponed capital gain will be triggered if the company leaves the group within six years of *receiving* the asset from another group member on a no gain/no loss basis. Section 179 of the TCGA 1992 provides that, on leaving a group, a company is treated as if it had sold and immediately re-acquired any asset which had been transferred to it from another member of the group within the previous six years. For the purpose of calculating the gain (or loss), this disposal and reacquisition is deemed to have taken place on the date the asset was last acquired intra-group. The gain or loss (often called a 'degrouping gain/loss') was previously borne by the company being sold out of the group (the 'departing company'). However, pursuant to the Finance Act 2011, different provisions now apply to degrouping charges which arise as a result of a disposal of shares. Any degrouping gain or loss will accrue to the company making the share disposal (ie the seller) and will be taken into account as part of the proceeds of the share disposal, although the departing company will continue to be deemed to have made the aforementioned disposal and immediate reacquisition of the asset.

Where there is a degrouping gain, therefore, the seller can apply its available reliefs and exemptions, most notably the substantial shareholding exemption if applicable (see **9.4.2.4**). The departing company will see an uplift in the base cost of the relevant asset (even if the gain proves to be exempt in the hands of the seller). On the other hand, if there is a degrouping loss this will not be available to the seller (ie to offset other gains) if the substantial shareholding exemption applies, and the departing company will see a reduction in the base cost of the capital asset.

EXAMPLE 7

A Ltd buys some land for £100,000 in 2012. A Ltd transfers the land in 2014 to its wholly-owned subsidiary, B Ltd, for £150,000 (its market value). B Ltd then transfers the land to C Ltd (B Ltd's wholly-owned subsidiary) in 2016 for £250,000 (its market value).

In 2018, B Ltd disposes of its entire shareholding in C Ltd, causing C Ltd to leave the group.

No corporation tax is paid on the transfer from A Ltd to B Ltd nor on the transfer from B Ltd to C Ltd. These transfers are deemed to be on a no gain/no loss basis.

C Ltd's exit from the group in 2018 triggers a degrouping charge since it leaves the group within six years of acquiring the land. C Ltd is deemed to have sold the land for its market value in 2016 (£250,000) (and immediately reacquired it at that value).

Ignoring indexation, the chargeable gain is £250,000 less the deemed acquisition cost of £100,000, ie £150,000. This gain will be taxable in the hands of B Ltd as part of its gain on the disposal of C Ltd, and will be subject to B Ltd's available reliefs and exemptions. B Ltd's entire gain, including the degrouping gain, is likely to be exempt from tax by virtue of the substantial shareholding exemption, provided it satisfies the relevant conditions.

Variation if asset transferred is shares

If shares are the asset being transferred then the substantial shareholdings exemption may be applied to the degrouping gain or loss if the company owning the substantial shareholding at the time of the degrouping would have been entitled to the exemption. When the holding is transferred intra-group, the company receiving the transfer is treated as having acquired it at the same time at which the transferor acquired it. If the shareholding has been held within the group for a continuous period of 12 months, the exiting company will qualify for the exemption. The company leaving the group is treated as if it had sold and then reacquired the shareholding immediately before the degrouping, though there will be no charge to tax, and the base cost of the shareholding following the deemed sale and reacquisition will be the market value of it immediately before the degrouping.

EXAMPLE 8

A Ltd has two subsidiaries, B Ltd and C Ltd. B Ltd holds shares in another subsidiary, D Ltd. These companies all form a defined group under s 170 of the TCGA 1992. In 2016, B Ltd transferred its entire shareholding in D Ltd to C Ltd for no gain/no loss. In 2018, the shares of C Ltd are sold by A Ltd and so C Ltd leaves the group. A degrouping charge will arise because C Ltd has left the group within six years of receiving a capital asset from another member of the group. However, as the asset transferred is a substantial shareholding held for the requisite length of time (12 months), C Ltd will qualify for the substantial shareholdings exemption. It is deemed to have sold and immediately reacquired the shareholding at the time it leaves the group, but there will be no tax to pay.

Although this gives a flavour of the interaction between intra-group provisions and other corporation tax reliefs, in practice it will be important to take specialist advice.

11.4.3.4 Transferring an asset out of the group

When a company transfers an asset out of the group, there is a charge to corporation tax on any gain that results. Here, the gain is the consideration received on transferring the asset out of the group *less* the price paid by the member who first brought the asset into the group.

So, using the figures from Example 8 in **11.4.3.3**, if C Ltd were to sell the land in 2018 for £300,000 (instead of leaving the group), the gain would be £300,000 less £100,000 (the price paid by A Ltd), ie £200,000. This gain is taxable in the hands of C Ltd, and it is free to apply any available capital tax reliefs, such as business asset roll-over relief, provided the relevant conditions are met.

11.4.4 Intangible assets and loan relationships

Provisions similar to those in relation to the transfer of capital assets apply to assets which are subject to the intangible assets regime (ie intangible assets such as intellectual property rights that were created or acquired from an unrelated party after 1 April 2002) under ss 775 and 776 of the CTA 2009. If such intangible assets are transferred within a defined group, the transfer will be deemed as tax neutral (ie so as to create neither a capital gain nor a capital loss). The defined group is substantially the same as that under s 170 of the TCGA 1992 for capital assets, and if the receiving company leaves the defined group it is subject to a degrouping charge based on the same criteria as those which relate to the transfer of a capital asset. However, there is one important distinction; rather than arising at the start of the accounting period in which it leaves the group, as for a capital asset, the resulting degrouping charge arises immediately before the transferee leaves the group.

It should also be noted that similar provisions apply in relation to the transfer of certain intra-group loans and debt securities, the details of which are outside the scope of this book.

11.4.5 Stamp duty and stamp duty land tax

Subject to certain anti-avoidance provisions, complete relief from stamp duty is available on a transfer of shares between companies where one company is a 75% subsidiary of the other or both are 75% subsidiaries of a third company (Finance Act 1930, s 42, as amended). In determining whether a company is a 75% subsidiary of another, direct or indirect shareholdings of ordinary shares are taken into account, and the economic ownership tests referred to at **11.4.1.4** must be satisfied.

For the purposes of SDLT, intra-group transactions are deemed to take place at market value regardless of the actual consideration given (Finance Act 2003, s 53). However, it is generally possible to claim group relief (subject to certain anti-avoidance provisions). The group relief for SDLT purposes is broadly the same as for stamp duty (Finance Act 2003, Sch 7). However, SDLT group relief can be clawed back if, within three years of the effective date of the intra-group land transaction, the transferee leaves the group of which it and the transferor were members and it, or a relevant associated company, holds the land that was transferred intra-group (Finance Act 2003, Sch 7, para 3).

The Finance Act 2008 introduced a further extension to the clawback rules. The Revenue had identified a number of schemes which allowed the transferor to leave the group first, thereby allowing the transferee company subsequently to leave the group without any clawback of group relief. The additional anti-avoidance provision will operate where the transferor company leaves the group and there is a subsequent change in control of the transferee within three years of the land being transferred.

Index